Market-based Instruments for Environmental Management

INTERNATIONAL STUDIES IN ENVIRONMENTAL POLICY MAKING

General Editor: Frank J. Convery, *Heritage Trust Professor of Environmental Studies and Director of the Environmental Institute at University College Dublin, Ireland*

This important series makes a significant contribution to the development of policies to combat environmental problems. It is the result of a Europe-wide study of the use of market-based instruments to formulate environmental policy and reduce degradation. International in scope, it addresses issues of current and future concern across the globe, in both East and West and in developed and developing countries.

This series provides a forum for the publication of a limited number of innovative, high quality volumes which extend and challenge the current literature. It demonstrates how economic analysis can make a contribution to understanding and resolving the environmental problems confronting the world in the twenty-first century.

Titles in the series include:

International Competitiveness and Environmental Policies
Edited by Terry Barker and Jonathan Köhler

Pollution for Sale
Emissions Trading and Joint Implementation
Edited by Steve Sorrell and Jim Skea

The Market and the Environment
The Effectiveness of Market Based Policy Instruments for
Environmental Reform
Edited by Thomas Sterner

Market-based Instruments for Environmental Management
Politics and Institutions
Edited by Mikael Skou Andersen and Rolf-Ulrich Sprenger

Market-based Instruments for Environmental Management

Politics and Institutions

Edited by

Mikael Skou Andersen

Associate Professor, Department of Political Science, University of Aarhus, Denmark

Rolf-Ulrich Sprenger

Director of the Environmental and Resource Economics Department, IFO Institute for Economic Research, Munich, Germany

INTERNATIONAL STUDIES IN ENVIRONMENTAL POLICY MAKING

Edward Elgar
Cheltenham, UK • Northampton, MA, USA

Published by
Edward Elgar Publishing Limited
Glensanda House
Montpellier Parade
Cheltenham
Glos GL50 1UA
UK

Edward Elgar Publishing, Inc.
136 West Street
Suite 202
Northampton
Massachusetts 01060
USA

A catalogue record for this book
is available from the British Library

Library of Congress Cataloguing in Publishing Data

Market-based instruments for environmental management: policies and institutions/
edited by Mikael Skou Andersen, Rolf-Ulrich Sprenger.
    (International studies in environmental policy making)
    1. Environmental impact charges — Europe — Congresses. 2. Environmental impact charges — Japan — Congresses. 3. Environmental management — Europe — Congresses. 4. Environmental management — Japan — Congresses.
I. Andersen, Mikael Skou. II. Sprenger, Rolf-Ulrich. III. Series.

HJ5403.5 . M37 2000
336.2 — dc21

                                          99-049220

ISBN 1 84064 039 1

Printed and bound in Great Britain by Bookcraft (Bath) Ltd

Contents

v

PART IV   IMPLEMENTATION PROBLEMS OF MBIs

Boxes

Figures

Tables

Contributors

Mikael Skou Andersen is an associate professor at the Department of Political Science, University of Aarhus, Universitetsparken, DK-8000 Århus, Denmark, and a member of The Centre for Social Science Research on the Environment, e-mail address: andersen@ps.au.dk

Bernard Barraqué is Research Director of the Centre Nationale de la Recherche Scientifique, CNRS, LATTS-ENPC, Paris, France, e-mail address: barraque@latts.enpc.fr

Stefan Brendstrup is a research assistant at The Centre for Social Science Research on the Environment, University of Aarhus; Gustav Wieds Vej 10, DK-8000 Aarhus, Denmark, e-mail address: cesamsb@au.dk

Hans Th. A. Bressers is Professor of Environmental Policy Studies at the University of Twente, The Netherlands, and Director of the Center for Clean Technology and Environmental Policy (CSTM), University of Twente-CSTM, e-mail address: j.t.a.bressers@cstm.utwente.nl

Carsten Daugbjerg is an Assistant Professor at the Department of Political Science and associated with the Centre for Social Science Research on the Environment, University of Aarhus, Denmark, e-mail address: cd@ps.au.dk

Martin Enevoldsen is a PhD student at the Centre for Social Science Research on the Environment, University of Aarhus; Gustav Wieds Vej 10, DK-8000 Aarhus, Denmark, e-mail address: cesamme@au.dk

Olivier Godard is Director of Research at the Centre National de la Recherche Scientifique (CNRS) and works at the Laboratoire d'Econométrie, a joint unit of CNRS and Ecole Polytechnique, 1 rue Descartes, F-75005 Paris, France, e-mail address: olivier.godard@wanadoo.fr

Dominic Hogg is Senior Consultant at ECOTEC Research and Consulting, Priestley House, 28-34 Albert Street, Birmingham B4 7UD, e-mail address: dominic_hogg@mailgate.ecotec.co.uk

Dave Huitema is a Research Associate and Lecturer at the Center for Clean Technology and Environmental Policy (CSTM), University of Twente-CSTM, e-mail address: d.huitema@cstm.utwente.nl

Martin Jänicke is Professor at Freie Universität Berlin, Environmental Policy Research Unit, Ihmestrasse 22, D-14195 Berlin-Dahlem, e-mail address: ffu@zedat.fu-berlin.de

Yu Matsuno is a Lecturer at the School of Business Administration, Meiji University, Kenkyuto 532, Kandasurugadai 1-1, Chiyoda-ku, Tokyo 101-8301, Japan, e-mail address: matsuno@kisc.meiji.ac.jp

Rolf-Ulrich Sprenger is Director of the Environmental and Resource Economics Department, IFO Institute for Economic Research, Munich, Germany, e-mail address: sprenger@ifo.de

Kazuhiro Ueta is a Professor at the Graduate School of Economics, Kyoto University, Yoshida-Honmachi, Sakyo-ku, Kyoto 606-01, Japan, e-mail address: ueta@econ.kyoto-u.ac.jp

Arild Vatn is Professor at the Department of Economics and Social Sciences, Agricultural University of Norway, PO Box 5033, N-1432 Aas, Norway, e-mail address: arild.vatn@ios.nlh.no

Preface

This book has been developed from the proceedings of a workshop 'The institutional aspects of economic instruments for environmental policy' held at Eigtveds Pakhus in Copenhagen in May 1997. The workshop was organized by the Centre for Social Science Research on the Environment (CESAM) at Aarhus University in Denmark in cooperation with IFO Institute Munich as part of a Concerted Action on 'Market-based Instruments for Sustainable Development' funded under the European Union research programme 'Human Dimensions of Environmental Change' and coordinated by Professor Frank Convery of University College, Dublin. The workshop received additional financial support from the Danish government's 'Strategic Environmental Research Programme'.

Denmark has been a pioneer in the application of economic instruments for environmental policy, and according to the latest Organization for Economic Co-operation and Development (OECD) survey it has the largest number of such instruments in operation. It is closely followed by the Netherlands and the other Nordic countries, who have chosen a similar approach. The experiences attained through the last decade or more with such instruments have provided new perspectives on the whole issue of market-based instruments and the associated green tax reforms.

From the scientific perspective countries which have ventured on the approach of market-based instruments can be regarded as 'laboratories of green taxes and green reform', from which the experiences and observations should lead to new reflections on the theories and methods of environmental economics. The workshop was a forum for a dialogue among environmental economists, political scientists and practitioners in the field, and this approach is reflected in the following chapters. The institutional approach pursued here refers to the issues associated with implementing the economic principles of environmental taxation in a regulatory and political setting which follows its own logic, and not necessarily one of efficiency or Pareto-optimality.

Although there is now a burgeoning literature on environmental taxation, relatively few *ex-post* evaluation studies of the effects of market-based instruments have so far been carried out. This book presents two such studies; an assessment of the Japanese SO_x charge (introduced in 1974) and an evaluation of the Danish waste tax (introduced in 1986). More *ex-post* evaluations are now being carried out, and the conceptual and theoretical perspective provided in a number of chapters may prove significant to improve the quality and rigour of such studies, as well as to improve the understanding of what insights can be obtained through the various approaches pursued by economists and political scientists.

The first part of the book contains an introduction to the subject. In the second part the political scientists offer new conceptual lenses through which to analyse and reflect on the role of environmental taxes and charges. In the third part a number of case studies are presented, based on various theoretical approaches, and they shed light on the problems of designing and introducing environmental taxes and charges. In the fourth part focus is on implementation and *ex-post* evaluation of experiences with economic instruments.

The reader will find that the book is mainly European in its perspective, and hence that the main focus is on taxes and charges, but it also contains a chapter on the Japanese experience. In an international context it will, therefore, complement the mainly american literature on tradeable pollution quotas. Experiences with taxes and charges for environmental policy have so far been rare in the Anglo-Saxon speaking countries, and the reader will find that nearly all of the contributions stem from authors and countries for whom English is not a native language. While one chapter has been translated for the purpose of the book, linguistic editorial assistance was provided for the remaining chapters. The editors believe that by bringing these experiences into the international literature a new stimulus can be provided to the important theoretical and practical debates on the use of market-based instruments for environmental policy.

The editors would like to thank Else Løvdal of the Department of Political Science at Aarhus University for her skilful secretarial assistance. We would also like to thank Professor Frank Convery at University College, Dublin, for initiating the European research network and hence to have provided the framework which made this book possible. Finally, we would like to thank Dymphna Evans and colleagues at Edward Elgar Publishing for their patience and smooth cooperation.

Århus and München, April 1999

PART I

Introduction

1. Market-based instruments in environmental policies: the lessons of experience

Rolf-Ulrich Sprenger

INTRODUCTION

Traditionally, environmental management has consisted of 'command-and-control' measures: regulations that set ambient, emission or technology targets and which impose penalties if those standards are not complied with. For decades, now, economists and other stakeholders have argued in favour of shifting the focus of this regulatory effort to market-based instruments (MBIs). Such instruments might include environmental taxes or charges, marketable permits, subsidies and so on. From a rather humble beginning these approaches have now been expanded in several countries and in different directions. This chapter describes this evolution, presents the experience with MBIs, and discusses which lessons can be learned from the fact that actual applications depart from the textbook ideal.

THE RATIONALE FOR MBIs IN ENVIRONMENTAL MANAGEMENT

Definition and Purpose of MBIs

In a broad sense, MBIs can be defined as proxies for market signals in the form of change to relative prices and/or a financial transfer between polluters and society. Unlike 'command-and-control' approaches, which place direct constraints on the polluter, an MBI acts via an economic signal or incentive to which the polluter responds.

MBIs are aimed at

- forcing producers and consumers to take account of the implications for the environment of their action;
- leaving them the freedom to choose and adapt their activities;

- enabling them to apply least-cost solutions;
- creating a dynamic which encourages the search for and application of better and cheaper means of maintaining and improving environmental quality.

Types of MBIs Employed for Environmental Purposes

Economic instruments employed for environmental purposes are commonly classified into five categories:

1. charges/taxes;
2. deposit-refund schemes;
3. market creations;
4. subsidies;
5. liability schemes.

Environmental charges/taxes

Environmental charges/taxes are commonly classified into four different categories:

1. emission charges/taxes;
2. product charges/taxes;
3. user charges;
4. sanction charges.

- Emission charges/taxes are payments on direct releases into the environment, based on pollutant characteristics and on the quantity of discharges.
- Product charges/taxes may be levied on products and services that involve pollution during production, consumption or at the disposal stage. Tax differentiation is also included in this category.
- User charges are payments for *inter alia* treatment and collection of effluent, such as sewage and solid waste. User charges related to such effluents are commonly governed by local authorities and may generally not be set in excess of prime cost.
- Sanction charges that punish non-compliance with established environmental norms may provide economic incentives for compliance. Such enforcement incentives include non-compliance fees, imposed when polluters do not comply with certain regulations and performance bonds, payments to authorities in expectation of compliance with imposed regulations. Refunding takes place when compliance has been achieved.

Deposit-refund schemes

Deposit surcharges may be placed on the sale of potentially polluting products. Such surcharges are refunded when certain conditions are satisfied, for example, when pollution is avoided upon redemption of used products or waste items to collection systems.

Market creations

Another category of MBIs for environmental protection is based on the creation of markets, in which environmental goods are indirectly given a positive price. Through the creation of certain kinds of market, pollution may thus be incorporated in the polluters' cost functions without the use of direct payments on polluting products or activities. Instruments for market creation include tradable permits and joint implementation.

Tradable permits are quotas, allowances or ceilings on pollution or resource use that, once initially allocated by the appropriate authority, can be traded subject to a set of prescribed rules. They are often called tradable permits or credits or emissions trading programmes. The units exchanged are referred to as credits, allowances or permits. Trades can be external (between different enterprises or countries) or internal (between different plants, products and so on of the same firm).

Joint implementation (JI) is referred to when countries cooperate in reaching certain environmental objectives: for example one country finances emission reductions in another country, where the costs of abatement are lower than in the investing country. The investing country can count the emission reductions achieved through JI, at least partly, as contributing to the fulfilment of is own abatement goal, whereas the receiving country benefits from JI by obtaining capital and/or technology. JI may be seen as a first step towards more cost-effective means of achieving international goals and may constitute a preceding phase for tradable permits.

Subsidies for environmental purposes

Environmental subsidies include various forms of financial assistance, intended either to encourage reductions in pollution, or to finance abatement measures. Different types of environmental subsidy include grants or transfer of payments, soft loans, tax allowances or charge reliefs.

Liability schemes

Liability schemes can be described as approaches slightly beyond economic incentives, but potentially with substantial environmental as well as economic significance. In fact, using liability is probably the oldest economic incentive. Compensation for environmental damage is normally provided by the law as a second-best remedy if the consequences of an injury or damage cannot be undone by the responsible person through restoration of the exact condition existing before the damaging event. The standard measure of compensation in such cases is the economic loss caused by the injury or damage.

Theoretical Features of MBIs

Theoretically, MBIs have several appealing properties, and if properly designed and effectively implemented, they have a number of advantages over traditional 'command-and-control' approaches:

- They allow the market agents themselves to decide upon the best way to reduce pollution, as only they have full information regarding their own cost functions (cost-effectiveness/static efficiency).
- They provide permanent incentives for technological improvements. While direct regulations usually provide few incentives for reducing pollution below the regulatory limits, economic instruments may entail continuous incentives for emission abatement (dynamic efficiency).
- They provide flexibility. For industry, freedom of choice is preserved. Polluters can choose the solution that best suits their interest. They may opt to pollute and pay for it or invest in pollution abatement or reduce pollution in some other cost-effective way. For the authorities, it is easier to modify and adjust a charge than to change legislation.
- They provide revenues which can be used to reinforce the incentive effects or to reduce other distortions in the economic system. Environmental taxes or charges or auctions of tradable permits may play an important role in the collection of funds, which can be reallocated to various purposes.
- They promote resource conservation and transmission to future generations (through appropriate resource pricing).

The Case for Using MBIs in Environmental Management

In principle, the justification for using MBIs in environmental policies may be supported by theoretical arguments and *ex-ante* assessments. However, the case for using MBIs can only be definitely assessed by *ex-post* evaluation of the actual performance of these instruments and by drawing conclusions from the evaluation evidence (OECD, 1997a).

Theoretical arguments
First, much of the initial advocacy of economic instruments has been based on theoretical or conceptual argument. Economic theory may be used to evaluate the costs and benefits of economic instruments and conventional 'command-

and-control' regulations, in the context of a theoretical model, representing the behaviour of profit-maximizing firms and a set of defined objectives for environmental policy. Analysis of this sort can indicate a range of relevant costs and benefits which will arise in the choice between different policy instruments, for the given set of assumptions about polluter behaviour. In some circumstances it may be possible to derive unambiguous conclusions about the merits of particular policy instruments, but more generally theoretical analysis can only indicate the range of conditions in which instruments or one set of policies would be preferable to another. Whether the particular conditions which would favour a particular instrument are satisfied in practice is an issue which cannot be resolved by theoretical argument, but depends on empirical evidence about the conditions existing in the practical application.

Ex-ante assessments

A second form of analysis regarding the costs and benefits of using economic instruments takes the form of *ex-ante* quantification of the potential benefits of different policy options, on the basis of data about the relevant environmental problems and economic context. Thus, it may be possible to evaluate some of the key parameters in advance of actual experience with economic instruments in environmental policy. The basis on which such *ex-ante* quantification may be made can include evidence of a number of different sorts. Thus, it may include data on the relative significance of various key magnitudes – if, for example, the 'static efficiency' case for economic instruments is stronger relative to command-and-control regulation, the greater the differences between polluters in the marginal costs of pollution abatement. It may also be possible to assess the likely strength of polluter responses to policy measures from evidence about polluter behaviour in similar economic circumstances. Thus, for example, evidence about the price elasticity of demand for energy, resulting from periods when the price of energy fluctuated as a result of changes in market supplies and demands, may be used to assess the likely response of energy users to imposition of higher energy taxes in the form of a carbon tax.

Ex-post evaluation

The case for using MBIs in environmental policy cannot be definitively assessed by theoretical and *ex-ante* analyses. Both theory and *ex-ante* quantitative analyses can only suggest the likely consequences of using economic instruments, on given assumptions about behaviour responses, and other relevant factors. Theoretical analyses depend on the assumption that the behaviour of polluters and other relevant parties will conform to that of a particular theoretical model of behaviour. Quantitative analyses based on *ex-ante* data, likewise, have to assume that responses will conform to predictions of theory, or to the patterns observed in response to other, analogous, episodes. *Ex-post* analysis of the experience of using economic instruments in practice can provide evidence of a fundamentally different sort, in that it can show the pattern of actual responses to economic instruments, and can provide data, based on experience, regarding a number of other issues (such as costs of administration and compliance) which are not easily evaluated on the basis of theoretical argument or *ex-ante* quantification.

THE EXPERIENCE WITH MBIs IN ENVIRONMENTAL POLICY

An evaluation of MBIs can be done on the basis of statistical analyses or fully-fledged evaluation studies using a set of well-defined criteria.

Statistical Analyses

The most widely applied approach to describing the use of MBIs has been statistical analysis. In various surveys the Organization for Economic Co-operation and Development (OECD) and other institutions have presented the extent of the use of MBIs in OECD countries.

A first OECD review was presented in 1987 (OECD, 1989). This covered five categories of instruments:

1. charges/taxes;
2. subsidies;
3. deposit-refund systems;
4. market creation instruments;
5. financial enforcement incentives.

The 1987 survey identifies 150 instances in 14 OECD countries where 'some form of economic arrangement had been made for the sake of improving environmental quality'. If subsidies, liability and administrative charges are excluded, the total number of economic instruments is reduced to around 100 (OECD, 1994). Basically then, in 1987, environmental policies in the OECD member countries were 'command and control policies with some financial and economic add-ons' (OECD, 1994, p. 22).

A second survey was conducted in 1992/3 with a narrower coverage of instruments (excluding subsidies, liability and administrative charges) but including a greater number of countries (OECD, 1994). The 1992/3 survey results suggest a rising trend in the use of economic instruments (Table 1.1).

Table 1.1   Economic instruments in OECD countries as of January 1992

Countries	Charges on emissions (of which user charges)	Charges on products (of which tax differentiations)	Deposit refunds	Tradable permits	Enforce-ment incentives
USA	*5 (2)	*6 (1)	*4	*4	2
Sweden	3 (2)	*11 (2)	*4		2
Canada	3 (2)	7 (3)	1	2	2
Denmark	3 (2)	10 (2)	2		
Finland	3 (2)	*10 (2)	2		
Norway	*4 (2)	8 (2)	3		
Australia	5 (2)	1 (0)	3	1	2
Germany	5 (2)	*3 (3)	*2	1	
Netherlands	5 (2)	4 (2)	2		
Austria	3 (1)	4 (2)	3		
Belgium	7 (2)	2 (2)	1		
Portugal	4 (1)	3 (1)	3		
France	5 (2)	*2 (1)			
Switzerland	3 (2)	2 (2)	1		
Italy	3 (2)	2 (0)			
Iceland	1 (1)	1 (1)	2		
Japan	3 (1)	1 (1)			
Ireland	2 (2)	1 (1)			
Greece		2 (1)	1		
Spain	3 (2)				
UK	1 (1)	1 (1)			
New Zealand	1 (1)				
Turkey			1		

Note: *Increase since 1987.

Source: OECD (1994).

Comparing the data for the eight best-documented countries, the number of economic instruments in use in 1992 was 25 per cent higher than in 1987. If the number brought into use in 1993 is also taken into account, the increase is nearly 50 per cent (OECD, 1994). During the period 1987–93, the main increases were in product charges and deposit-refund schemes.

In summary, over the period from the mid-1980s to the present, the use of economic instruments in OECD countries has grown significantly, rather than dramatically, and to a varying extent in different member countries.

Subsequently, the OECD reviewed the use made of environmentally-related taxes and charges in OECD countries at the beginning of 1995 (OECD, 1996)

Table 1.2   *The use of environment-related taxes or charges in the OECD member states*

Countries	January 1992*	January 1995	January 1997
Austria	7	3	9
Belgium	9	12	19
Denmark	13	20	23
Finland	13	17	21
France	7	6	12
Germany	8	12	13
Greece	2	3	5
Ireland	3	6	6
Italy	5	6	6
Luxembourg	–	3	3
Netherlands	9	10	16
Portugal	7	11	11
Spain	3	8	8
Sweden	14	18	21
UK	2	8	8
Sub-total EU	102	143	181
Australia	6	15	15
Canada	10	7	7
Iceland	2	9	9
Japan	4	3	6
Mexico	–	7	10
New Zealand	1	2	2
Norway	12	22	22
Switzerland	5	9	12
Turkey	–	6	6
USA	11	14	14
Sub-total non-EU	51	94	103
Total OECD	153	237	284

Note: *Surveys are not directly comparable.

Sources: OECD (1994), (1996) and (1997b).

and in 1997 (OECD, 1997b). Although these studies are not directly comparable with the 1992/3 survey, it is possible to derive some general trends from the data (Tables 1.2 and 1.3). The comparison has shown two main trends. One group of countries has radically restructured their tax systems, shifting the tax burden away from income to consumption taxes, including environmental taxes. As a consequence, explicit environmental considerations tend to play a more prominent role in the design of tax reforms in such member countries as Denmark, Finland, Norway, the Netherlands and Sweden. A second group of member countries – including Austria, Germany, Belgium, France and Switzerland – have made increased use of environmental taxes, both new and existing, but within a narrower framework than one of a comprehensive tax reform.

Table 1.3   The use of environment-related taxes or charges in the OECD* and EU member states

Tax or charge on:	January 1995 OECD	EU	January 1997 OECD	EU	Difference 1997/1995 OECD	EU
Motor fuels	56	36	61	40	5	4
Other energy products	30	21	35	26	5	5
Vehicles	31	17	35	20	4	3
Agricultural inputs	6	4	6	4	0	0
Other goods	21	12	25	15	4	3
Direct tax provision	19	10	28	17	9	7
Air transport	12	6	14	7	2	1
Water	24	13	39	24	15	11
Waste disposal and management	38	24	41	28	3	4
Total	237	143	284	181	47	38

Note: *Excluding Czech Republic, Hungary and Poland.

Sources: OECD (1996) and (1997b).

The use of tradable permits developed significantly in the USA. However, tradable permit programmes to control air pollution in the USA have undergone a considerable evolution from their earliest incarnations (Tietenberg, 1998). Tracing this evolution reveals considerable variety in the implemented programmes. Some (such as the Ozone Depleting Gas and Lead Phaseout Programs) were designed to eliminate pollutants, while others were designed to stabilize (Emissions Trading) or reduce (Sulphur Allowance and RECLAIM) emissions. While most programmes (Emissions Trading, Sulphur Allowance, Ozone Depleting Gas and Lead Phaseout) were created by the federal government, newer programmes (OTC Budget, RECLAIM) were created by regional or state authorities. While earlier programmes (Emissions Trading, Lead Phaseout) tended to complement traditional regulation, newer programmes (Sulphur Allowance and RECLAIM) tend to replace it.

As regards subsidies for environmental purposes survey results are shown in an IFO study aimed at taking stock of different types of such subsidies in the EU-12 (IFO, 1994).

Data in Table 1.4 show the media orientation of the state aids included in the study. Horizontal support measures are the most important subsidy, representing 91 out of 247 schemes identified. A significant fraction of support schemes (68 out of 247) subsidize activities in the field of energy saving and the production or use of renewable energies. The data available suggest that subsidies for other policy areas such as air pollution control, waste management and waste water treatment are by far less important. There is, however, considerable variation across the European Union (EU) countries.

Grants are on the whole the most important component of subsidization for environmental purposes. According to the country data, soft loans are the

Table 1.4   Subsidy programmes for environmental purposes in the EU (1994)

Countries	Energy	Wastewater	Waste	Air/noise	General	Total
Belgium	2	1	–	–	11	14
Denmark	9	–	3	3	6	21
France	–	2	–	2	1	5
Germany	32	14	10	13	32	101
Greece	–	–	–	4	–	4
Ireland	2	1	2	–	1	6
Italy	2	1	1	1	5	10
Luxembourg	2	2	–	4	4	12
Portugal	9	–	–	–	5	14
Spain	2	1	5	–	8	16
Netherlands	5	3	3	7	13	31
UK	3	2	3	–	5	13
Total	68	27	27	34	91	247

Source: IFO (1994).

second most important subsidy instrument. Some countries report tax concessions, although they appear to be as insignificant as loan guarantees. As indicated in Table 1.4, there is again considerable variation across countries.

The major area of concentrated support has been 'integrated pollution control' including subsidies for clean technologies. However, a significant fraction of the subsidy schemes reported still support the traditional end-of-pipe technologies. Subsidies for environmentally friendly products still only account for an insignificant fraction of all schemes.

The IFO study was not intended to evaluate identified subsidies, to draw conclusions from the inventory and to make specific recommendations to promote the subsequent modification or withdrawal of specific subsidy schemes. Its first and only purpose was to establish a reliable database for comparisons to other EU member states and thus to facilitate further evaluation.

Compared to other MBIs, subsidies may only be a second-best solution in situations where the polluter-pays principle is not yet fully applied. Therefore, the broad use of state aids for environmental purposes in the EU cannot be dubbed a success story.

The current practice in the use of MBIs also has to be considered in the context of the general regulatory framework. Taking a closer look at the mix of regulatory and MBIs in Germany, the number of MBIs appears to be of little significance (Box 1.1). Broadly speaking, therefore, the way in which environmental policy in Germany worked was through measures of the 'command-and-control' type.

To conclude, the statistical evidence on the use of MBIs in the environmental policies of OECD member states shows that increasing use has been made of environmental taxes and subsidies for environmental purposes. The greatest increases were in product charges, whereas the use of tradable permits has been confined to the USA.

Evaluation Studies

Although it is possible to derive some general trends from the OECD surveys, these statistics do not reflect the actual performance of the MBIs which have been identified. Therefore, existing evaluation evidence on MBIs in environmental policy has to be considered.

There are undoubtedly numerous studies on a number of different MBIs in practice. However, it is beyond the scope of this study to attempt to provide a comprehensive coverage of all evaluation evidence from both official and published studies. Nevertheless, the evaluation results discussed cover the major European initiatives in the area of environmental charges and taxes and the US experience with tradable permits. The evaluation studies have been

BOX 1.1   THE MIX OF REGULATORY AND MBIs FOR
           ENVIRONMENTAL MANAGEMENT: THE CASE
           OF GERMANY

1.   *Command-and-control*
     800 acts, 2800 ordinances and
     4700 technical instructions
2.   *Pollution charges or taxes*
     Wastewater: uniform scheme for all states
     Hazardous waste: three states
     Air pollution: tax differentiation for leaded and unleaded
     petrol
3.   *User charges*
     Groundwater: 14 state schemes
     Wastewater: local schemes
     Waste disposal: local schemes
4.   *Deposit-refund schemes*
     Mostly for beverage containers
5.   *Tradable permits*
     Air pollution control: offset provisions
6.   *Voluntary agreements*
     More than 90 since the early 1970s
7.   *Subsidies*
     Direct grants, soft loans, tax allowances; loan guarantees
     Twenty-three programmes at federal level
     124 programmes at state level
8.   *Strict liability*
     For classified industrial plants

Source: Sprenger (1996).

chosen because they summarize the *ex-post* performance of relatively well-established MBIs, for which enough time has elapsed for experience and data on actual performance to be available.

Results from existing studies on a number of charge or tax mechanisms in Europe are summarized in Boxes 1.2–1.4. As regards the evaluation evidence (OECD, 1994) on environmental charges and taxes the majority of emissions charges still seemed to be designed mainly as revenue-raising devices, but, overall, the incentive role of economic instruments appeared to have become more prominent. In some 45 per cent of cases, economic instruments appeared

BOX 1.2 EUROPEAN EXPERIENCE WITH INCENTIVE CHARGES

Instrument	Environmental Function	Environmental Effects	Incentive Effects
Tax differentiation on leaded petrol (Sweden)	To increase penetration of unleaded petrol	Emissions of lead dropped by about 80% between 1988–93	Tax differential exceeds additional production costs of unleaded petrol
Tax differentiation for diesel (Sweden)	To increase penetration of low-pollution diesel fuels	75% reduction of S emissions by diesel cars; 95% in cities; reduced emissions of particles, smoke, No$_x$, hydrocarbons and PAC expected but not quantified	Tax differential higher than additional production costs of classes I and II
Toxic waste charge (Germany)	To reduce the amount of toxic waste	Reduction of toxic waste generation of 20–45% between 1991–93	Tax rate increased average dumping and incineration costs by at least 5–15%; rate doubled in 1993 increasing this cost to 10–30%; otherwise unknown
No$_x$-charge (Sweden)	To speed up reduction of No$_x$ emissions from large combustion plants	Main cause of the reduction by 9000 tons in 1992 (35% of liable emissions)	Charge rate of SEK40 exceeds average abatement costs of SEK10
Fertilizer charge (Sweden)	To reduce the demand for fertilizer	N down by 25%; P down by 65% between 1980 and 1992; charge was one of the factors	Unknown
Water pollution charge (France)	To stimulate adoption of in-plant wastewater treatment measures and building of treatment plants	Modest	Charge rate considerably lower than average pollution abatement costs
Water pollution charge (Germany)	To support adoption of water pollution abatement in permit application process	Early announcement contributed to stepping up construction of wastewater treatment capacity	Original relation between charge rate and marginal abatement costs were not implemented

Source: European Environmental Agency (EEA) (1996).

BOX 1.3   EUROPEAN EXPERIENCE WITH FISCAL ENVIRONMENTAL TAXES AND CHARGES

Instrument	Environmental Function	Environmental Effects	Incentive Effects
Sulphur tax (Sweden)	To increase penetration of low-S fuels and adoption of S-abatement measures	Reduction of 6000 tons of S corresponding to 6% reduction of total S emissions, reduction of S content of oil by 40% on average; 25% of taxpayers reduced S emissions by 70% on average	Average abatement costs were about SEK10, lower than the tax rate of SEK40 therefore strong incentive effect
CO_2 tax (Sweden)	To reduce CO_2 emissions	Hard to evaluate due to short period of operation; possible shifts in fuels and increased competitiveness of combined heat and power plant	Unknown
CO_2 tax (Norway)	To reduce CO_2 emissions	CO_2 emissions dropped by 3–4% in 1991–93 from arising trend	Price of heating oil increased 15% and price of petrol increased 10%; otherwise unknown
Tax on domestic flights (Sweden)	To reduce emissions by nationally operated air transport	Unknown, but most likely very small	Unknown
Waste charge (Denmark)	To reduce waste generation and increase recycling and reuse	Reused fraction of demolition waste increased from 12% to 82%; contributed to an increase in reuse and recycling rate of 20–30% between 1985–93	Tax rate doubles average cost of waste dumping and increases cost of incineration by 70% on average, otherwise unknown

Source: European Environmental Agency (EEA) (1996).

BOX 1.4   EUROPEAN EXPERIENCE WITH USER CHARGES (1) AND EARMARKED CHARGES (2)

(1)

Instrument	Environmental Function	Environmental Effects	Incentive Effects
Water pollution charge (Netherlands)	To finance wastewater treatment plants	Water pollution (BOD) down to 5% for households and for industry	Average charge slightly lower than average pollution abatement costs
Household waste charge (Netherlands)	To promote a fair distribution of waste management costs over users	10–20% less household waste supply in 'pay-per-bag' villages	Unknown

(2)

Instrument	Environmental Function	Environmental Effects	Incentive Effects
Battery charges (Sweden)	To cover costs of collection and disposal and of information	Collection of lead batteries 95%; decreasing share of small Hg and NiCd batteries	Charge renders recycling of Pb-batteries feasible
Aircraft noise charge (Netherlands)	To finance insulation and redevelopment programmes around airports	Insulation of buildings around airport areas	Very low

Source: European Environmental Agency (1996).

to be intended to have an incentive effect (as compared to 30 per cent of cases where an incentive effect was explicitly not sought). As far as the performance of the instruments is concerned, however, the study found little evidence about the existence of incentive effects; in 90 per cent of cases, information on incentive effects was inconclusive or unavailable. One of the main conclusions of the study concerned the absence of clear evidence on the incentive performance of economic instruments in practice.

A more recent study (OECD, 1997b) concludes that theoretically achievable efficiency gains of environmental charges and taxes have not always been realized in practice for a number of reasons:

1. Charges may not be set at the appropriate level to achieve the environmental quality target (for example, they may be set at too low a level to have a sufficient incentive effect): see
   Box 1.2 European experience with incentive charges
   Box 1.3 European experience with fiscal environmental taxes and charges
   Box 1.4 European experience with user charges (1) and earmarked charges (2).
2. The 'command-and-control' benchmark may have been wrongly specified (for example, it may have more flexibility than assumed so that strictly uniform standards may not be applied).
3. Economic instruments may not stimulate technical change and innovation if the financial incentives are set at too low a level.
4. Differences in other costs between the two schemes (for example, set up, administration, monitoring and compliance costs) may require revisions of the above estimates.

Evaluation evidence regarding the use of tradable permits is available for the USA. Hahn and Hester (1989) have summarized the experience with the Emissions Trading Program for the late 1970s and early 1980s (Table 1.5).

The main conclusions of various evaluation efforts for these programmes are the following:

- The environment has not been significantly affected by the emissions trading programmes in the USA.
- Actual cost savings have been significant to individual companies. This has been demonstrated in cases involving air and water emissions and phasing out material inputs.
- The largest actual cost savings to companies in the USA have come from an ability to make internal trades to meet a standard for an entire plant.

Table 1.5   Summary of US emissions trading activity

Activity	Estimated number of internal transactions	Estimated number of external transactions	Estimated cost savings (millions)	Environmental quality impact
Netting	5000–12 000	None	$25–$300 in permitting costs. $500–$12 000 in emission control costs	Insignificant in individual cases; probably insignificant in aggregate
Offsets	1800	200	Not easily estimated; probably hundreds of millions of $	Probably insignificant
Bubbles				
Federally approved	40	2	$300	Insignificant
State approved	89	0	$135	Insignificant
Banking	<100	<20	Small	Insignificant

Source: Hahn and Hester (1989).

- The total cost savings may have been somewhat less than 10 per cent of the cost of the stationary source air emissions programme.
- Economic approaches do not seem to have a direct effect on technological change although the recent interest in pollution prevention that pays may be an indirect impact of administrative and economic instruments.
- Actual cost savings are likely to be significantly less in total than the maximum cost savings predicted from a pure economic instrument in a world with no transactions costs. This has been demonstrated in simulation models and in the level of observed use of economic instruments (Farrow, 1995).

The more recent experience with trading programmes concludes that:

- by shifting the focus of control from the source to the aggregate level of

emissions greater control has been gained over total emissions;
- the tradable commodity has changed from a credit to an allowance (Tietenberg, 1998).

LESSONS TO BE LEARNED FROM EVALUATION EVIDENCE

This section briefly considers what lessons can be learned from the various efforts made to identify and evaluate the use of MBIs in practice:

Lesson 1 *There is far too little evaluation evidence to arrive at valid conclusions* Taking a closer look at the existing literature, it appears obvious that there is little tradition for *ex-post* evaluation, as compared with *ex-ante* assessment, that has been studied extensively since the early days of cost-benefit analysis. *Ex-post* policy evaluation is a common activity in the field of government finance, where accounting conventions facilitate policy assessment. *Ex-post* policy evaluation is less common in other policy fields, including environmental policy, although some initiatives can be recorded.

One of the reasons for the limited interest shown by some stakeholders such as government authorities and industry may be that policy evaluation might be able to uncover in detail the policy-making process, or the process in which instruments are brought to operationality. This is not always a positive result, as it may weaken the positions of policy-makers in related policy decision processes.

While quantitative or partly quantitative performance criteria were regularly employed for *ex-ante* evaluation of environmental policy instruments, there is far too little empirical evidence to arrive at a systematic *ex-post* evaluation of the significance of instruments as used in practice. Much of the available evidence reflects 'incidental observations' and 'observation-driven intuitions' (OECD, 1994). Further work to develop evaluation methodologies and collect evidence is needed. Without such work, the often-heard arguments of ineffectiveness or low elasticity will continue to be heard and constitute obstacles to a rational application of economic incentives. The same holds for the issue of administrative implementability; there is no a priori case that economic incentives are more difficult to implement, but this could be supported by much more empirical evidence (OECD, 1994).

Lesson 2 *Data and resource constraints may induce a bias in concentrating on easily measurable impacts* Both data constraints and resource constraints have often limited the scope of analysis to those aspects of the use of MBIs which could be readily observed, measured or quantified. To conclude, partial or superficial evaluation may result in incomplete, or even incorrect, conclusions which may impede successful instrument practice.

The limitations placed on the scope of evaluation studies by resources and the availability of information need to be borne in mind in interpreting the results. There is an obvious danger of bias in concentrating solely on those aspects which can be measured and ignoring considerations which are not readily amenable to evaluation. Some of the aspects of the effects of particular instruments may be inherently difficult to measure or quantify. As already noted, for example, it is unlikely that evaluation studies will be able to provide robust *ex-post* evidence of the effect of the dynamic efficiency incentive from MBIs. The difficulty of obtaining evidence on these dynamic effects does not, however, mean that these effects are negligible, or that they can be ignored in comparing the relative merits of different instruments.

Frequently, policy considerations have called for evaluations to be undertaken soon after a policy is initiated, so as to produce results and conclusions which can help in the modification and adjustment of the policy. Such early evaluations can only reflect the short-term effects of policy, and cannot provide evidence on longer-term consequences.

This means that evidence is more often available concerning effects such as the short-term effects on static costs, initial environmental effects, and initial wider economic consequences; only few evaluations provide good evidence about long-term environmental effects, macroeconomic adjustments, and long-term technology decisions.

Lesson 3 *In many cases it is difficult, if not impossible, to separate the impact of MBIs from other parts of an instrument mix* MBIs are not operated in isolation; they are generally used within the regulatory framework. There are many cases where specific economic instruments are applied in conjunction with other instruments (mixed approaches). Combinations of an MBI and direct regulation are quite common, either to reinforce such regulations or to provide for necessary funds.

There is an obvious difficulty in assessing the effects of an MBI where it is combined in a package of instruments. Separating the impact of the MBI from the impacts of other parallel instruments is difficult in principle. In many cases it is simply impossible to disentangle the individual contribution of an MBI implemented as part of the package. Therefore, the evaluation will often have to be content with evidence on the joint effect of all the elements of the instrument mix taken together.

Lesson 4 *Attributing all effects after introduction of an MBI to that instrument risks ignoring the impact of other significant factors* Presenting the effects after introduction of a new instrument does not necessarily reflect the effects that can be attributed to other factors. Sometimes it is more the announcement effect of a planned introduction of an MBI than the actual implementation itself. In the light of the New Policy Research the instrument choice can hardly explain the results of a policy change. In most cases the effects of MBIs appear to have been secondary in their contribution to changes compared to the effects of a broader policy package. To avoid a bias by attributing impacts to one single instrument one has to consider all changes that took place as a result of the policy style and the economic, political and institutional context of environmental decision-making (Jänicke, this volume, Chapter 3).

Similarly, it is unlikely to be the case that all effects after the introduction of an MBI can be attributed to the effects of that instrument; some of the changes might have occurred in any case, regardless of whether environmental policy had changed or not. What would have happened in the absence of the policy change must, therefore, be assessed as the baseline against which the effectiveness of a particular policy (instrument) is to be judged.

To conclude, policy choices based on evaluation results that overexpose instruments compared to other factors and policy variables appear to be overly 'instrumentalist' and thus run the risk of failing.

Lesson 5   *Since the performance of specific instruments will vary depending on the evaluation criteria applied, policy choice will depend on the weighting of individual evaluation criteria*   Any environmental problem can be managed by a variety of alternative instruments, but it appears that no single instrument is best for all situations. Only through a systematic evaluation of the many alternative instruments available for any given problem and an explicit trade-off of the many conflicting effects of any chosen instrument is the desired environmental quality likely to be achieved in an effective, efficient and equitable manner.

Before any judgements can be made about the merits or drawbacks of MBIs, it is necessary to establish some criteria on which to base the evaluation. Such criteria should be useful to the extent that they help assess the actual advantages and disadvantages of the MBI relative to the (existing) command-and-control approach.

Although many criteria are possible, the following list seems to encompass the most pertinent considerations for the evaluation of instruments:

- environmental effectiveness;
- static and dynamic efficiency;
- wider economic effects (for example, employment, competitiveness);
- revenue effects;
- equity;

- compatibility with administrative and institutional framework;
- enforceability;
- political acceptability;
- ease of adjustment;
- capacity-building effects.

These criteria are subject to further development and refinement, but they provide an initial necessary framework for the analysis of any environmental policy. Evaluations of any subset of these criteria, therefore, should be regarded as incomplete.

The individual criteria are directed at conflicting goals which must be balanced to achieve effective policy. For example, a specific MBI may achieve higher marks for encouraging cost-effectiveness but may suffer on environmental quality grounds; it may provide strong incentives for innovations in pollution control technology but may prove difficult to enforce.

Therefore, the final step in evaluating an MBI would be to combine the ratings on the individual criteria. This process involves assigning relative weight to the individual criteria. However, it is difficult to identify a weighted or even an ordinal relationship between these criteria.

Aside from the difficulties in assigning relative weight to the individual criteria, it must be recognized that this process is the responsibility of decision-makers, not of analysts of government policy. It is also useful to note that, as programmes mature and priorities shift, the relative weight given to the criteria can change, requiring modifications of the existing approach.

Lesson 6 *There are a lot of missed opportunities for the successful use of MBIs because decision-makers have often ignored the political economy of instrument choice* Since the various actors and interest groups involved in environmental decision-making assign different weights to the above-mentioned evaluation criteria, the results of the instrument choice will depend on the relative weight and power of the relevant 'players'.

Even though the present 'command-and-control' approaches have obvious drawbacks, these schemes tend to persist (Howe, 1993).

The literature suggests the following reasons:

- lawyers write the rules and they are trained to believe in regulations;
- legislators appear to believe that a system of rules with enforcement is more reliable and more equitable than systems based on economic motivation;
- environmental groups sometimes resist economic instruments because 'they treat the environment like property';
- established firms like the biases against new firms that must meet the

higher 'new source pollution standards'; and
● the present value of costs to the firm may be lower under the current system (purchase of equipment plus operating costs) than under charges or tradable permits (equipment plus operating costs plus charges or purchase of permits).

On the other hand, why are MBIs not more widely used? Again the literature suggests the following reasons:

● uncertainty on the parts of both authorities and polluters about the effects of untried systems, especially taxes;
● possible high transactions costs in discharge permit trading;
● administrators and legislators' fear of 'losing control'.

BIBLIOGRAPHY

European Environmental Agency (EEA) (1996), *Environmental Taxes, Implementation and Environmental Effectiveness*, Copenhagen: EEA.
Farrow, S. (1995), 'Comparing economic and administrative methods: the US experience', Proceedings of the Economics Instruments for Sustainable Development Workshop, Prague: Ministry of the Environment of the Czech Republic.
Hahn, R.W. and G.L. Hester (1989), 'Marketable permits: lessons for theory and practice', *Ecology Law Quarterly*, **16**, 361–406.
Howe, C.W. (1993), 'The US environmental policy experience: a critique with suggestions for the European Community', *Environmental Resource Economics*, **3**, 359–79.
IFO (Institute for Economic Research) (1994), 'Inventory on subsidies for environmental purposes', draft final report, on behalf of The Commission of the European Union.
OECD (1989), *Economic Instruments for Environmental Protection*, Paris: OECD.
OECD (1991), *Environmental Policy: How to Apply Economic Instruments*, Paris: OECD.
OECD (1993), *Taxation and Environment: Complementary Policies*, Paris: OECD.
OECD (1994), *Managing the Environment: the Role of Economic Instruments*, Paris: OECD.
OECD (1995), *Environmental Taxes in OECD Countries: Progress in the 1990s*, Paris: OECD.
OECD (1996), *Implementation Strategies for Environmental Taxes*, Paris: OECD.
OECD (1997a), *Evaluating Economic Instruments for Environmental Policy*, Paris: OECD.
OECD (1997b), *Environmental Taxes and Green Tax Reform*, Paris: OECD.
Sprenger, R.U. (1996), 'The use of taxes and charges in environmental policy: the case of Germany', paper presented at the National Tax Association Panel Discussion on the Prospects for Environmental Taxation, San Francisco.
Tietenberg, T.H. (1998), 'Tradable permits and the control of air pollution – lessons from the United States', *Zeitschrift für angewandte Umweltforschung*, **9**, 11–31.

PART II

Politics and institutions

2. Designing and introducing green taxes: institutional dimensions

Mikael Skou Andersen

Unlike theorists, policy analysts are not free to make simplifying assumptions but must consider how policy instruments are effectively constrained by political, administrative and other institutional factors – and by people's attempts to manipulate these factors in their favour (Majone, 1989).

INTRODUCTION

Economic and market-based instruments (MBIs) like taxes and charges were not commonly applied for environmental protection purposes until the end of the 20th century. Japan was a well-known pioneer in this field, as a successful tax on SO_2-emissions was introduced in 1974 (Weidner, 1986; Nishimura, 1989; Matsuno and Ueta, this volume, Chapter 10). However, mainly west European countries such as the Netherlands, the Nordic countries and, to some extent also France, began to more systematically explore and use economic instruments during the 1980s and 1990s, partly in response to the implementation deficits of traditional methods of environmental regulation, but also to raise money for environmental protection purposes (Organisation for Economic Co-operation and Development (OECD), 1994a; 1995). Since their conversion to market economies around 1990 the east European countries also entered into the field of environmental management by incentives (OECD, 1994b). Finally, on the brink of the 1990s major European countries like Germany, the UK and Italy gradually ventured towards more systematic increases of taxation of energy and pollution (Tindale and Holtham, 1996; *Environment Watch Western Europe* (*EWWE*), 1999). The introduction of green taxes and charges has nevertheless rarely gone unnoticed, as the dispute to some extent has shifted from the ends to the means of environmental policy.

While support for the introduction of such instruments has been fairly broad, mainly in the expectation of more effective alleviation of environmental problems, interest groups of varying economic origin have objected to the specific distribution of tax burdens and their possible side-effects (AIM, 1996; Freeman, 1996; Walcot and Kohlhase, 1996). Concerns have been raised about the impact on the competitiveness of enterprises subject to environmental taxation, and target groups have frequently succeeded in achieving exemptions or influencing the design of environmental taxes in order to diminish their own burden. In addition, policy-makers have generally entrusted tax authorities, often unfamiliar with environmental technicalities, with the responsibility for designing the new taxes and charges and to provide proposals for the rates, and they have often merged fiscal, environmental and administrative considerations in a rather pragmatic way. Ministries of Finance appreciate the new flow of revenue into their treasuries generated by environmental taxes and charges (in some countries more than 10 per cent of public revenue), but have also been inclined to find ways to avoid the tax erosion effect that could result from significant environmental improvements.

On this background it is hardly surprising that a number of environmental taxes and charges have failed to deliver fully on their promises. With a few notable exceptions, the entire process of designing and implementing green taxes and charges has boldly contrasted the simple blackboard exercises used by environmental economists to estimate externalities and impose taxes. It may be recalled that, according to a more textbook loyal approach, an environmental tax should reflect as accurately as possible the marginal external damage to the environment, as determined in a valuation procedure (Baumol and Oates, 1988; Pearce and Turner, 1990; Perman *et al.*, 1997). The tax should then be fixed at a uniform rate per unit of pollutant, in order to ensure an efficient response at the corresponding level of marginal abatement costs. In this way the external costs of environmental degradation can be internalized in market transactions, and allow the economic actors to calculate such costs into their market transactions. In the medium and long term the changes in prices thus induced can lead to technological innovations (dynamic efficiency) which may eventually create new employment opportunities and improve competitiveness (the so-called double dividend) (Bohm, 1997; O'Riordan, 1997).

Environmental economists have been surprised to learn how difficult it has been to maintain a supposedly straightforward approach in the design and introduction of economic instruments (OECD, 1994c, 1997). To the economist, the political and administrative processes through which environmental taxes are introduced often seem to be 'intractable, chaotic and even haphazard' (to paraphrase one experienced OECD consultant). However, the difficulties of properly implementing economic incentives relate not only to the political circumstances but also to certain core difficulties with neoclassical environmental economics and its assumptions.

From the point of view of the political scientist the actual creation and operation of green market incentives has been, in fact, a somewhat less casual process than what an intuitive observation may suggest. What may appear irrational at first glance is, in fact, an outcome characterized by specific patterns of interaction among the actors and institutions of public regulation involved. A number of useful concepts and theories can be applied to improve our understanding of some of the possible difficulties connected with the application of green taxes and charges. First, however, it is useful to consider some of the shortcomings of environmental economics.

INSTITUTIONAL COMPLEXITIES

Policy Failures

While the initial background for the use of economic instruments was the theory of market failures – pollution externalities representing such failures – it has become clear that next to market failures, also policy failures are significant in generating environmental externalities (Mitnick, 1980; Jänicke, 1990; OECD, 1992). Policy failures, for example, within agriculture, transport and energy policies which involve massive transfers of subsidies, are liable to engender perverse structural effects that tend to multiply the external effects that accrue from market failures *per se*. Even environmental policy itself has at times served to reinforce rather than reduce pollution (policies of dilution by longer pipes and so on).

Among environmental economists there is now increasing concern about the perverse effects of subsidies, and the standard response is to seek to remove such distortions. However, this approach does not seem to fully recognize that, within sectoral policy domains like agricultural policies, energy policies or transport policies, the 'clients' of public policies have acquired substantial definition powers that make it difficult to remove subsidies. It is, therefore, complicated to introduce economic instruments without an appropriate analysis and understanding of the incentives and rewards such instruments may deduce in the complex settings of regulations and subsidies. Consider the example of a fertilizer tax, which will provide farmers with an incentive to reduce nitrate flows. In practice, such a tax would be up against the incentives of the entire Common Agricultural Policy of the European Union (EU) with its emphasis on specialization and intensification. It is fair to question whether relatively minor price changes will be sufficient to induce the desired change of behaviour. Institutions, that is, planning procedures, property rights or intervention prices, clearly restrict the desired responses to environmental taxation.

The rational decision-maker

Second, policies and instruments – environmental or otherwise – are not designed by a single decision-maker possessing complete information. Clifford Russell, former Chair of the American Association of Environmental Economists, has pointed out how environmental economics as a discipline originated in the US water resource economics of the early 1960s. In that context, and in a (pre-Vietnam) period of unquestioned executive decision-making, there was a natural tendency to drift into a set of assumptions regarding the single decision-maker (Russell, 1994).

However, the main problem is that there is no single decision-maker who can decide to apply specific policy instruments in accordance with a coherent and rational analysis. Many different actors, with different perceptions and interests, are engaged in policy-making. Each acts according to his or her own perception of rationality. To paraphrase Allison (1971), the decision-maker 'stands where he sits', which is to say that his or her position largely depends on his or her institutional or organizational affiliation. As a result there will be conflicting views about what constitutes the proper use and design of policy instruments, and the outcome is more often than not an ambiguous compromise. In the joint process of decision-making, policy-makers may decide to design policies and apply instruments in ways that no individual policy-maker would regard as suitable or rational.

Packages of policy instruments

Third, the expectations regarding economic efficiency are based on achieving an optimum by using the environmental tax as a single policy instrument, without additional instruments or administrative arrangements. While this assumption has unquestionably facilitated the formal analysis, Baumol and Oates (1988, p. 22) may have gone too far by claiming that the formal analysis was 'not meant to be theory for theory's sake. (The) prime concern is policy'. Ordinary markets do not function in a vacuum, and simulated markets with green taxes and charges are, therefore, unlikely to do so either. It is not a regrettable circumstance that economic instruments are used in combination with other policy instruments, but rather an inevitable fact.

Environmental taxes and charges are not introduced in a vacuum, because other regulations and basic institutions are already in place. The background to these regulations and institutions is often a certain historical development which lead to the institutionalization of vested interests. Among political scientists it is acknowledged that choice of policy instrument is context bound (Vogel, 1986; Linder and Peters, 1989; Howlett, 1991). The choice of a particular policy instrument for a given purpose tends to reflect the institutional background of specific political systems and their traditions or paths of regulatory development. The same rule applied in two different contexts is likely to have different impacts, just as the same relative price change on two different markets would be likely to have different effects (North, 1990). In either case the institutional preconditions will vary, and since the change, whether of the rule or the price, is only marginal, the outcome is also most likely to differ. On this background political scientists see few chances for developing a grand policy instrument theory, valid at all times and in all places.

For a more successful application of environmental taxes and charges we need to pay more attention to some of those dimensions that have thus far not been addressed by mainstream environmental economics, that is, the political, administrative and other institutional factors (Andersen, 1994, 1999). It is on this background that an institutional approach to the application of environmental taxes and charges is presented, and not least in recognition of the positive potential impact that well-designed environmental taxes and charges may have on sustainable development. A more systematic understanding of the political economy of instrument choice can, therefore, be helpful.

THE ROLE OF INSTITUTIONS

New theoretical perspectives on the relationship between the economy and the natural environment have been developed in recent years, but mainly within the rather loose paradigm of so-called ecological economics (Daly and Cobb, 1994). Environmental economics as such is a sub-discipline which has remained rather firmly anchored in the tradition of neoclassical economics. The new institutional economics, which has penetrated into other sub-disciplines like industrial economics, has barely made an impact on the development of environmental economics. The reason for this development is probably that environmental economics, although not an entirely young sub-discipline, still faces numerous challenges in developing its core methodologies for valuation of externalities and in building econometric and general equilibrium models for forecasts, as well as in dealing with a number of innovative issues such as the 'double dividend' of environmental taxation. The shift of perspective from a closed economy to an open and global economy has provided sufficient challenges, and there has been little reason for departing from the mainstream approach (Carraro and Siniscalco, 1997).

The absence of institutional reflections in environmental economics is striking, since the work of Ronald Coase on property rights and environmental externalities counts as one of the primary sources of new institutional economics (Coase, 1960, 1988). While Coase's argument provided the theoretical basis for the development of tradable pollution permits, the differences between tradable permits and tax/charge instruments have been explored chiefly within the neoclassical paradigm and without considering the more far-reaching implications of the institutional approach, although a few exceptions to this general pattern can be found (Bromley, 1991; Vatn, this volume, Chapter 6).

Coase, who belongs to the law and economics tradition, pointed out that market mechanisms (to which green taxes present a correction) do not function in a vacuum, but that institutions, in particular property rights, need to be defined first. Property rights represent an institutional mechanism which defines who owns or controls what resources, and hence who is subject to and who the cause of so-called externalities. Coase distinguished between private and common property rights, as did Garrett Hardin (1968), and this distinction was extended by Bromley (1991), who clarified that common property could have three meanings: state property rights, open access (lack of property rights), and true common property, that is, shared ownership. Although these contributions were significant in demonstrating the role of institutions, they were primarily concerned with one type of institution, that is, property rights. A more comprehensive institutional approach is needed in order to extend the list of institutional factors and to specify the relations between the political and economic actors and such institutions.

In order to achieve this purpose it is necessary to differentiate among different types of institutions. New economic institutionalism draws on insights from sociological institutionalism as both traditions make a distinction between formal and informal institutions. The formal institutions encompass rules, for instance procedures, conventions and organizations (March and Olsen, 1989). In new economic institutionalism a further distinction is made between political institutions like constitutions and legislation, which in turn settle the economic institutions, such as property rights (North, 1990). The informal institutions are beliefs, paradigms, codes and culture (March and Olsen, 1989), or routines, habits, traditions and culture (North, 1990) (Table 2.1). In the broadest sense institutions refer to rules which constrain the choices available to decision-makers. Institutions create transaction costs, that is, the search, information, bargaining and decision costs, as well as the costs of compliance and enforcement.

The institutional approach recognizes that individual actors, whether operating in the market-place or in the political system, are constrained by institutionalized practices (Hall and Taylor, 1996). The rationality of individual actors is further constrained by limited time, resources and mental capacity to consider available options and satisficing rather than optimizing is in reality the leading criterion (Simon, 1957; North, 1993).

The path of institutional change that influences long-term evolution 'is shaped by constraints derived from the past and the sometimes unanticipated consequences of the innumerable incremental choices of entrepreneurs, which

Table 2.1   Formal and informal institutions in new institutionalism

	Formal institutions	Informal institutions
New sociological institutionalism	Procedures Conventions Organizations	Beliefs Paradigms Codes Culture
New economic institutionalism	*Political* Constitutions Legislation *Economic* Property rights	Routines Habits Traditions Culture

Sources: North (1990); March and Olsen (1989).

continually modify these constraints' (North, 1989, p. 259). Thus there is also an opportunity structure associated with institutions. Institutions may serve to reduce transaction costs, both in the economic and the political system, by providing a set of templates for action and choice. Institutions may in some instances serve as comfortable vehicles for change if new instruments and solutions are developed along lines that conform to the more or less standard operating procedures of regulation. It is this very duality of constraints and possibilities which is so intriguing to explore.

Before the possible influence of institutions on economic instruments for environmental policy is considered, a necessary distinction is put forward here. Because different institutions are at play it is proposed to differentiate between the decision-making process, where economic instruments are agreed upon and designed by policy-makers, and the implementation phase, where economic instruments are introduced with certain expectations regarding the response of the economic agents. The distinction is essentially between the political process, where economic instruments are introduced and negotiated, and the economic process, where adaptations to price incentives take place. It may seem ambitious to comprehend both the political and the economic processes under the same theoretical perspective, but by distinguishing between decision-making and implementation we believe it is possible. In addition, it is important to clarify the difference between interests and institutions, as economists tend to confuse interest groups with institutions.

Consider the cost-benefit ratio of participation in the policy process. Wilson (1980) has pointed out that environmental regulation belongs to a category of public intervention in which the costs tend to be concentrated on specific groups, while the benefits (of a cleaner environment) are diffused onto the entire electorate or corps of taxpayers. In more traditional types of regulation, for instance agriculture or business, costs and benefits are distributed in the reverse; while the benefits (of regulation) are concentrated on a specific group, the costs are dispersed. For traditional regulations this asymmetric distribution has often caused a client-like relationship to develop between regulators and regulatees – the concentration of benefits in certain target groups provides a strong incentive for these to become involved in legislative activity (for example, Italian pasta producers on the EU intervention price for durum wheat), while the general public does not care much. Wilson argues that it is rational for average taxpayers not to involve themselves in decision-making because their direct personal benefits of diminished transfers to the clients of public regulation will be insignificant. According to Wilson, a conventional client-like relationship among the target groups and the environmental regulators does not exist; in fact, the emergence of environmental regulation requires the presence of collective policy entrepreneurs demanding public intervention.

The perceived concentration of the costs associated with environmental taxes and charges on specific target groups provides a strong case for lobbyism from such groups, while the dispersal of the expected benefits provide few incentives for other groups to become strongly involved in the details of environmental taxation. The improved environmental quality which results from any tax will be marginal to an individual member of society. Collective groups like environmental NGOs that act as policy entrepreneurs or watchdogs have more incentives to engage in legislative activity, but they will often lack the sufficiently detailed knowledge needed to successfully influence decision-making.

Although they may affect decision-making in quite significant ways, political and economic interests do not in themselves constitute institutions, according to mainstream political science. Interests are not rules, but over time interests become institutionalized. When different interests bargain about public policies, each of them will search for outcomes that can help secure a stronger position in future negotiations. In the give-and-take process of public policy-making, vested interests will seek to consolidate their position by ensuring that procedures, norms or organizations will strengthen their future bargaining power. Vested interests can, for instance, demand influence on the implementation processes, or they can ensure that organizations are established that will be beneficial to their own interests. Institutions are rules, and decision-making is to some extent also a question of making the rules for future political games.

Policy-makers who want to introduce economic instruments do not operate on a clean slate, but act on the background of regulatory realities that represent the compromises of the past which are not easily reshuffled. In some cases such regulatory realities are linked with more deep-seated national policy styles and express institutionalized patterns of interaction among regulatory authorities and private entities, as well as between different levels of government (Vogel, 1986; Andersen, 1994). The transaction costs of renegotiating entire regulatory packages or traditions generally tend to preclude more comprehensive reforms of regulatory structures, which is why economic instruments are often introduced only at the margins, that is, as supplements to existing regulations.

In accordance with North (1989; 1990; 1993), it is proposed to view the economic market as being, to a large extent, shaped by political decisions and regulations, and not as an independent and 'free' market *per se*. Public regulations, mainly belonging to the category of formal institutions, affect and constrain transactions among individual market actors and affect relative price levels – and they also constrain the scope for the adaptation of market actors to green taxes and charges. MBIs may indeed provide incentives, but the absence of regulatory review may cause existing regulations to create a filter which, in turn, reduces the intended incentive to be generated by the green tax or charge.

In addition to the set of institutions set up by the political and regulatory system there are meso- and micro-level institutions and institutionalized practices which refer to individual sectors of the economy or even individual firms.

Essentially, environmental economics assumes that the actor subject to the environmental tax is unitary, rational and profit-maximizing. It may be stipulated that rational action (that is, response to the environmental tax or charge) is constrained by available time, resources and mental capacity needed to consider all available options, and that satisficing rather than profit-maximization is thus the leading criterion. It may also be noted that many companies and households subject to environmental taxes are in effect collective, rather than individual unitary actors, and hence that different individuals with varying perceptions and interests are engaged in making decisions on how to respond to the imposed environmental taxes or charges. This perspective allows us to extend the analysis of decision-making to market-place actors in general, and to observe that they, too, are biased towards standard operating procedures. A company, a farm or even a household is an organization, not an individual, and their response to price signals will depend on collective decisions or at least collective behaviour. Within a company there are different departments or units who all make claims on available resources for investments or increased staff. Although the overall target is to maximize profits, there will be different ideas about how to achieve that target, depending on the position and experiences of individual decision-makers.

DESIGN PROBLEMS: SOME COMMON SYNDROMES

What guidance does environmental economics offer concerning the design of environmental taxes? Generally speaking only little, because, as Hahn (1996, p. 129) points out, environmental economics 'often emphasises elegance at the expense of realism'. The Cambridge environmental economist, Terry Barker (1996, p. xv), maintains that:

> Only those problems capable of a developed mathematical treatment of a rather limited kind are represented. It is quite possible, and in my view likely, that much of economic life is incapable of being represented in a mathematical formulation that uses the tools adopted by most economists today.

In order to introduce an environmental tax, decisions need to be taken on at least five significant issues: the tax base, the tax rate, the revenue disposal, the tax agent and linkage with other policy instruments (Andersen, 1995) (Table 2.2). Neoclassical environmental economics offers little guidance on these issues, except on tax rate and to some extent revenue disposal. However, there are opportunities for various interests and institutions to influence decisions on all five items.

The tendency towards granting exemptions to the largest polluters, while the small and less influential 'baker-masters' are taxed more heavily, follows from Wilson's basic interest group asymmetry. Indeed in the Netherlands, the energy tax applies only to 'small-users', while large energy-intensive industries are exempted (Vermeend and van der Vaart, 1998, p. 25). Although such exemptions might be helpful in maintaining a level playing-field for export-oriented industries, the exemptions are believed to cause distortions. Opportunities for pollution reductions are not exploited at the same marginal costs. The same can be said about the Belgian pesticide tax which applies to individual consumers, but not to farmers (De Clercq, 1997). In Denmark the CO_2-tax operates with different rates for different parts of industry (Ministry of Finance, 1995). Although no outright exemptions have been granted, the result may, nevertheless, impact on the socio-economic effectiveness of the scheme. The baker-master syndrome may be seen mainly as a result of effective lobbying by large and powerful firms, and as a result of institutionalized patterns of regulation for export-oriented industries.

A related phenomenon is the recurrent tendency to distort the tax base (twist syndrome). The initial motivation for an environmental tax may get lost or watered down in the process of designing the tax base. The tendency to tax

Table 2.2   Design syndromes of green taxes and charges

Tax base	*Baker-master syndrome* Differentiation of tax base which exempts large and politically powerful polluters, but not small or middle-sized polluters (at baker-master level)
	Twist syndrome Tax base adopted according to administrative feasibility, but the twist in tax base distorts desired environmental incentive
Tax rate	*Fiscal syndrome* Rate of tax is set to raise a specific revenue fixed by the fiscal authorities; the tax rate does not reflect external costs or the intention to reach a specific environmental target
Revenue disposal	*Linkage syndrome* In return for acceptance of a tax or charge the revenue is hypothecated, so that it remains under the control of those liable to the tax
Tax agent	*Agent syndrome* Competence for tax collection assigned to public authority with little or no experience in such matters, or who regard green taxes and charges as peripheral to their core business
Link with other policy instruments	*Entangling syndrome* Neglect of interplay with and entangling in other policy instruments, such as planning requirements, defined competencies or subsidies. Economic instruments added 'at the margin' of existing regulations, thus causing a filter on the desired price incentive

electricity consumption at the consumer level, rather than taxing specific fuels according to their CO_2-content at power plant level, represents a prominent and frequent type of tax base twist. In Denmark the pesticide tax has become value-based, thus not reflecting the toxicity of various pesticides. It was modelled on the basis of experiences with the perfumery tax which was value-based and had been in place for more than 50 years. The tax nevertheless requires a comprehensive system of official seals on each container of pesticide sold. Bureaucratic interests (familiarity with standard operating procedures in the Tax and Customs Agency) appears to explain this outcome (Andersen, 1995). The problem with the value-based tax is that if older pesticides tend to be cheaper than newer ones (with uncovered research and development expenditures), it may provide an unintended incentive not to apply innovative and potentially less harmful pesticides.

Frequently, environmental tax rates are set according to the fiscal requirements, not according to a valuation of environmental externalities or a desired environmental target (fiscal syndrome). Against the opposition to environmental taxes and charges by various target groups, the main governmental motivation is to secure a specific revenue, either for the general budget or for specific expenditures. Gasoline prices, for instance, are fixed somewhere between the fiscal needs and the fear of negative voter reactions.

The linkage syndrome refers to a counterbalancing mechanism employed against the opposition to specific environmental taxes and charges. The revenue from many environmental taxes and charges have been hypothecated or earmarked for specific purposes, either directly for environmental-purpose funds, or indirectly to lower other distortionary taxes. However, the linkage syndrome refers to the tendency for subgroups among those liable to the environmental tax to seek to obtain 'their' compensation in an almost overscrupulous way, matching as exactly as possible the costs imposed by the tax. The negotiations on the use of the revenue from the UK landfill tax and the design of the recent German energy tax are examples of this tendency.

The agent syndrome refers to the choice of tax agent, that is, the authority charged with the collection of the tax. The collection of the historical water charges in France and the Netherlands were vested in special-purpose water agencies, who had a long-standing experience both in water management and in collecting payments (Andersen, 1994, 1999). However, in more recent cases the collection of environmental taxes and charges has been turned over to authorities with little capacity to deal with the technicalities of such taxes, or who regard it as a relatively minor activity. In Sweden the Environmental Protection Agency was notoriously ineffective in their collection of a battery charge, because that agency had no previous experience in tax collection (Ministry of the Environment and National Resources, 1994). In other cases national tax inspectorates have failed to perform professionally because they regarded the revenue flows from such taxes as insignificant.

Finally, the entangling syndrome refers to the lack of thorough analyses of the interplay between economic instruments and other types of policy instrument. The reason that decision-makers tend to abstain from a more general review and reform of the regulations surrounding a specific tax seems to be that such a reform would rip open established compromises and challenge established interests. Such an approach would increase the transaction costs associated with introducing economic instruments. Waste taxes, for instance, are often imposed according to weight and collected at landfills and incinerators, who are expected to pass on both costs and incentive to their customers. However, as many customers pay according to a fixed volume of waste (the size of their garbage bin), the tax is not reflected in the costs of individual waste producers. In fact, existing waste regulations more or less preclude payment on a per weight basis. These regulations reflect a fine-tuned regulatory waste management scheme based on an understanding with the local municipalities, who are sceptical about national waste taxes, and will not be easy to change without their consent (Andersen, this volume, Chapter 12).

Not all these syndromes apply equally or simultaneously to all environmental taxes and charges. On the other hand, they do seem to constitute a well-known pattern, and on the basis of previous experience it is fair to state that hardly any environmental taxes or charges are not subject to one or more of the design syndromes. The political economy of economic instruments seems to explain why such design failures are relatively common.

IMPLEMENTATION PROBLEMS: THE MATRIX OF POSSIBLE RESPONSES

On the basis of the design failures of green taxes and charges it is both tempting and rather common to conclude that such deficiencies will prevent MBIs from achieving the desired internalization of environmental damages in market transactions. However, it is essential to acknowledge that such *ex-ante* expectations are based on the strict rational choice assumption of neoclassical economics, and that some of the design failures may prove to be less detrimental if it is considered how institutions can affect the behaviour of market actors in the economic sphere.

Figure 2.1 provides an overview of available response options according to the rational actor model of target group behaviour (Goldstone, 1982). It should first be noted that within the rational actor model paradigm several response options are available, other than the direct reduction of pollution or consumption of natural resources in response to an environmental tax or charge. The table differentiates between industry response, market response and actor response. Companies do not have to undertake pollution control in response to an economic incentive; they are also able to pass on the tax to their customers (in particular where a monopoly or oligopoly exists, for example, in the domestic market), or to absorb it. Consumers also have several options and the market can adapt in a number of ways. It, therefore, seems to be important to note that it cannot be concluded from the possible absence of environmental effects that the tax was not succesfully internalized in market transactions. A number of response options must be considered.

Now, if the rational actor model in the market sphere is relaxed in the same way as in the political sphere, to what extent will this have implications for the

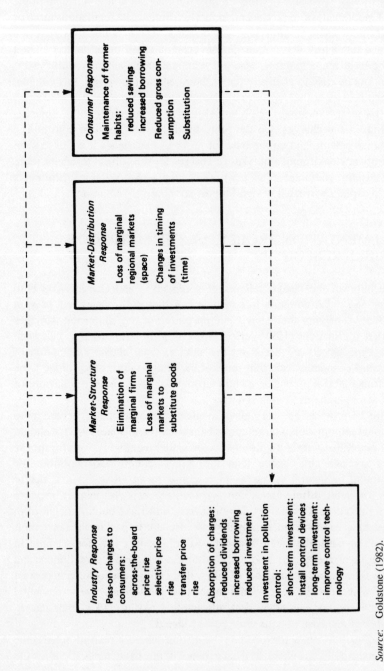

Industry Response
Pass-on charges to consumers:
across-the-board price rise
selective price rise
transfer price rise

Absorption of charges:
reduced dividends
increased borrowing
reduced investment

Investment in pollution control:
short-term investment: install control devices
long-term investment: improve control technology

Market-Structure Response
Elimination of marginal firms
Loss of marginal markets to substitute goods

Market-Distribution Response
Loss of marginal regional markets (space)
Changes in timing of investments (time)

Consumer Response
Maintenance of former habits:
reduced savings
increased borrowing
Reduced gross consumption
Substitution

Source: Goldstone (1982).

Figure 2.1 Response options for evaluating the consequences of pollution charges

expectations on the effects of economic instruments? A company environ-mental manager will have to compete with other departments for resources. The sales manager may perhaps argue that reduced profits can be offset by increased prices or marketing efforts, in particular if the rate of the environmental tax is modest. If the company is small and its production technology supplier-dominated, it is not likely that responses based on innovation can be achieved within the framework of the firm itself. Behind the menu of response options in Figure 2.1 stand different stakeholders who are likely to opt for different response strategies.

If the company does not have an environmental manager or management system, it probably does not have information procedures on environmental costings, and the general management may thus lack the information required to make a rational allocation of resources according to internal pay-off. There are many companies in which individual production units have little or no information about the production costs related to items like energy consumption and waste disposal, and who hence lack the incentive for or possibility to respond in a cost-effective manner to green taxes and charges. Even in a household individual members may lack information or incentives to reduce the use of energy, water or waste disposal facilities (teenagers may care less about the amount of time they shower than does the parent who pays the water and heating bills). There is a strong tendency towards inertia, that is, to stick to standard operating procedures. Indeed, when the Cellule de Prospective of Commission President, Jacques Delors, investigated produc-tion management and environmental management in a number of European and Japanese companies, they were surprised to learn that even large companies were prone to Downs' cycle of organizational rigidity as long as no external shocks required a change in procedures (Rogers, 1996). Research of waste management practices in individual firms has confirmed that many companies lack even the most simple information systems necessary to respond rationally to waste taxes and charges (Andersen, Dengsø and Brendstrup, 1997).

Thus, transaction costs are involved when collective units adapt to changed price signals. The magnitude of these transaction costs, or even the perception of their magnitude, may alter the balance between what pays off and what does not. Faced with an energy tax or a waste disposal tax a company may choose not to respond if it assumes that the transaction costs of responding will consume possible dividends in the short term, or simply that the risk of such an imbalance is considered too great or burdensome.

The prediction is that individuals act as rationally as they can on the basis of their perceived interests, previous experiences and institutional background (Knott and Miller, 1987). Simple problems, complete information, repetitive situations and high motivation will increase the chances that their behaviour corresponds to that predicted by rational choice (North, 1993). Since environmental taxation is innovative, decision-makers have to review their procedures from a completely new perspective, a circumstance that is likely to increase search and information costs. Problems of appropriate environmental management are far from simple; they require new procedures for information-gathering, they confront companies or households with new challenges and motivations differ according to level of environmental awareness. Hence at least in the initial stages of environmental taxation, we should be careful not to expect that rational choices will automatically prevail.

WHY AND HOW SHOULD WE EXPECT ENVIRONMENTAL TAXES AND CHARGES TO WORK AT ALL?

How can one expect environmental taxes and charges marked by substantial exemptions or reductions, the tax rates of which tend to be rather low, where the revenue is under the control of target groups, which are managed by not always competent agencies, that are poorly integrated with other policy instruments and whose effects are constrained by formal and informal institutions to work?

If the significance of institutions and transaction costs is acknowledged, specific aspects of current types of environmental taxation can begin to be appreciated. Consider the interaction between the six design syndromes and the path-dependent constrained rational actor, and the following observations can be made.

According to the principle of abatement at equal marginal cost we would expect exemptions (baker-master syndrome) to tap into possible cost-effective responses to environmental taxation. Since large companies are generally more energy and resource-intensive, they have historically paid more attention to energy and material efficiency, whereas this has been a less pressing problem for many small and middle-sized companies. Empirical research has shown that, counterintuitively, the marginal abatement costs for CO_2-control are actually lower for small and middle-sized companies compared to industries in chemicals and steel production. A similar tendency is reported for waste management. Hence, the greater share of the potential internalization of external costs seems to be available to those companies that are least frequently subject to exemptions from the tax base. The reason appears to be that the search for energy and material efficiency is more of a standard operating procedure among large companies, that is, a repetitive consideration, and they also have more established routines of environmental management. Since many tax rates are rather low, their effect may be to provide a psychological signal to polluters to pay more attention to their external effects, rather than a fully-fledged pricing of externalities. The twist syndrome is actually more of a problem because it distorts the desired incentives towards changing behaviour.

Environmentalists and industrialists complain that the dividend of environmental taxes accrue to the treasury (fiscal syndrome). Environmental economists are often disappointed to find that environmental taxes are fixed according to the need for revenue, and not on the basis of a valuation of environmental goods and evils. They neglect that valuation methods remain in their infantry and do not yet allow for a more precise valuation that could lead to the setting of more precise environmental tax rates. The few valuation exercises on specific environmental taxes have been thoroughly disputed. They tend to simplify the actual number and complexity of external effects to those that can be quantified in monetary terms. Important externalities such as effects on biodiversity and human health are disregarded. The alternative is to employ the Baumol and Oates second-best solution which prescribes that tax rates be fixed in order to ensure the attainment of specific emission targets. This method is complicated by the absence of information on relevant elasticities.

These circumstances leave few choices but to fix tax rates in a pragmatic way. A particular tax rate could be perceived rather as an experiment in a longer trial-and-error process, in which governments can adjust such rates in accordance with the degree of attainment of specific targets. Once Ministries of Finance have come to appreciate the revenue flow into the treasury of green taxes and charges, this appreciation generates its own institutional dynamic in securing an adjustment of rates in an upward direction.

Robert Hahn (1991; Bressers and Huitema, this volume, Chapter 4) has argued that environmentalists and industrialists have a common interest in earmarking or hypothecation of revenue from environmental taxes and/or charges. From the point of view of policy-makers this may also serve to relax opposition (linkage syndrome). From an economic point of view an actual shift in taxation objects, that is, the replacement of employers' social security contributions with environmental taxes is regarded as more beneficial because of differences in the associated distortions. From the point of view of industry (and labour) a direct tax shift is more attractive than hypothecation because the degree of freedom for revenue disposal is greater. From an environmental point of view, however, hypothecation or earmarking can provide an effective lubrication of the response mechanisms to environmental taxes and charges. If the revenue is earmarked for information mechanisms it serves to reduce transaction costs, as was the case with the French water charges which were rather low and insignificant, but provided revenue for a concerted and very effective effort among the largest polluters and the French river basin agencies in the control of waste water (Andersen, 1994; Barraqué, this volume, Chapter

11). Essentially, the reduction of transaction costs will tend to increase the elasticities of response functions, and hence enable lower tax rates than would otherwise have been levied. In turn lower tax rates will ease political acceptability.

The choice of tax agent depends to a large extent on traditional methods of tax collection, but also on whether taxes are fiscal or hypothecated. Despite the merits of hypothecated taxes in easing transaction costs, the possible opportunities can be forgone if the right agent is not chosen (agent syndrome). There are a number of examples of new special-purpose agencies having been established to assume responsibility for the collection of environmental charges without having the required professionalism (such as French ADEME (Agence de l'Environnement et de la Maîtrise de l'Energie) for waste management). Much seems to depend on national standard operating procedures for tax collection, a payment much prone to free-riding, according to the taxation literature. In countries with effective national tax agencies, the collection of environmental taxes and charges may benefit from their often quite rigorous approach. The difference between the power and position of the tax inspector as compared to that of the environmental inspector provides an independent institutional explanation for the strength of economic incentives versus the rule-obeying approach. However, there is also a danger that tax inspectors regard environmental charges and taxes as a marginal and somewhat peculiar field of activity, and to which they, therefore, devote less attention.

Negligence of the regulatory framework implies that the incentive of the tax may have to pass through a comprehensive filter which distorts and impairs the price signal (entangling syndrome), but the constructive solution is not a dismantling of regulations, but a well-designed interplay between price incentives and rules. The rules are necessary to define the terms of transactions and will depend on the type of market concerned, for example, the sector of the economy being targeted. Rules involve a range of issues from property rights to distribution of competence. There are few cases of a non-intentional constructive interplay between price incentives and rules; rule-making tends to represent a somewhat rigid institutionalization of the compromises of the past. The elasticity of response to energy taxation will be higher, for instance, if there are specific rules that define the premises for the use and marketing of renewables, for example, support for wind energy. In the absence of such rules transaction costs may impair some of the desired responses.

CONCLUSIONS

It can be useful to simplify assumptions for the purpose of constructing theories. However, the standard approach in environmental economics, which depicts environmental quality as an economic resource allocation problem, is, in fact, a '*normative* theory of environmental regulation' (Cropper and Oates, 1992, p. 678). It was not meant to be theory for the sake of theory. The difficulties arise when deducing from theory to practice if too little attention is paid to the original simplifications. Freeman III *et al.* (1973, p. 10) depicted the attainment of environmental quality as both an economic and a political resource allocation problem, the resolution of which requires major changes in economic, political and legal institutions (ibid., pp. v, 45). Despite this insight in early environmental economics, 'it had by the end of the 1980s become clear that much of the original debate on economic instruments had remained too remote from the realities of the economic process and the policy arena' (OECD, 1994c, p. 35). Cropper and Oates indeed frankly acknowledge that the policy structure and analysis of applied environmental economics is a good deal more complicated than standard textbooks would suggest (Cropper and Oates, 1992, p. 700).

The purpose of this study has been to contrast the perceived design syndromes of environmental taxes and charges with insights from political science and new institutional economics. The conventional neoclassical framework of environmental economics, which involves setting one independent policy goal and the equivalent single policy instrument, imply only that economic instruments can provide economic efficiency and cost-effectiveness in a closed economy. When a shift is made from the rational actor assumption to an assumption of bounded rationality constrained by institutions, it has significant implications for the understanding of the design difficulties and the subsequent implementation capacity of economic instruments.

REFERENCES

AIM (European Brands Association) (1996), 'Economic instruments in environmental policy', paper presented at the Conference on Environmental Economic Policies: Competitiveness and Employment, Dublin, 16–17 October 1996, Brussels: AIM.

Allison, Graham T. (1971), *Essence of Decision – Explaining the Cuban Missile Crisis*, Boston: Little, Brown and Company.

Andersen, M. Skou (1994), *Governance by Green Taxes: Making Pollution Prevention Pay*, Manchester and New York: Manchester University Press.

Andersen, M. Skou (1995), 'The importance of institutions in the design and implementation of economic instruments in environmental policy', *ENV/EPOC/GEEI(95)2*, Paris: OECD Environment Directorate.

Andersen, M. Skou (1999), 'Governance by green taxes: implementing clean water policies in Europe 1970–1990', *Environmental Economics and Policy Studies*, **2** (1), 39–64.

Andersen, M.S., N. Dengsø and S. Brendstrup (1997), 'Affaldsafgiften – en *ex-post* evaluering af incitamenter og miljreffekter?', Arbejdsrapport fra Miljøstyrelsen, nr. 96, København. ('The waste tax – an *ex-post* evaluation of incentives and environmental effects', Report from Danish Environmental Protection Agency, no. 96, Copenhagen.)

Barker, T. (1996), *Space-time Economics*, Cambridge: Cambridge Econometrics.

Baumol, W.J. and W.E. Oates (1988), *The Theory of Environmental Policy*, Cambridge: Cambridge University Press.

Bohm, P. (1997), 'Environmental taxation and the double dividend: fact or fallacy?', in T. O'Riordan (ed.), *Ecotaxation*, London: Earthscan, pp. 106–24.

Bromley, Daniel W. (1991), *Environment and Economy: Property Rights and Public Policy*, Oxford: Basil Blackwell.

Carraro, C. and D. Siniscalco (eds) (1997), *New Directions in the Economic Theory of the Environment*, Cambridge: Cambridge University Press.

Coase, R.H. (1988), *The Firm, the Market and the Law*, Chicago: University of Chicago Press.

Coase, Ronald H. (1960), 'The problem of social cost', *Journal of Law and Economics*, **3**, 1–44.

Cropper, Maureen L. and Wallace E. Oates (1992), 'Environmental economics: a survey', *Journal of Economic Literature*, **XXX** (June), 675–740.

Daly, H.E. and J.B. Cobb (1994), *For the Common Good: Redirecting the Economy Toward Community, the Environment and a Sustainable Future*, Boston: Beacon Press.

De Clercq, M. (1996), 'The implementation of green taxes: the Belgian experience', in *Environmental Taxes and Charges: National Experiences and Plans*, Dublin: European Foundation for the Improvement of Living and Working Conditions, pp. 45–66.

EWWE (Environment Watch Western Europe) (1999), 'German energy tax takes effect', **8** (7), p. 9.

Freeman, R.D. (1996), 'Economic growth and industrial employment', paper presented at the Conference on Environmental Economic Policies: Competitiveness and Employment, Dublin, 16-17 October 1996, Imperial Chemical Industries PLC.

Freeman III, A. Myrick, R. Haveman and A. Kneese (1973), *The Economics of Environmental Policy*, New York: John Wiley.

Goldstone, J. (1982), 'Response options for evaluating the consequences of pollution charges', in D. Mann (ed.), *Environmental Policy Implementation*, Lexington: D.C. Heath, pp. 185–92.

Hahn, R.W. (1991), *A Primer on Environmental Policy Design*, London: Harwood Academic Publishers.

Hahn, R.W. (1996), 'Economic prescriptions for environmental problems: lessons from the United States and continental Europe', in R. Eckersley (ed.), *Markets, the State and the Environment*, London: Macmillan, pp. 129–56.

Hall, P. and R. Taylor (1996), 'Political science and the three new institutionalisms', *Political Studies*, **XLIV**, 936–57.

Hardin, Garrett (1968), 'The Tragedy of the Commons', *Science*, **162** (1), pp. 1243–8.

Howlett, Michael (1991), 'Policy instruments, policy styles and policy implementation: national approaches to theories of instrument choice', *Policy Studies Journal*, **19** (2), 1–21.

Jänicke, Martin (1990), *State Failure: the Impotence of Politics in Industrial Society*, Cambridge: Polity Press.

Knott, J. and G. Miller (1987), *Reforming Bureaucracy: the Politics of Institutional Choice*, Englewood Cliffs, NJ: Prentice-Hall.

Linder, Stephen H. and Guy Peters (1989), 'Instruments of government: perceptions and contexts', *Journal of Public Policy*, **9**, 35–58.

Majone, Giandomenico (1989), *Evidence, Argument and Persuasion in the Policy Process*, London: Yale.

March, J. and J.P. Olsen (1989), *Re-discovering Institutions*, New York: The Free Press.

Matsuno, Y. and K. Ueta (1999), 'A socio-economic evaluation of the SO$_x$ charge in Japan', this volume, Chapter 10.

Ministry of the Environment and Natural Resource (1994), *The Swedish Experience – Taxes and Charges in Environmental Policy*, Stockholm: Ministry of the Environment and Natural Resources.

Ministry of Finance (1995), *Energy Tax on Industry in Denmark*, Copenhagen: Ministry of Finance.

Mitnick, Barry (1980), *The Political Economy of Regulation*, New York: Columbia University Press.

Nishimura, H. (ed.) (1989), *How to Conquer Air Pollution: a Japanese Experience*, Amsterdam: Elsevier.

North, Douglass C. (1989), 'A transaction cost approach to historical development of politics and economies', *Journal of Institutional and Theoretical Economics*, **145**, 661–8.

North, Douglass C. (1990), *Institutions, Institutional Change, and Economic Performance*, Cambridge: Cambridge University Press.

North, Douglass C. (1993), 'What do we mean by rationality', *Public Choice*, **77**, 159–62.

OECD (1992), *Market and Government Failures in Environmental Management: the Case of Transport*, Paris: OECD.

OECD (1994a), *Environment and Taxation: the Cases of the Netherlands, Sweden and the United States*, Paris: OECD.

OECD (1994b), 'Taxation and the environment in European economies in transition', *OECD GD(94)42*, Paris: OECD

OECD (1994c), *Managing the Environment: the Role of Economic Instruments*, Paris: OECD.

OECD (1995), *Environmental Taxes in OECD Countries*, Paris: OECD.

OECD (1997), *Evaluating Economic Instruments for Environmental Policy*, Paris: OECD.

O'Riordan, T. (ed.) (1997), *Ecotaxation*, London: Earthscan.

Pearce, D. and K. Turner (1990), *Economics of Natural Resources and the Environment*, New York: Harvester Wheatsheaf.

Perman, R., Y. Ma and J. McGilvray (1997), *Natural Resource and Environmental Economics*, London: Longman.

Rogers, M. (1996), 'Micro-economic case studies on the field of business and the environment', paper presented at the Conference on Environmental Economic Policies: Competitiveness and Employment, Dublin, 16–17 October 1996.

Russell, Clifford S. (1994), 'Complex regulation and the environment: an economist's view', opening plenary speech, Governing Our Environment Conference, 17–18 November, Copenhagen.

Simon, H. (1957), *Administrative Behavior: A Study of Decision-making Processes in Administrative Organizations*, 2nd edition, New York: Macmillan.

Tindale, S. and G. Holtham (1996), *Green Tax Reform: Pollution Payments and Labour Tax Cuts*, London: Institute for Public Policy Research.

Vermeend, W. and J. van der Vaart (1998), *Greening Taxes: the Dutch Model*, Deventer: Kluwer.

Vogel, David (1986), *National Styles of Regulation: Environmental Policy in Great Britain and the United States*, Ithaca: Cornell University Press.

Walcot, C. and K. Kohlhase (1996), 'Environmental economic instruments: a business perspective', paper presented at the Conference on Environmental Economic Policies: Competitiveness and Employment, Dublin, 16–17 October 1996, European Roundtable of Industrialists.

Weidner, H. (1986), 'Japan: The success and limitations of technocratic environmental policy', *IIUG pre 86-1*, Berlin: Wissenschaftszentrum.

Wilson, James Q. (1980), *The Politics of Regulation*, New York: Basic Books.

3. Environmental innovations from the standpoint of policy analysis: from an instrumental to a strategic approach in environmental policy*

Martin Jänicke

INTRODUCTION

Theses

- When attributing specific effects on innovation to specific policy instruments, it is assumed that the state has the capability of detailed control. This idea was abandoned long ago by empirical policy research. As a rule, innovations can neither be caused nor explained (least of all on the basis of model calculations) by detailed state control.
- Nevertheless, a government's interest in the effects of its policies on innovation is highly legitimate, not least with respect to environmental protection. This interest is best served by research projects that focus on answering the question as to how the dynamic complexity of conditions promoting innovation can be influenced by environmental policy. Regulatory patterns are better explanatory tools than instruments.
- The entire process of policy formulation is of importance as far as the effectiveness of government measures is concerned. Technical innovations are more strongly induced in advance of political decisions – above all during the process of formulating objectives – than when government measures are implemented. The latter phase, however, is highly significant for the diffusion process. Both phases of the political process can be optimized with regard to a strategy of ecological modernization.

*This chapter was developed within the framework of the BMBF (German Ministry of Science) project 'Assessment of the effects of environmental policy instruments on innovation' and updated in 1999. Translated by V. Schildhauer.

Politics and institutions

Policy analysis does not concern itself with the political system as such ('polity') and its decision-making processes ('politics'), but focuses on the concrete contents of government activity ('policy'). It primarily looks at the control and management aspects of politics, and has a certain affinity to the science of public administration.

The main area of interest of policy analysis or evaluation research is the effectiveness or efficiency of political measures and programmes (Héritier, 1993; Rossi and Freeman, 1993; Prittwitz, 1994; Fischer, 1995; Bussmann *et al.*, 1997). A special area of evaluation research is concerned with the conditions needed to ensure the success of environmental policy (Kitschelt, 1983; Mayntz, 1983; Knoepfel, 1993; Jänicke and Weidner, 1995; Ricken, 1995; Wallace, 1995; Bressers and Huitema, 1996; Jänicke, 1996; Conrad, 1998) and, in this connection, takes as its subject innovations in environmental technology. The promotion of integrated environmental technology is the subject of special evaluation studies (Widmer, 1991; Balthasar and Knoepfel, 1994; Andersen and Joergensen, 1995; Coenen *et al.*, 1995).

The issue of the success conditions for action concerning environmental policy is closely related to the conditions for governmental promotion of innovations. Just like empirical innovation research, modern policy studies also emphasize the complexity and dynamics of interactions of political conditions as regards success and innovation. According to this and other studies, it is quite evident that successful environmental policy is not only the result of systematic (governmental and non-governmental) action, but of the dynamic interaction of complex conditions of action (Bressers and Klok, 1991; Jänicke and Weidner, 1995; Conrad, 1998). Central aspects are institutional context, constellation of actors, the policy learning in communications networks and systems of negotiation, policy style, the context aspect of politics and the structure of the problem to be solved (Mayntz, 1983; Jänicke, 1996).

Thus, empirical policy studies that concentrate on the success criteria of environmental policy are in contrast with established top-down concepts of political control that prevailed in the past debate on the instruments of environmental policy. This applies in particular to the effects of government policy on innovation. Recent policy studies show that government promotion of innovation is not conceivable through detailed control.

Authors like Luhmann and Willke criticized such mechanistic concepts of control at an early stage. In his essay on 'ecological communication' (1986), Luhmann pointed out the difficulties encountered by political control functions when it attempted to strike the 'response conditions' of its political addressees and do justice to their individual logic, codes and programmes. As early as 1983, Renate Mayntz pointed out that the success of a regulation, apart from the problem itself, depended on the formulated 'programme' and the interaction between the regulators and the regulated (the 'intervention field'), and that the significance of an instrument decreased when the parties involved agreed on the target (Mayntz, 1983). 'Cooperative government' and 'decentralized context control' were used as substitute formulas. In the meantime, policy analysis no longer applies the dichotomy of controlling institution and controlled object, as it is known from the customary 'perspective of legislators' (Mayntz and Scharpf, 1995).

Based on studies of the success criteria of environmental policy and empirical innovation studies (Dodgson and Rothwell, 1994; Kemp *et al.*, 1994; Hemmelskamp, 1996; Klemmer, 1999), the following research topic can be formulated. How can objectives of environmental policy be realized by means of a government innovation strategy, and which means can the government apply to significantly increase the speed of technical progress and developments that contribute to saving the environment? How can an innovation policy, which is strongly oriented towards environmental aspects (Both, 1993), do justice to the dynamic complexity of the factors of influence associated with technical change?

The question of the methods chosen by a government is also a subject of social scientific analysis. Evidently, the selection of instruments as such is less critical as regards the result than has been assumed until now, and, as a rule, it is hardly possible to make an adequate methodological distinction betwen the contribution of one single instrument and other influencing factors (or influence levels).

TWO APPROACHES OF POLICY IMPACT ANALYSIS

There are two predominant approaches to the analysis of the effectiveness of government actions: (1) the model-theoretical approach of economy; and (2) the approach of evaluation research or empirical policy analysis. The first approach generally studies the effects of political measures *ex-ante* and top-down, that is, from the point of view of the government institution issuing the measure (Sabatier, 1986). This is not usually an empirical manner of proceeding. When looked at critically, it could be said that the approach operates with too few variables and calls upon too much plausibility. The selected assumptions are open to all kinds of influences; therefore, the controversy about corresponding studies is so widespread.

Frequently, impact studies of policy analysis also begin *ex-ante* and top-down, but in their core they empirically evaluate past effects *ex-post*. They were purely accompanying research for political measures for a long time, and, consequently, related to government actions. More recent approaches, however, place the bottom-up approach entirely in the forefront and actually study the development from the effects to the causes. Thus, the evaluation is methodically open to any kind of influence factors, be they government actions or other determining factors. One possibly ensuing problem may be how to handle the high complexity, which usually is excessively simplified by the economic approach.

Policy analysis, which tries to explain the success or failure of policies *ex-post*, not only resembles the approach of empirical innovation studies but frequently relates to them. Combining the two approaches seems self-evident, in which case the policy approach would centre on policy and the innovation research would concentrate on companies. The conditions and logic of both fields of action could then be related to one another systematically. The conditions promoting innovation by companies may then be referred to as success conditions of environmental policy.

METHODOLOGICAL PROBLEMS OF MODEL CALCULATIONS

The decisive problem of the economic *ex-ante* top-down model lies in making forecasts about the effect of individual government measures. What this means will be illustrated below through an extreme example taken from one of our studies.

From 1974 to the end of the 1980s, Japanese industry had a progressive electricity tariff which, moreover, headed the list of an Organization for Economic Co-operation and Development (OECD) comparison for a long time. The reasons – expensive energy imports and capacity shortages of the power industry – are not of interest in this context.

What would an *ex-ante* economic model analysis have told us about this in 1973? Most likely, serious cost-induced competition problems would have been forecast for highly electricity-intensive industries (chemical, metallurgical industries and so on). In fact, the growth level of the chemical industry was higher than the industrial average from 1971 to 1987 (see Figure 3.1). However, electricity consumption barely increased. This is a completely atypical development when viewed in an international context (Jänicke *et al.*, 1993), and the only explanation is massive innovations. And, in this case, such innovations can primarily be attributed to the structure of the electricity tariffs, which can be compared to the influence of taxes or charges.

How can this be simulated in model calculations? A subsequent bottom-up evaluation that takes into account the actual influential factors would find this a much simpler task, naturally, since it is carried out subsequently.

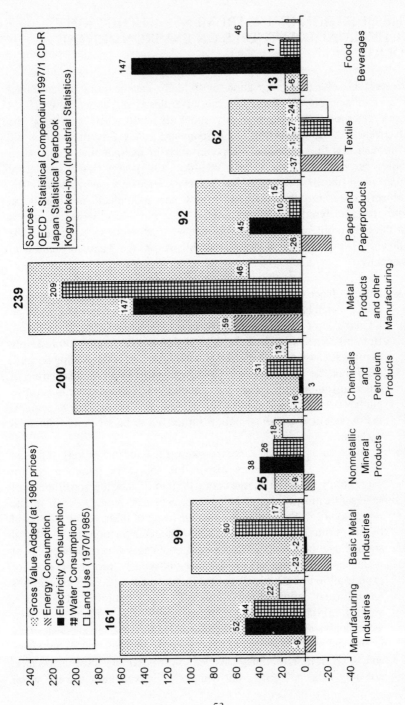

Figure 3.1 Percentage change by indicator and branch, 1971–87: Japan

THE QUESTION OF INSTRUMENTS IN THE LIGHT OF EVALUATION STUDIES ON ENVIRONMENTAL POLICY

Whereas the effect of innovation most likely can actually be attributed to a dominant control factor in the case described above, this is, as a rule, methodically incomparably more difficult when analysing the effectiveness of the instruments of environmental policy. First of all this is due to the fact that there is usually a policy mix. In international comparative studies carried out (Jänicke and Weidner, 1995) very few cases were found where the desired effect was achieved with only one measure. The problem concerning this method is how can individual instruments be isolated and analysed as regards cause and effect in a mix? However, that is not the only problem with respect to methods that needs to be solved. The following list illustrates additional problems on the basis of empirical examples:

- At first glance the high reduction in sulphur dioxide emissions in Japan can be traced back to the imposition of regulations (up to 1974) and then a charge (up to 1988) that served to compensate victims of pollution. Both instruments can even be delimited from one another impressively as regards cause and effect. The picture, however, is misleading because studies on the subject proved the effectiveness of a broad spectrum of other instruments, for example, voluntary agreements, administrative guidance and ecological information. And, finally, the energy savings, that is, not environmental policy, turned out to be a central influential variable.

- In other cases, similar successes were achieved using very different means. The Dutch agency responsible for water pollution control successfully enforced charges after 1970 to finance the construction of sewage treatment plants. In contrast Swedish pioneer work in the protection of waters (1960–80) was the result of massive subsidies paid by the central government towards the construction of municipal sewage treatment plants. However, in both cases government policy of imposing regulations was involved simultaneously. Moreover, a poll of experts attributed the success of the Dutch water conservation measures to informal administrative actions (negotiations, discussions, consulting) and inspections. Interestingly, the influence of new technology was considered insignificant. In fact, the sewage water levy in Holland more likely led to a diffusion of conventional technologies and, apart from that, it may have led to excessive investments, because not only local authorities but companies as well built sewage water treatment plants. The Swedish programme of subsidies in connection with ambitious cleaning regulations probably had a greater innovative effect. Yet, that can hardly be put forward as an argument for one or the other instrument in the face of the current state of research (Jänicke and Weidner, 1995).

- Frequently, it is not the definite choice of instrument that counts the most, but the signalizing effect of a measure as such. What is important in this respect are processes of information and communications triggered by intervention. One example of this is that 85 per cent of PCB users in Dutch industry decided to phase out their use of this product. According to a study this phase-out was not as stimulated by subsidies – which a quarter of the companies did not even claim – as by appropriate communicative and informative side-effects (Jänicke and Weidner, 1995).

- In particular, cases of environmental improvements that cannot be attributed directly to government measures, yet could be connected to informal administrative actions, give reason for methodic caution. Following the prohibition of cadmium in Sweden, increasingly critical discussions arose in Germany and German industry seriously began developing substitutes for cadmium after 1980. We have now reached a decisive point concerning the aspect of innovation. Substitutions and processes of innovative adaptation by industry often occur before the government issues a formal measure (Figure 3.2) and there is still considerable room for research in this respect. The Free University conducted a study of more than 60 hazardous substances, the production of which was limited or substituted. Only in a very few of these cases could environmentally desirable, perhaps innovative, developments be attributed to direct government measures (Jacob and Jänicke, 1996).

- Consequently, the government is often neither the only nor the decisive influential factor for promoting significant innovations in connection with environmental policy. A poll of managers in Germany and three Scandinavian countries provided the following information on external influences that caused them to actively undertake pro-ecological actions: (1) Government environmental institutions were always mentioned first, followed by (in varying order) (2) environmental associations, (3) the media, and (4) customers (Brinkmann and Kirchgeorg, 1995; Gothenburg Research Institute, 1995). The system of 'chain management', known from the trade sector, evidently plays an important role in this respect today, and it may resemble the control impulses given by the political administrative system. In many OECD countries, environmental associations have more members than do the

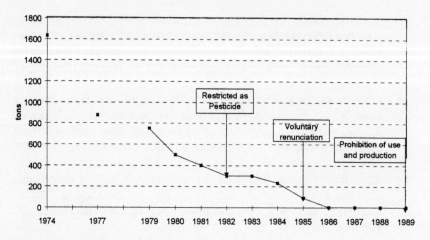

Source: Jacob and Jänicke (1998).

Figure 3.2   Consumption and regulation of PCP/PCP-na in Germany,
*   1974-89*

political parties; in fact, in some cases their membership figures can be
compared to those of trade unions (Switzerland) or go far beyond them
(the Netherlands). And they increasingly interact directly with
companies and branches of trade. Thus, the mechanistic image of
government control needs to be revised, also because of the
differentiated structures of the actors involved.

- The constellation of the actors also seems to be very significant with
  regard to innovation. Thus, for example, changes in the configuration of
  actors in the Federal Republic of Germany since 1969 also appears to
  have improved the conditions of innovation (Jänicke and Weidner,
  1997; for the USA, see Hoffmann, 1994).
- As regards the aspect of innovation, the policy style, that is, the manner
  of government intervention, may be more significant than the actual
  measure itself. In an international comparison it can be ascertained that
  successful environmental protection is most often connected with the
  imposition of regulations, permits and prohibitions (Widmer, 1991;
  Low, 1992; Jänicke and Weidner, 1995, 1997; OECD, 1996). Yet they
  have weaknesses that have been discussed in the relevant literature: low
  cost-efficiency, insufficient utilization of innovative scope, resistance of
  the groups targeted by a policy and so on. When, however, the
  imposition of a requirement is merely announced and negotiated 'in the
  hierarchical shadows', thereby avoiding, moreover, the complicated
  decision-making process, such a – prospective – regulative instrument

may offer considerable advantages. This has, meanwhile, become customary in many countries (as administrative guidance, negotiated rule-making and so on). In recent studies on innovation the flexible, business-compatible forms of environmental regulations for the most part receive quite positive evaluations (Porter and van der Linde, 1995; Wallace, 1995).

• In the light of strategy analyses, the issue of instruments must also take into account that actors learn (policy learning) in the course of time; particularly the flexibility of the instruments applied can, therefore, be decisive.

• Modern public management increasingly emphasizes the goals rather than the means (Damkowski and Precht, 1995). A corresponding orientation based on 'environmental performance goals' (OECD, 1997b, p. 19) or 'management by objectives (MbO)' (Damkowski and Precht, 1995, p. 169f.; Ministry of the Environment, 1997) is becoming prevalent in environmental policy. The flexibility shown in employing various means is a central aspect of this approach. How the targets are defined to begin with is significant with respect to the political result. If the targets are set with the consent of the most important actors, implementation will be determined and simplified accordingly. Following the Conference of Rio (1992), such processes of defining objectives gained significance (OECD, 1995; Jänicke *et al.*, 1997), primarily in cooperative environmental planning (Agenda 21). This also takes into account the circumstance that considerable social efforts are called for if an environmental policy is to be effective in future, too, and that it is neither limited to government action, nor implemented with simple patterns of action.

• Defined objectives of environmental policy, as established in national environmental policy plans, international agreements or voluntary agreements, are most likely very important with respect to promoting innovation. They define the direction of innovation and reduce the investment risks associated with technical innovations. Dialogue structures and information networks, which – as experience has shown – are important to innovation, have also been created in connection with recent cooperative environmental planning. Based on specified, scientifically founded environmental objectives and time schedules, the innovation requirements of companies can be anticipated, and being able to anticipate government measures is already of considerable importance to corporate environmental management. Cooperative target-setting processes, in turn, modify the issue of instruments or place it in a more comprehensive context.

• All in all, the effect of government instruments cannot be viewed

separately from the political process – from the time an issue becomes
a political subject (agenda-setting) to its implementation (Bressers and
Klok, 1991). Innovators in the target group can respond as the targets
are being defined, and negotiated solutions ('negotiated rule-making')
offer greater chances of success than when resistance in the target group
cannot be overcome.

TOP-DOWN AND BOTTOM-UP: POSSIBLE MEDIATION

Accordingly, a paradigmatic change is called for – and already taking place –
in connection with the question of instruments, and this also indicates an
extensive need for research on new forms of government controls. From the
standpoint of empirical evaluation of the success of environmental actions, a
highly differentiated picture of the instruments available to governments
arises. This is different from the one that is obtained with the model analyses
of individual instruments. Recently, both the OECD and the European
Environmental Agency (EEA) also underscored this with respect to the
analysis of the impact of environmental taxes and charges (EEA, 1996;
OECD, 1997a). Thus, for example, moderate taxes or charges in
combination with other instruments may have a greater control effect than is
shown by model calculations with specified elasticity assumptions.
Nevertheless, thanks to the past debate on instruments the awareness of
possible options of action open to government environmental institutions has
been improved.

Combining this top-down approach with the knowledge of evaluation
research, which proceeds from the empirical success case, appears to be
particularly meaningful if concern is shown with the impact of government
actions on innovation. Several proposals on this issue are presented in the
following section.

It should be emphasized the explorative character of the statements and the
corresponding need for further research.

INSTRUMENTS OF ENVIRONMENTAL POLICY IN THE CONTEXT OF NATIONAL POLICY PATTERNS

It is believed that the term 'policy pattern' could be useful in discussing the
empirical question concerning the impact of measures of environmental
protection undertaken by the government on innovation. Using this term may
attempt to link the complexity and dynamics of the action conditions in
environmental policy with the narrower approach offered by instrument

analysis in such a way that an empirical relation to the effects on innovation appears promising.

The concept of policy pattern should at least comprise the following three influential factors (Table 3.1):

1. The structure of the instruments (or 'programme') in relation to specific environmental goals.
2. The policy style of government institutions on environmental issues.
3. The political-institutional context of the actors and actions.

'Policy pattern' can be defined as the sum of all calculable rules, manners of proceeding and contexts of action within an area that is subject to government control. For example, one can speak about a policy pattern for climate protection in a country. Within this area, the impact of action on innovation can then be ascribed to all these levels of influence, with special importance attached to the mix of instruments (including their relative dominance).

As far as the instruments are concerned, therefore, the individual instruments are not what count, but rather the sum of measures, in which individual instruments can, however, play a special part. Thus, an ecological tax or subsidy may be a necessary condition for ensuring that 'soft' administrative influential measures (administrative guidance) or structures of discourse in networks become sufficiently significant to be adequate criteria. Another essential point with respect to modernizing environmental policy is

Table 3.1   Policy patterns of environmental policy

Instruments (1)	Policy style (2)	Political-institutional context of action (3)
Dominant instruments in the mix Degree of determining behaviour Punctual versus strategic approach	Form of target-setting Flexibility in applying the instruments Timing of the measure Orientation towards consensus Legalization, bureaucratization Calculability	Competence and influence of the regulating body(s) Role of other policies (policy integration!) Relation between regulators and regulatees Role of non-governmental environmental institutions

whether the measure is part of an integrated or strategic procedure and, for example, is based on negotiated and comprehensive targets, or whether it takes the selective approach known from the traditional debate on instruments and relies on the effect of one instrument.

The institutional context refers to the structure and professionalism of environmental institutions, legal structures and spheres of competence but also, for example, to the importance of other policies relevant to the area to be regulated (climate protection is not just a matter of environmental administration). Taking as an example the German Packaging Ordinance, the significance of another organizational framework can be illustrated. The resulting policy does not so much depend on the choice of instruments as on the structure of the 'dual system' in Germany and its role in the functional structure of government and private waste management organizations and policies.

The configuration of actors concerns the question as to with whom government agencies usually clarify, define and implement targets, whether the relevant political network is pluralistic and inclusive, for example, and includes environmental interests or whether it is exclusive and favours the interests of certain polluters, whether the constellation of actors consists of cooperative networks or opposing blocks and so on.

Richardson was the first to emphasize the significance of policy style (1982). How the instruments are applied may have a considerable impact on the resulting policy. Particularly, the target-setting process, the flexibility, the timing and the advisory process accompanying a measure are of considerable importance for innovation strategies (Porter and van der Linde, 1995). An international comparison of environmental policy would provide many examples that the announcement of a measure already can have an impact whereby the tiresome path through the political decision-making bodies potentially can be avoided. Innovators in the target group anticipated the measure in the interest of their investments and, thus, developed their own dynamics to reach the target (Jänicke and Weidner, 1995; Jacob and Jänicke, 1996).

Hypotheses: Target Definition and Instruments of a Target Group Strategy that Promotes Innovation

Up until now government environmental policy evidently has tended to contribute more towards the diffusion of advanced technology than to innovation. It has probably stimulated more innovations leading to improvements than basic innovations. Usually environmental policy has followed environmental technology. Governmental 'technology forcing' (for example, through exhaust emission standards) was the exception (Kern, 1997). Although oil price shocks or high costs of waste disposal have the same effect, they are less calculable than planned government actions.

So how may a government environmental strategy that promotes innovation be conceived instrumentally? Several hypotheses are given below:

- The effectiveness of political instruments is determined by the political process as a whole, and this, in turn, is characterized by the stages of problem definition, definition of goals, decision-making, (flexible) implementation and impact control; that is, it does not begin with implementation.

- Innovators react to early phases in the political process of opinion-forming and decision-making, whereas the diffusion of advanced technology tends to come after measures have been agreed upon. Innovation strategies should primarily be concerned with the policy formulation process and less with its result ('public choice'). Nevertheless, a strategy of ecological modernization (which comprises innovation and diffusion) involves both phases of the political process and should optimize them accordingly (Figure 3.3).

- Based on the current state of environmental policy research, a target-group policy related to polluters is to be preferred to an approach based on ecological media (water, air, soil). Target-group policy implies a strategy for dialogue with polluters and aims for a high degree of mutual information. Initially, potential innovators will be the decisive addressees within the target group, because environmental-friendly innovations can significantly affect the situation within the target group as they tend to pressure competitors to adapt. Thus, they make it easier to implement environmental goals or diffuse problem solutions. The sequence of actions runs from the innovators to the companies that first adapt, to the adapting majority (Rogers, 1995), to companies finding it difficult to adapt for economic reasons – and requiring subsidies – and, finally, to the real opponents, who are the last addressees of governmental coercive measures (Cohen and Kamieniecki, 1991).

- As regards innovation processes, an early and clear-cut definition of targets by the government accompanied by calculable medium-term sequences of action seems to be just as important as the measures (instruments) themselves. The effectiveness and efficiency of environmental policy measures seem to be highest when they minimize the investment risk of (potential) innovators within the target group by means of clear-cut specifications, while offering informational as well as other innovation incentives. An early, reliable announcement is very important in this connection. Even a strategy of technology forcing has a firmer basis when it utilizes the early phases of the political process to make a reliable announcement of, if necessary, strict medium-term

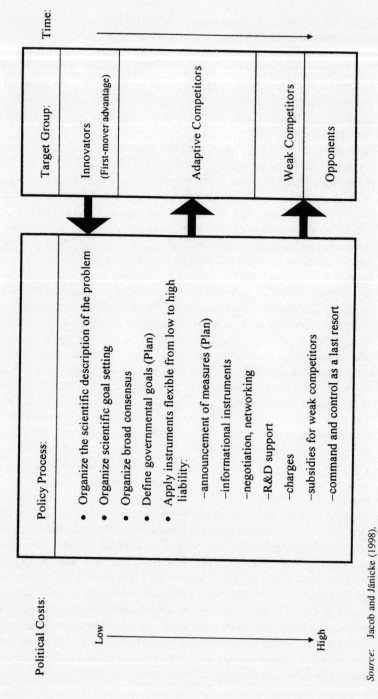

Source: Jacob and Jänicke (1998).

Figure 3.3   A policy model for ecological modernization

regulations, but leaves open the periods of time necessary for the innovation process, that is, from research to the decision to make an appropriate investment.

- The subsequent diffusion of corresponding technological innovations will be achieved with a minimum of political costs if the government's specification of goals is followed by a flexible application of instruments that continuously and calculably increases the pressure to adapt, that is, imposes binding standards as a last resort. The conflict costs of the political process are thus minimized; only in borderline cases where adaptation is stubbornly refused should recourse be taken to use force or impose coercive measures. The threat of 'command and control' can also help avoid complicated decision-making processes in the government (see above). Today 'threat and control' (Jänicke and Weidner, 1995) is a tactical variant frequently applied in environmental policy in many industrial countries (Wallace, 1995).
- The effectiveness of political instruments also depends on the negotiations conducted with the target group. Ideally, the result of the negotiations will be a voluntary agreement, including an obligation to report, with controls and credible threats of standards being used as a last resort.
- The chances for reaching solutions by negotiation can be assessed by means of *ex-ante* restriction analyses. The question that needs to be answered is: what are the available resources of the target group needed to realize, ignore or sabotage the specified target (Cohen and Kamieniecki, 1991)?
- It is self-evident that a strategy of innovation in connection with an environmental policy striving for ecological modernization is not appropriate for all types of problem, for example, neither for warding off dangers nor for environmental problems that cannot be remedied by means of standard technological solutions, such as the problems of land use and loss of species.

Nonetheless, the remaining wide scope of application of a strategy oriented towards innovation is worth the strategic reorientation.

REFERENCES

Andersen, M.S. and U. Joergensen (1995), 'Evaluation of the cleaner technology programme 1987–1992', translated by D. Barry, *Environmental Review*, **14** (1997), Copenhagen: Danish Environmental Protection Agency.

Balthasar, A. and C. Knoepfel (1994), *Umweltpolitik und technische Entwicklung. Eine politikwissenschaftliche Evaluation am Beispiel der Heizungen*, Basel, Frankfurt/M: Helbing & Lichtenhahn.

Both, P. (1993), *Umweltorientierte Innovationspolitik. Untersuchungen und Perspektiven für die Schweiz*, ETH Zürich: ORL-Bericht 83.

Bressers, J. Th. A. and P.J. Klok (1991), *The Explanation of Policy Effectiveness*, University of Twente: Ms. Centre for Clean Technology and Environmental Policy.

Bressers, J. Th. A. and D. Huitema (1996), 'Politics as usual: the effect of policy-making on the design of economic policy instruments', paper presented at the International Conference on Environment and Climate, Rome, 4–8 March.

Brinkmann, J. and M. Kirchgeorg (1995), 'Umweltorientiertes Unternehmens-verhalten', *Zeitschrift für Umweltpolitik und Umweltrecht*, **18** (3), 377–90.

Bussmann, W., U. Klöti and P. Knoepfel (eds) (1997), *Einführung in die Politikevaluation*, Basel, Frankfurt/M: Helbing & Lichtenhahn.

Coenen, R., S. Klein-Vielheuer and R. Meyer (1995), TA-Projekt 'Umwelttechnik und wirtschaftliche Entwicklung', *TAB Arbeitsbericht Nr. 35*, Bonn.

Cohen, St. and S. Kamieniecki (1991), *Environmental Regulation Through Strategic Planning*, Boulder, CO: Westview Press.

Conrad, J. (1998), *Successful Environmental Management in European Companies*, Amsterdam: Gordon and Breach.

Damkowski, W. and C. Precht (1995), *Public Management. Neuere Steuerungs-konzepte für den öffentlichen Sektor*, Stuttgart, Berlin, Köln: Kohlhammer.

Dodgson, M. and R. Rothwell (eds) (1994), *The Handbook of Industrial Innovation*, Aldershot: Edward Elgar.

European Environment Agency (EEA) (1996), *Environmental Taxes. Implementation and Environmental Effectiveness*, Copenhagen: EE.

Fischer, F. (1995), *Evaluating Public Policy*, Chicago: Nelson-Hall.

Gothenburg Research Institute (1995), *The Nordic Business Environmental Barometer*, Oslo: Bedriftsoekonomens Forlag.

Hemmelskamp, J. (1996), *Umweltpolitik und Innovation – Grundlegende Begriffe und Zusammenhänge*, Discussion Paper No. 96–23, ZEW Mannheim.

Héritier, A. (ed.) (1993), 'Policy-Analyse. Kritik und Neuorientierung', *Politische Vierteljahresschrift*, special issue **24**, Opladen: Westdeutscher Verlag.

Hoffmann, A.J. (1994), 'The environmental transformation of American indusry: an institutional account of environmental strategies in the chemical and petroleum industries', paper, Sloan School of Management, MIT.

Jacob, K. and M. Jänicke (1996), 'Eco-restructuring in the German chemical industry: who causes changes, why, and how?', paper presented at the Greening of Industry Network Conference, Heidelberg, 24–27 November.

Jacob, K. and M. Jänicke (1998), 'Ökologische Innovationen in der chemischen Industrie: Umweltentlastung ohne Staat? Eine Untersuchung und kommentierung zu 182 Gefahrstoffen', *Zeitschrift für Umweltpolitik und Umweltrecht (ZfU)*, December, **21**, pp. 519-47.

Jänicke, M. (1990), *State Failure. The Impotence of Politics in Industrial Society*, Cambridge: Polity Press.

Jänicke, M. (ed.) (1996), *Umweltpolitik der Industrieländer*, Berlin: Edition Sigma.

Jänicke, M. and H. Weidner (eds) (1995), *Successful Environmental Policy: A Critical Evaluation of 24 Cases*, Berlin: Edition Sigma.

Jänicke, M., H. Mönch, M. Binder *et al.* (1993), *Umweltentlastung durch industriellen Strukturwandel?*, Berlin: Edition Sigma.

Jänicke, M., A. Carius and H. Jörgens (1997), *Nationale Umweltpläne in ausgewählten*

OECD-Ländern, Berlin: Springer Verlag.

Kemp, R., O. Xander, F. Oosterhuis and H. Verbruggen (1994), 'Policy instruments to stimulate cleaner technologies', in H. Opschoor and K. Turner (eds), *Economic Incentives and Environmental Policies*, Dordrecht: Kluwer, pp. 275–300.

Kern, K. (1997): 'Ansätze einer innovativen und integrativen Mobilitätspolitik in den USA', in L. Mez and M. Jänicke (eds), *Sektorale Umweltpolitik. Analysen im Industrieländernvergleich*, Berlin: Edition Sigma, pp. 270–79.

Kitschelt, H. (1983), *Politik und Energie. Energie-Technologiepolitiken in den USA, der Bundesrepublik Deutschland, Frankreich und Schweden*, Frankfurt/M., New York: Campus Verlag.

Klemmer, P. (ed.) (1999), *Innovation und Umwelt. Fallstudien zum Anpassungsverhalten in Wirtschaft und Gesellschaft*, Berlin: Analytica.

Knoepfel, P. (1993), 'Bedingungen einer wirksamen Umsetzung umweltpolitischer Programme – Erfahrungen aus westeuropäischen Staaten', *Cahiers de l'IDEHEAP*, **108**, Lausanne: Institut des Hautes Etudes en Administration Publique.

Low, P. (ed.) (1992), *International Trade and the Environment*, Washington, DC: World Bank Discussion Papers, no. 1959.

Luhmann, N. (1986), *Ökologische Kommunikation*, Opladen: Westdeutscher Verlag.

Mayntz, R. (1983), 'Zur Einleitung: Probleme der Theoriebildung in der Implementationsforschung', in R. Mayntz (ed.), *Implementation politischer Programme*, Opladen: Westdeutscher Verlag.

Mayntz, R. and F.W. Scharpf (1995), 'Steuerung und Selbstrorganisation in staatsnahen Sektoren', in R. Mayntz and F. W. Scharpf (eds), *Gesellschaftliche Selbstregulierung und politische Steuerung*, Frankfurt/New York: Campus Verlag.

Ministry of the Environment (1997), 'Environmental policy for a sustainable development: joint efforts for the future', report to the Storting, no. 58, Oslo.

OECD (1995), *Planning for Sustainable Development. Country Experiences*, Paris: OECD.

OECD (1996), *Integrating Environment and Economy. Progress in the 1990s*, Paris, OECD.

OECD (1997a), *Environmental Taxes and Green Tax Reform*, Paris: OECD.

OECD (1997b), *Reforming Environmental Regulation in OECD Countries*, Paris: OECD.

Porter, M.E. and C. van der Linde (1995), 'Green and competitive: ending the stalemate', *Harvard Business Review*, September–October, 120–34.

Prittwitz, V. v. (1994), *Politikanalyse*, Opladen: UTB.

Richardson, J.J. (ed.) (1982), *Policy Styles in Western Europe*, London: Allen and Unwin.

Ricken, C. (1995), 'Nationaler Politikstil, Netzwerkstrukturen sowie ökonomischer Entwicklungsstand als Determinanten einer effektiven Umweltpolitik – Ein empirischer Industrieländervergleich', *Zeitschrift für Umweltpolitik und Umweltrecht*, **4**, 481–501.

Rogers, E.M. (1995), *Diffusion of Innovations*, 4th edn., New York, London: Free Press.

Rossi, P.H. and H.E. Freeman (1993), *Evaluation. A Systematic Approach*, 5th edn., Newbury Park, London, New Delhi: Sage Publications.

Sabatier, P. A. (1986), 'Top-down and bottom-up approaches to implementation research', *Journal of Public Policy*, **6** (1), 21–48.

Sabatier, P.A. (1993), 'Advocacy-Koalitionen, Policy-Wandel und Policy-Lernen. Eine Alternative zur Phasenheuristik', in Adrienne Héritier (ed.), *Policy-Analyse*.

Kritik und Neuorientierung, Politische Vierteljahresschrift, special edition, Opladen: Westdeutscher Verlag, pp. 116–48.

Wallace, D. (1995), *Environmental Policy and Industrial Innovation: Strategies in Europe, the USA and Japan*, London: Earthscan.

Widmer, Th. (1991), *Evaluation von Maßmahmen zur Luftreinhaltepolitik in der Schweiz*, Zürich: Verlag Rüegger.

4. What the doctor should know: politicians are special patients. The impact of the policy-making process on the design of economic instruments*

Hans Th. A. Bressers and Dave Huitema

ABSTRACT

Economic instruments appear to be a promising alternative to regulations as instruments of environmental policy. From what some call 'the fairyland of microeconomics' the expectation arises that this type of instrument will put market forces to work for the achievement of environmental goals, thus achieving targets at much lower costs. In practice, however, economic instruments often do not resemble the ones proposed by the underlying economic theory. As one observer of the debate put it: 'the patient has not followed the doctor's orders' (Hahn, 1989). The notion of cost-effectiveness which dominates considerations in economic theory is only one of many criteria which policy-makers take into account in the real world. This is not a question of 'good science' versus 'bad politics', but a recognition of the fact that politics has a rationality of its own. It is argued, therefore argue that lessons learned from analyses of policy-making and implementation deserve attention equal to the presupposed behavioural reactions of key target groups. Issues to be taken into account include the interests of the actors involved, the institutional contexts of both policy-making and implementation and finally, policy-learning. Such factors are discussed by using them to explain observed deviations in instrument design from economic theory.

INTRODUCTION

In the view of economists, the environmental degradation which has taken place during and after the industrialization of the West implies that 'resources' provided by our natural environment have been and still are being over-exploited. The argument is that overexploitation arises because no adequate markets exist for these resources, therefore, their scarcity is not recognized, or at least not fully so (Daly, 1977; Kneese and Sweeney, 1985). One solution implies that government and other institutions should calculate the prices of raw materials, commodities, consumer goods or various types of pollution and apply these as surtaxes. The effect would be to get 'the price right', thus providing an incentive to change people's behaviour, and creating sustainable development (von Weizsäcker, 1994; Vos, 1997). The argument is elegant, attractive and receives public acclaim. President Clinton of the USA, for instance, spoke of 'harnessing market forces' so that companies would incorporate 'environmental incentives into daily production decisions' (Dryzek, 1997, p. 103). The World Watch Institute, to mention another influential voice, advocates assessing some 1000 billion dollars in green taxes from the total amount of income tax and company tax paid annually world-wide (approximately 7500 billion dollars) (Brown *et al.*, 1996). It seems fair to state that the 'polluter-pays-principle' has become one of the leading mottos of environmental protection.

Ever since the 1970s the regulating power of economic policy instruments has been the subject of much scientific literature, particularly in the field of environmental economics. The conclusion is almost always that economic instruments, such as charges and emissions trading, have great potential to decrease the dilemma of choosing between ecological and economic interests, because they would allow environmental goals to be attained at much lower costs. In this sense, economic instruments are expected to be much more cost effective than other types of instrument, regulations in particular, which are condescendingly labelled 'command-and-control'.[1] The debate on economic instruments, however, has long remained an exchange of theoretical arguments concerning their advantages, put forward in the blind assumption that such instruments could be politically feasible and applied completely and correctly to the policy target groups. Problems relating to policy formulation and implementation were largely ignored.

In fact, when studying 'legal', 'communicative' and 'economic' policy instruments, it is found that economic policy instruments are the ones least implemented in practice (Opschoor, Vos and de Savornin Lohman, 1994). There are, of course, examples of effective economic instruments in use. Well-known examples from the Netherlands, for instance, are the water-quality charge (Bressers, 1983, 1988, 1995) and tax differentiation for cleaner cars and unleaded petrol (Schrama and Klok, 1995). In these cases some of the theoretical arguments about the effectiveness of economic instruments were proved correct.

Despite such positive examples, the introduction of economic policy instruments in environmental policy appears to be an uphill struggle and has made 'glacial progress' (Dryzek, 1997, p. 116). Naturally, this makes environmental economists unhappy, as well as others who have high expectations for this type of instrument. Apparently, the political feasibility of economic policy instruments in environmental policy depends on other factors than the hypothetical advantages for policy effectiveness, the cost of the instruments, or the practical results achieved in some sub-areas.

In this study, the consequences of these other factors for the use of economic policy instruments are examined. If there is one thing which is striking about the surveys of existing economic policy instruments used in the environmental policies of OECD countries (Opschoor, Vos and de Savornin Lohman, 1994), it is that political decision-making also has a major impact on the final design of the instrument. This means that there are two main differences between that which many environmental economists advocate and that which is actually accepted in practice. Environmental policy has relatively few economic instruments, and those that are introduced are often designed in such a way as to be unsuitable for actually realizing the expected cost-effective benefits. Here the focus is primarily on the issue of design.

Many of the benefits ascribed to economic policy instruments depend on assumptions, particularly with respect to policy instruments (Stavins, 1994a; Andersen, 1995). One such assumption underlying the view of cost-effective economic instruments is that economic agents are 'utility-maximizers', except for the responsible regulators who set the goals to be achieved (Dryzek, 1997). Another is that they can be compared with an inflexible form of direct regulation called command and control (Peeters, 1992). Such assumptions, although they can be very much contested, are not the present subject. Instead, another major assumption is looked at which remains implicit in many discussions of economic policy instruments, namely that economic instruments are also feasible in the policy-making process, once their attractiveness in terms of cost-effectiveness has been demonstrated.

In the following section certain criteria are described which, in addition to cost-effectiveness, are important to the feasibility of instruments in the policy-making process. Next an indication is given of ways in which these criteria can cause economic policy instruments to deviate in use from the ideal typical design, which is usually assumed in theory development, along with the consequences of these deviations for the expected cost-effectiveness of the instruments chosen. Examples from various countries are used to illustrate the point. Then an attempt is made to provide a contribution to theory development on policy-making with regard to economic instruments, before offering some general conclusions.

MULTIPLE CRITERIA IN THE POLICY PROCESS

Only recently has it been realized that policy implementation and policy-making matter to the adoption of economic instruments (Keohane *et al.*, 1997). This implies a shift of focus. The role of the institutions, for example, and the role of interest groups and other actors in the policy-making process, are now receiving greater attention (Andersen, 1994, p. 5). It is increasingly recognized by economists that other requirements apply to policy instruments than just cost-effectiveness. Specifically, there is a growing awareness of the importance of distribution issues in the policy-making process and of the transaction costs that accompany the application of the instruments. Economists are no strangers to these issues, but their reservations have not been broadly promulgated, however, and this may partly explain why economists receive little response to their proposals in practice. For instance, within the Organization for Economic Cooperation and Development (OECD) and the staff of the US Congress, cookbook-style manuals have been written in which, in a more or less straightforward way, policy instruments are linked to certain problem situations or policy targets, ignoring the political and administrative context of the policy process (OECD, 1991; US Congress, Office for Technology Assessment, 1995). In general, little attention is paid to the effects of the political process and to the role of the bureaucracy in the design of the policy instruments introduced. It seems fair to state that in most studies or recommendations, policy-making is seen mainly as the 'address' to which recommendations are sent, and not as a necessary element of the field of study. Often this is combined with a strong emphasis on the presumed cost-effectiveness advantages.

However, what happens when the advice of the economists, failing to take into account issues of implementation and feasibility, arrives at the intended address? As Dryzek (1997, p. 117) observes: '. . . proposals for economic instruments can never enter in the clean and straightforward fashion of the economics textbooks. Instead, their entry and so their design is heavily dependent on the configuration of political forces'. And 'The fairyland of neoclassical microeconomics in which economic rationalist argument for market-oriented policy instruments is rooted is very different from the real world'. Most students of politics will acknowledge that cost-effectiveness is not necessarily the primary, or even a major, concern for bureaucrats or politicians when they choose instruments for implementation. Numerous other criteria are normally applied, explicitly or implicitly, to test proposals for both policy-making and realization, for example:

- effects on competitiveness at home and abroad;
- distribution effects: which groups are burdened with the costs of policy

initially and which ones at later stages (can costs be translated into the prices of goods and services)?

- the 'implementability' of the proposal: is a well-motivated and well-equipped implementing regime available? Are the costs of implementation on the part of the government and other transaction costs for both sides possibly too high? What are the objectives and resources of the target group?

- existing regulations and regulating traditions: does the policy instrument correspond with already existing practices? Is much change in environmental law required?

- flexibility of the instrument: what is the extent to which it can be adapted to different circumstances of time and place, and to uncertainties?

Weighing the relative 'scores' of instruments according to these criteria is far from easy. It is quite possible, for example, for a negative score on one criterion to coexist with, or even be caused by, a positive score on another criterion. Further, what is negative along one dimension can be positive along another, and priority-setting in policy-making is definitively a multi-actor interaction process. Partly because of this, it is not just the actual properties of the instruments which are of importance to the actors during policy-making, but also the perceptions and subjective evaluations of them.

The issue of perception also draws attention to the fact that for actors within policy-making processes the visibility of effects is important. It can be shown that an increase in the price of petrol, for example, is certainly effective in the long run to reduce emissions from cars (Sterner, 1990). However, if policy-makers or the public at large do not believe this to be the case, since quite often there has been no reversal of the rising trend of the number of kilometres driven by car, this argument carries little weight during policy-making.

In addition, it is not just considerations with regard to these proposals that play a part during policy-making, but also considerations as to whether the outcomes of the decision-making process weaken or strengthen an actor's position in view of other issues, and whether such issues are at stake simultaneously or at a later date. The image of the responsible regulator vanishes quickly in the real world. Having a say in the debate on the introduction of economic instruments may provide leverage for influencing other policy initiatives as well. Power is, in Deutsch's terms (1970, p. 23), both 'a net and a fish'.

Policy-makers are thus often 'rational' in numerous ways differing from the cost-effective logic, primarily because of the different criteria of relevance for their behaviour, such as their concern for budgets and electoral results. It is, therefore, not surprising that when politicians and bureaucrats are considering various alternative instruments, decisions are often taken which clearly are not optimal from the point of view of cost-effectiveness.

THE DESIGN OF ECONOMIC INSTRUMENTS IN PRACTICE

This section summarizes the effects of the policy-making process on the final design of economic instruments. The differences between the ideal types usually assumed in economic theory are described, and the instruments that actually survived the policy-making process.

1. Insufficient Stimuli

The actual level of the stimulus imparted by economic instruments is hardly ever as high as it should be according to economic theory. This is largely due to the fact that most of the levies actually introduced are not intended to achieve a change in behaviour, but to generate revenues. OECD reviews show that revenue-raising is often the main purpose of environmental taxes in member-countries (Opschoor, Vos and de Savornin Lohman, 1994). The implication is that there is seldom a clear relation between the amount of the sum to be paid and the targeted behaviour. Waste tariffs for households, for instance, usually do not vary in proportion to the amount of waste produced and, therefore, cannot accurately reflect environmental damage, even if it is known how to calculate this damage.

Sweden is at the forefront of environmental taxes and, therefore, deserves some attention here. Although the introduction of a number of environmental taxes in Sweden took place in a favourable political climate, and the charges imposed are quite high, internationally speaking, these charges are still too low to accurately reflect environmental costs. The fact that the Swedish charges could rise to a relatively high level is largely due to strong public support for environmental policy at the time their introduction was being discussed, and also to the fact that a linkage was made to the reduction of a number of (income and business) tax rates (Lövgren, 1994; Sterner, 1994). The fact that this instrument was relatively unfamiliar to industry has also been pointed out.[2]

In summary, only under special conditions is it feasible to openly attach an explicit incentive character to tax measures. Even in such cases, however, the level of the charges imposed is generally too low.

2. Slow Progression to Fully-fledged Stimulus

New 'economic' instruments are often based on existing legal instruments and, therefore, take a long time to develop into a fully-fledged market-oriented approach. This effect can be seen, for example, in the introduction of 'emissions trading' in the USA where, at first, the exchange of emissions from different chimneys was permitted within the same firm, then exchange between firms and, finally, the saving up of emission rights for later years. Because the design of the existing legal instruments is not such that it can be easily transformed into a more market-oriented approach, it has aspects that impede the impact or even the realization of the new approach. Such effects may also occur for charges initially instituted as retributions. In calculating the Dutch water quality fee, for example, much attention was at first paid to factors which affected the cost of purification, but were not related to the firms' environmental behaviour.

A trend noted by Hahn (1991, p. 49) is that once they have been introduced, fees tend to increase faster than inflation because they were instituted at a very low level, in order to keep political resistance at a moderate level. The Dutch water-quality surcharge, now one of the highest environmental taxes in the world, was introduced gradually and at a very low level during the first half of the 1970s. Even then it was only accepted because it was seen as compensation for services rendered, namely water purification. The fact that this was linked to the expensive water-purification process subsequently increased the fee more and more, leading eventually to an exceptional degree of effectiveness.

The implication is, therefore, that even when a choice is made in favour of economic instruments, it often takes a relatively long time before the instruments achieve a design which enables them to make an optimum contribution to a cost-effective environmental policy.

3. Earmarking Revenues

A third effect is apparent in the way in which revenues from surcharges are spent. In principle, the most rational approach, economically speaking, is not to treat these revenues differently than other forms of governmental income, and to choose their most effective destination based on the preferences of the democratically elected government. As it happens, however, they are quite often used to subsidize activities intended to reduce environmental pollution, such as major investments in, for example, waste processing and sewage water purification. Revenues are then earmarked and often used to subsidize improvements in the behaviour of specific target groups, usually the ones that paid the tax in the first place. When this is done several negative characteristics, which are observed in subsidies, may arise. Howe (1991, p. 7), for instance, found that many subsidies are aimed at the introduction of so-called 'end-of-pipe' techniques, where pollution is not prevented but only purified afterwards. These techniques are not often the most cost-effective ones. A high effectiveness expectation, therefore, is not the main reason for introducing environmental subsidies. In a study of US environmental policy in various states, Brierly (1992) even found that subsidies on emission reductions resulted in higher levels of economic activity in environmentally polluting sectors, when compared to direct regulation.

In summary, the way in which revenues from environmental taxes are spent is often not aimed at an optimum contribution to the policy target or to the general good of society, but rather at making the extra charges acceptable by reducing (re)allocation effects as much as possible, regardless of the overall economic rationality of the process.

4. 'Grandfathering' Tradable Permits

When a tradable permit market is initiated, the permits naturally acquire monetary value. They achieve importance for the firm not only because they serve as a legal justification of the firm's behaviour but – assuming a decline in the firm's pollution level – they also serve as (potentially quite valuable) trading goods. Firms wishing to enter the market have to start by buying the required permits from already existing firms. If the initial allocation takes place on the basis of actual pollution in a given year, rather than on the basis of an equally strict pollution standard for all actors, free allocation also means that firms which already did their best in the past to reduce pollution as much as possible are disadvantaged, compared to firms which so far have invested little in the environment – a 'first remiss, then rich' effect.

According to economic theory (the Coase theorem) it makes no difference, from the point of view of cost-effectiveness, how pollution rights are initially allocated. Nevertheless, it will be clear that the allocation of pollution rights does affect income distribution in society. In this way forerunners can be punished for their progressiveness. Because managers are not only interested in maximizing utility, but are also capable of human reactions, such policies can have a discouraging effect. Furthermore, Stavins (1994b) has shown that in a market with transaction costs, the initial allocation of pollution rights certainly does affect the market's cost-effectiveness. Transaction costs are made by market parties in order to find one another, to gather information, to negotiate and make decisions, and to verify whether agreements are being complied with.

All this indicates that the allocation effects of tradable permits tend to be such that effects on already existing firms will be minimized, even at the expense of the cost-effectiveness or fairness of the instrument.

5. Limiting or Supplementing Direct Regulation

Regulations tend to affect the flexibility of economic instruments. Especially under a tradable permit scheme, a concentration of pollution may occur in specific areas ('hot spots'). This is because all permits may be bought by firms in one single area. To prevent this from happening, mechanisms are incorporated which enable the government to intervene in the market. An approval procedure for an exchange of permit rights is thus standard for permit markets.

Also in the case of surcharges, politicians will want to have as much certainty about the time and place of the emission reductions as they think they have with traditional (non-tradable) permits. The fact that this certainty is partly an illusion in the light of the failing implementation and effectiveness of many permit schemes does not really matter (see the earlier discussion about the importance of perceptions). Usually, surcharges do not replace existing regulations, which remain in place as a 'safety net' or if the charge is only a revenue-raising device, it might even be the 'official' policy instrument. From the perspective of an optimally functioning market system, many of these supplementary rules and procedures are impediments.

Approval procedures for trades between firms imply that firms willing to trade have to make costs before trading. This reduces their potential cost savings. Less trade takes place than would be possible. Hahn and Hester (1989, p. 376) find that transaction costs constitute the main factor in explaining the success or failure of permit markets. In practice, their effect is that trade in emission rights takes place mostly between the branch offices of various firms, and hardly at all between the firms. When trading internally, transaction costs are far lower. The extent of the limiting effect of transaction costs and the consequent uncertainty about cost-effectiveness depends, among other things, on the number of firms participating in the market (Stavins, 1994a, p. 11). Summarizing, Hahn (1989, p. 51) concludes that cost savings from both charges and from marketable permits have remained 'far below their theoretical potential'.

In summary, economic policy instruments are rarely given the chance to create a 'free' market. Additional requirements and procedures, whether or not they are justified in themselves, interfere with the economic mechanism that the economic policy instruments are intended to realize.

6. Exceptions and Exemptions

Because of factors such as international competitiveness, firms may claim that they deserve to be exempted when an instrument is introduced at the national level. Politicians tend to be very sensitive to such arguments. Therefore, they often limit the target group of the instrument and thus its scope by allowing exceptions and exemptions.

There is evidence that it is too easily assumed that higher environmental costs automatically involve less competitiveness. Since the 1970s the Netherlands have had by far the highest water pollution charges in the world, the revenue being used to pay for waste water treatment. Of all branches of industry, the Dutch paper industry was probably the most vulnerable. It operates in an international market: its products generally do not have brand names; it initially produced one of the highest quantities of pollution in proportion to the size of the sector; and it was required, therefore, to pay relatively high taxes. In Belgium, water-quality policy was initiated only at the end of the 1980s. Thus, the Belgian paper industry was able to economize both on the cost of the charges and on the cost of purification measures during this period. Yet the Belgian paper industry fared no better during the 1970s and 1980s than its Dutch counterpart.

Indications exist that the pressure to which the Dutch firms were subjected to led to their beginning to modernize more quickly (De la Fuente, 1994). In certain cases, therefore, environmental taxes may also result in a competitive advantage. In short, the criterion of (international) competitiveness can lead to exemptions for specific businesses, which, in turn, can reduce the (cost) effectiveness of the economic instruments employed.

7.   Sub-optimal Scale

One consequence of the existence of the nation state and its sovereignty is that environmental issues frequently are not dealt with at the right level with respect to the scale of the environmental issue at stake. The emission of a number of substances causes environmental damage at the supranational (either regional or global) rather than the national level, causing further problems for national cost-effective instruments. Individual countries have, therefore, stressed the need for the introduction of economic instruments at the international level. At the same time, however, there is considerable resistance concerning attempts to tax at the supranational level, because of national fear of losing sovereignty to international organizations. In spite of support from the European Parliament and the European Commission, the European Union has had great difficulty in trying to arrive at an effective carbon-emissions tax (Liberatore, 1995).

In short, the potential for cost-effective instruments in terms of both rationale and popular support is peculiarly bound up with the logic of sovereign national actors.

This section concludes by stating that because other criteria than the optimization of cost-effectiveness are applied during policy-making, economic policy is usually designed in such a way as to deviate in many respects from the ideal types of the instrument as grounded, explicitly or implicitly, in applied economic theory.

Starting from this conclusion, the process can lead in at least three directions. First, the lack of vision of policy-makers, who seem to be insufficiently aware of the enormous potential of economic instruments of control, can be moaned about. Second, it is also possible to turn away completely from economic policy instruments as a serious option for environmental policy. Or, finally, admit that the development of theory as to the application of economic instruments cannot be meaningfully limited to the way in which citizens and firms are likely to respond to the actually chosen and correctly applied policy instruments. The third course has been chosen. In the next section, therefore, an initial attempt is made to supplement theories of instrument application with perspectives from policy analysis.

SELECTING INSTRUMENTS AS A MULTIPLE ACTOR PROCESS

So far, the implicit assumption in this study has been that governnment intervention is a conscious, well-considered choice by a single central actor. However, this is hardly realistic. Theory development about the choice of instrument must be a highly complex matter due to the numerous factors influencing the decision-making process. There are few models or theories that capture the entire complexity of this process, however, despite many partial explanations of the choice of instruments. Traditions relating to the choice of instruments have already been mentioned, but also other factors such as bureaucratic culture (Andersen, 1995); the effects of various arenas (de Savornin Lohman, 1994); institutional, procedural and structural obstacles (Larrue, 1995); 'captive agencies'; communist strongholds (Nentjes quoted in Sliggers, 1995); and overall uncertainty as to ultimate effects (Opschoor and Turner, 1994, pp. 33–7).

An alternative approach from 'political economics' is now examined, one which is believed to offer more relevant points of contact for the phenomena listed above. The approach with key perspectives is supplemented from policy science.

Robert Hahn

The concept of utility maximization is central to political economy. The simplest policy models in this tradition assume that a single actor determines the mode of instrument application to be employed, and that the instrument chosen is that which maximizes the utility of the actor in question. More developed models also leave room for the influence of interest groups such as the regulated branches of industry and the environmental movement. Hahn

(1989, 1991) offers a relatively well-structured survey of the status, building on existing insights and constructing a 'state-of-the-art' model, while indicating the defects of existing theories. It is believed that this survey is still accurate.

Hahn posits an essential contrast between the environmental movement and industry, with industry mainly concerned with profits and the environmental movement with the quality of the environment. He assumes that decisions about instruments are taken by a single political actor who pursues utility maximization and who, for this reason, is mainly bent on acquiring political support. This political support can be obtained by the actor by choosing those objectives of environmental policy that most appeal to both interest groups. Hahn shows that the optimum of political support is located wherever stricter targets are applied to new firms ('new firms don't vote'), and more lenient rules are applied to existing firms.

It is further assumed that, in essence, instruments differ in the extent of their market orientation. Generally speaking, industries prefer market-oriented instruments over direct regulation, because these involve lower costs to the industry; the more influential an industry is, the more often a choice will be made in favour of this type of instrument. Furthermore, industry prefers a weaker to a stronger stimulus, while the reverse is true for the environmental movement. Both have in common that they feel that the earmarking of the revenues from surcharges is an attractive option: the environmental movement because they are in favour of an adjustment of environmental taxes; industry because the same revenues are a sign of its efforts with respect to the environment. This means that when a charge is introduced, it will soon yield earmarked revenues.

Furthermore, Hahn discusses the visibility of the cost of instruments and the importance of symbolic politics. Politicians generally tend to prefer instruments which entail little visible cost to industry and appear to stimulate employment. Economic instruments have a bad score on both counts because they entail rather visible extra costs for industry and offer few visible positive effects on employment. Hahn also models the importance that may be attached to symbols by interest groups. He assumes that the environmental movement is, in fact, in favour of symbolic policies, mainly because such policies set unrealistically high targets, which can be utilized in the long run as a basis for demanding ever stricter policies and which, moreover, can enhance the perception of the environmental problem on the part of the general public.

On the basis of the model outlined above, a number of the previously identified effects of the policy-making process on the design of economic instruments can be explained. The lack of an effective stimulus (Effect 1 above) can be explained by resistance on the part of industry. The same also partly applies to the earmarking of revenues from taxes (Effect 3), at least if this involves the earmarking of subsidies. Based on Hahn's conclusion, the fact that marketable permits are generally allotted free of charge (Effect 4) can be understood to mean that old firms will be privileged *vis-à-vis* new ones ('new firms don't vote'). The fact that all sorts of supplementary regulations remain in place (Effect 5) could be explained by the interest that the environmental movement is purported to attach to the symbolic aspect of the policy. This explanation is, however, only partially satisfactory. Providing for full or partial exemptions (Effect 6) may be partly due to the general resistance on the part of industry and partly to the fact that existing firms are granted privileges.

Other aspects of the policy-making process are more difficult to discern from Hahn's model: why economic policy instruments develop so gradually in many cases (Effect 2); why government expenditures are often financed through direct assessments rather than subsidies (which would, after all, make both politicians and industrialists happy (Sub-effect 3); why so many supplementary rules continue to exist when an economic instrument has been chosen (Effect 5); and why the use of instruments at a supranational level is generally not feasible (Effect 7).

Compared to the model of policy-making as a process of choice for a single actor's pursuit of maximum cost-effectiveness, Hahn's model is more realistic since it takes into account both the rationality of the political actor and that of others involved in the policy-making process. Also, the introduction of the possibility that a policy can be purely symbolic is interesting and rarely seen elsewhere, although it can be quite realistic and rational from the perspective of politicians (Gustafsson and Richardson, 1979).

Yet theory development on the choice of instruments in political economy, where Hahn's work can be viewed as 'state of the art', has a number of limitations, many of which are recognized by the author himself. The most important of these are:

- an over-simplification of reality by limiting the number of parties involved in policy-making to a single decision-maker who allows him or herself to be influenced by only two interest groups, each of which has only a few motives;
- too little attention paid to the learning effects of past experiences with certain types of policy instrument;
- too little attention paid to the institutional component of policy-making.

A Diversity of Actors and Motives

Interesting theoretical supplements are to be found for the three defects we have identified in the policy science and political science literature. To begin with the first one: in a study on the influence of selected groups on US air-quality policy, Svoboda (1992) shows that at least four groups exerted influence: the bureaucracy, the environmental movement, industry and political élites. According to the 'captive-agency' theory, the influence of industry should be dominant, but Svoboda's study shows that it is only marginal. The role of political élites and the bureaucracy, which is largely ignored in Hahn's model, is striking, however. Therefore, when developing theories on policy-making, it hardly seems wise to limit complexity by reducing the number of actors in the analysis. A large number of actors or factors in the analysis, on the other hand, quickly makes it impossible to arrive at a predictive model (Bressers and Klok, 1988). A possible solution which permits the number of actors in the analysis not to be limited and still constructs a controllable theoretical framework, is to place the actors in a limited number of 'coalitions' (see below). This approach was chosen by Bressers (1998) in the construction of a model of the relation between the nature of policy networks and the choice of instruments.

Supplementing the model with additional actors and their motives makes it easier to understand the use of the revenues from charges in financing government activities (Sub-effect 3). Bureaucracy in particular is interested in a high level of activities, and the revenues from charges offer opportunities in this respect, and they are all the more interesting because many other tax tariffs have been subject to pressure since the 1980s. The example of the Polish mining sector, in which subsidies were not just a response to general resistance from industry but were precisely intended to influence the allocation between industries, also becomes easier to explain by identifying actually existing coalitions in the policy-making game instead of using categories such as 'industry' or 'the environmental movement'. Also full and partial exemptions (Effect 6) can be adapted in order to reduce to such differences between various groups of firms. Limiting or supplementing regulations (Effect 5) can be partly understood as an attempt on the part of the bureaucracy and political élites to limit the loss of capacity and to directly influence the behaviour of firms which accompanies the use of general economic instruments.

Learning Effects

Existing theories pay scant attention to learning effects. Such effects are quite often observed in practice, however. An example is the system of marketable permits which was set up recently in the USA with respect to acidification. Under this system a portion of pollution rights is not allocated among existing polluters, but is sold annually at public auction. The gradually increasing introduction of market elements in the US emissions trading programme itself can be seen as a result of policy learning. Furthermore, following the US example, 'emissions trading' is now being considered and applied in other countries as well. Another observation is that the level of charges applied is often adjusted regularly to maximize environmental impact.

A theoretical framework which is suitable for the study of policy changes is Sabatier's 'advocacy coalition' approach (Sabatier and Jenkins-Smith, 1993, 1997). This approach sees changes in policy as being a function of (1) the interaction of competing coalitions in a sub-system of the political system and (2) external changes, such as changes in the socio-economic situation, against a background of (3) a number of stable parameters, including constitutional rules. This theoretical framework is based on the assumption that decisions about certain policy fields are made within sub-systems of the political system, and that within such a sub-system, coalitions are created which oppose one another. Here coalition formation is based on shared values, shared problem perceptions and shared causal assumptions. Coalitions are bent on manipulating the rules that concern government organizations, which they want to use to achieve their aims. Coalitions try to obtain this influence in three different ways: (1) by gathering and using information; (2) by trying to manipulate the forum where decisions are being made; and (3) by supporting politicians who sympathize with the coalition. Here, policy changes can be realized by means of compromise; through external factors which may change the resources of actors; through policy experiments and policy evaluation; and through changing insights within the coalitions. Information-gathering and learning from past experiences, in particular, are seen as driving forces behind policy changes.

An interesting idea in this perspective is the thought that the policy style of the US Environmental Protection Agency (EPA) may well have been a decisive factor underlying the introduction of economic policy instruments. Vogel (1986) has shown that this agency functioned in a very bureaucratic manner, with extremely little room for consultation and a highly formal attitude. This forced firms to go to a great deal of expense, and there was a strong stimulus to obtain more freedom of action. A similar process can be seen in Poland, where the energy sector aims to reduce interference on the part of the local authorities, and is, therefore, advocating a permits market at the national level.

Differences in policy styles may also serve to partly explain the European lack of interest in economic policy instruments. In European countries such as the Netherlands, the dominant policy style in environmental policy has more of a consensus orientation. Many of the possible cost-benefits of economic policy instruments in the USA are already being realized in various European countries through wider negotiations during the permit procedure.

In addition to having a positive or negative influence on the choice of policy instruments, learning effects can also affect the design of instruments. This is reflected particularly in the gradual growth of the instruments towards more adequate economic stimuli (Effect 2). This perspective also makes it clear why such policy improvements reflect a gradual process whereby numerous different factors must interact positively to bring about a shift in policy.

Institutional Factors

In the above, the third item has already briefly been indicated: the lack of attention paid to institutional factors in existing theories on policy-making. Although this factor is mentioned in many partial explanations of the choice of instruments (Larrue, 1995), it is rarely incorporated in more extensive theories on policy-making. Majone pointed out as early as 1976 that many theories on policy-making do not take into account the attempts made by actors to change the institutions within which they operate. The 'advocacy-coalition' concept provides considerably more leeway for this, and further additions can be found in the work of Ostrom and others (Kiser and Ostrom, 1982; Ostrom, 1990; Tang, 1992).

The approach is based on the idea that institutions can be seen as rules, and that institutions have a layered structure. There are at least three levels of rules which can influence the actions of actors who operate within set regulations: the constitutional level, the collective level, and the operational level. The actions of actors at these levels depend on their motives and their resources (Klok, 1995). The rules that determine decision-making at the level in question, however, limit the actors' latitude. Other limiting factors are the culture of the society and physical circumstances. Together, these factors determine the so-called 'arena of action' in which the actors find themselves.

The introduction of several levels of regulation and arenas appears to constitute a particularly promising addition to existing theories about the choice of economic policy instruments. De Savornin Lohman (1994) points out that the choice of economic policy instruments often takes place in arenas other than those involved in the choice of legal instruments. Due to the nature of their subject matter, choice here often involves other actors, such as the Ministry of Finance. These actors may, in fact, introduce motives which are prejudicial to the selection of economic instruments, for example, the pursuit of fiscal neutrality. Precisely because the rules of the game have a layered structure and vary for each arena, actors may also try to manipulate the situation. Under the rule of fiscal neutrality, the chance that economic instruments will be adopted is relatively poor. Not just the game, but also the rules of the game can be manipulated, such as rules providing access and role responsibility. This implies, of course, that theory development on policy-making must be sensitive to differing rules at different levels of the game.

Supplementing this with an institutional perspective provides further insight into the question of why growth towards 'real' economic stimuli (Effect 2) often happens so slowly. There are many formal and informal rules that need to be changed, and the impact of the instrument often affects institutions which habitually pursue fiscal neutrality rather than maximum behavioural effect. A similar point applies to the existence of external delimiting and supplemental regulations (Effect 5). Many of these regulations may not have resulted from the process that led to the choice of the economic instrument, but were already present as a result of previous decision-making, sometimes even as a framework which had to be adhered to during policy-making. In Europe, the limitation of the impact of the instrument (Effect 6) may also have something to do with the fact that agreements had already been made with various branches of industry about the reduction of environmental pollution, in which case high tax assessments are seen as violating the principle of legal security. Finally, international covenants and supranational organizations may provide a basis both for economic instruments and for their realization, or hinder the choice of the optimum scale level (Effect 7).

In summary, it is argued that a combination of state-of-the-art political economy, allowing for greater complexity than that associated with classical rational choice models, supplemented by insights from theories of policy analysis in political science, can produce more adequate explanations of the phenomena described in the previous section.

CONCLUSION

This study started with the observation that economic instruments are, in theory, very attractive because of their cost-effectiveness. The innate appeal of this feature is that there exists a viable short-cut on the road to sustainable development.

A less appealing perspective has been stressed, however, by pointing out that in the real world of policy-making more criteria are taken into account than that of cost-effectiveness. Because of this, the design of economic instruments often fails to satisfy the ideal model outlined in environmental economics. Various types of effect may be distinguished, including effects on the level of the stimulus applied by the instrumentarium, the direction of the stimulus applied and the target group at which the instrumentarium is aimed. The consequences are that the constellation of economic instruments falls far short of flight-manual expectations. These expectations are frequently unrealistic because they assume an ideally designed instrument functioning within the confines of a well-functioning market. Unfortunately, too many economists still seem to view policy-making as just another domain for their instrumental recommendations, rather than an independent arena which requires its own mode of scientific analysis.

Here the basic principle might be that the choice of instruments at the operational level is influenced not only by the features of the problem situation and the basic conflicts of interest with regard to the problem and the way it is handled, but also by a multitude of actors with different motives who tend to 'learn by doing'. The context for decision-making with respect to sustainable development is thus seen as both highly flexible and contingent. Actors who are involved in decision-making also try to influence the 'rules of the game', most tellingly by demanding to be admitted to the decision-making arena itself, but also by insisting on defining what the arena and borders for instrumental change are to encompass.

It is felt that the issues raised in this study have implications for both academics and policy practitioners. Despite this critique, economic instruments are viewed as a potentially attractive option for pursuing sustainable development, provided the matching of contextual factors and operational premises is more thoroughly explored and integrated.

NOTES

* Different versions of this study have been published in Boorsma, P.B., K. Aarts and A.E. Steenge (eds), *Public Priority; Rules and Costs*, Kluwer Academic Publishers, Dordrecht, 1997 and a special issue on sustainability in the *International Political Science Review*, pp. 181–200 (Spring, 1999). Kind permission was granted by Kluwer Academic Publishers to republish the material.
1. For a critique of this label, see Dryzek (1997).
2. Telephone interview (1 September 1994) with Mrs K. Lövgren, MISTRA (Stiftelsen för miljöstrategisk forskning), Stockholm, Sweden.

REFERENCES

Andersen, M.S. (1994), 'Economic instruments and clean water: why institutions and policy design matter', *PUMA/REG (94) 5*, Paris: OECD Public Management Service.

Andersen, M. Skou (1995), 'The importance of institutions in the design and implementation of economic instruments in environmental policy', *ENV/EPOC/GEEI (95) 2*, Paris: OECD Environment Directorate.

Bressers, J. Th. A. (1983), 'The role of effluent charges in Dutch water quality policy', in P.B. Downing and K. Hanf (eds), *International Comparisons in Implementing Pollution Laws*, Boston: Kluwer-Nijhof, pp. 143–68.

Bressers, J. Th. A. (1988), 'A comparison of the effectiveness of incentives and directives: the case of Dutch water quality policy', *Policy Studies Review*, **7** (3), 500–518.

Bressers, J. Th. A. (1995), 'The impact of effluent charges: a Dutch success story', in

M. Jänicke and H. Weidner (eds), *Successful Environmental Policy*, Berlin: Sigma, pp. 10–26.

Bressers, J. Th. A. (1998), 'Policy networks and choice of instruments', in B. Guy Peters and Frans K.M. van Nispen (eds), *Public Policy Instruments: Evaluating the Tools of Public Administration*, Cheltenham, UK and Northampton, MA, USA: Edward Elgar.

Bressers, J. Th. A. and P.-J. Klok (1988), 'Fundamentals for a theory of policy instruments', *International Journal of Social Economics*, **15** (3–4), 22–41.

Brierly, A.B. (1992), 'Assessing environmental policy strategies: the effects of pollution control subsidies and regulatory standards on economic growth in the American States', mimeo, University of Northern Iowa.

Brown, L.R. *et al.* (eds) (1996), *State of the World 1996*, Washington, DC: World Watch Institute.

Daly, H.E. (1977), *Steady-state Economics*, San Francisco: W.H. Freeman.

De la Fuente, M. (1994), 'De relatie tussen waterkosten en concurrentiepositie. Een onderzoek in de Nederlandse en Belgische papier- en karton industrie', masters' thesis, University of Twente.

De Savornin Lohman, L. (1994), 'Incentive charges in environmental policies: why are they white ravens?,' in H. Opschoor and K. Turner (eds), *Economic Incentives and Environmental Policies*, Dordrecht: Kluwer Academic Publishers, pp. 55–69.

Deutsch, K.W. (1970), *Politics and Government*, Boston: Houghton Mifflin.

Dryzek, J.S. (1997), *The Politics of the Earth. Environmental Discourses*, Oxford: Oxford University Press.

Gustafsson, G. and J.J. Richardson (1979), 'Concepts of rationality and the policy process', *European Journal of Political Research*, **7**, 415–36.

Hahn, R.W. (1989), 'Economic presciptions for environmental problems: how the patient followed the doctor's orders', *Journal of Economic Perspectives*, **3** (3), 95–114.

Hahn, R.W. (1991), *A Primer on Environmental Policy Design*, London: Harwood Academic Publishers.

Hahn, R.W. and G.L. Hester (1989), 'Marketable permits: lessons for theory and practice', *Ecology Law Quarterly*, **16**, 361–406.

Howe, C.W. (1991), *Taxes Versus Tradable Permits: The Views from Europe and the United States*, Wageningen: Agricultural University.

Keohane, N.O., R.L. Revesz and R.N. Stavins (1997), 'The positive political economy of instrument choice in environmental policy', paper presented at the 1997 Allied Social Science Associations Meeting, New Orleans, 4–6 January.

Kiser, L.L. and E. Ostrom (1982), 'The three worlds of action: a metatheoretical synthesis of institutional approaches', in E. Ostrom (ed.), *Strategies of Political Inquiry*, Beverly Hills: Sage, pp. 179–222.

Klok, P.-J. (1995), 'A classification of instruments for environmental policy', in B. Dente (ed.), *Environmental Policy in Search of New Instruments*, Dordrecht: Kluwer Academic Publishers, pp. 21–36.

Kneese, A.V. and J.L. Sweeney (1985), *Handbook of Natural Resource and Energy Economics*, vol. 1, Amsterdam: North Holland.

Larrue, C. (1995), 'The political (un)feasibility of environmental economic instruments', in B. Dente (ed.), *Environmental Policy in Search of New Instruments*, Dordrecht: Kluwer Academic Publishers, pp. 37–54.

Liberatore, A. (1995), 'Arguments, assumptions and the choice of policy instruments: the case of the debate on the CO-2/energy tax in the European Community', in B.

Dente (ed.), *Environmental Policy in Search of New Instruments*, Dordrecht: Kluwer Academic Publishers, pp. 55–71.

Lövgren, K. (1994), 'Economic instruments for air pollution control in Sweden', in F. Forsund and G. Klaassen (eds), *Economic Instruments for Air Pollution Control*, Solna.

OECD (1991), *Environmental Policy: How to Apply Economic Instruments*, Paris: OECD.

Opschoor, J.B. and K. Turner (1994), *Economic Incentives and Environmental Policies*, Dordrecht: Kluwer Academic Publishers.

Opschoor, J.B., H.B. Vos and L. de Savornin Lohman (1994), *Managing the Environment: The Role of Economic Instruments*, Paris: OECD.

Ostrom, E. (1990), *Governing the Commons: The Evolution of Institutions for Collective Action*, New York: Cambridge University Press.

Peeters, M. (1992), 'Marktconform milieurecht? Een rechtsvergelijkende studie naar de verhandelbaarheid van emissierechten', dissertation, Zwolle: W.E.J. Tjeenk Willink.

Sabatier, P.A. and H.C. Jenkins-Smith (eds) (1993), *Policy Change and Learning: An Advocacy Coalition Approach*, Boulder: Westview Press.

Sabatier, P.A. and H.C. Jenkins-Smith (1997), 'The advocacy coalition framework: an assessment', in F. Forsund and G. Klaassen (eds), *Theories of the Policy Process*, Boulder: Westview Press (forthcoming – version as of April 1997).

Schrama, G.J.I. and P.-J. Klok (1995), 'The swift introduction of "Clean Cars" in the Netherlands, 1986–1992: the origin and effect of incentive measures', in M. Jänicke and H. Weidner (eds), *Successful Environmental Policy*, Berlin: Edition Sigma, pp. 203–22.

Sliggers, C.J. (1995), 'Verhandelbare emissierechten en verzuring: Nederland wint van Amerika', *Milieu*, **9**, 17–18.

Stavins, R.N. (1994a), 'Transaction costs and tradeable permits', Faculty Research Working Paper Series, John F. Kennedy School of Government, Harvard University.

Stavins, R.N. (1994b), 'Tradeable Permits for Environmental Protection', presentation for the Ministry of Environmental Protection, Warsaw.

Sterner, T. (1990), *The Pricing of and Demand for Gasoline*, Stockholm: Swedish Transport Research Board.

Sterner, T. (1994), 'Environmental tax reform: the Swedish experience', mimeo, Stockholm.

Svoboda, C.J. (1992), 'Examining state air pollution regulations', paper prepared for the Annual Meeting of the Southern Political Science Association, Atlanta.

Tang, S.Y. (1992), *Institutions and Collective Action: Self Governance in Irrigation*, San Francisco: Institute for Contemporary Studies Press.

US Congress, Office of Technology Assessment (1995), *Environmental Policy Tools: A User's Guide*, Washington, DC: The United States Congress.

Vogel, D. (1986), *National Styles of Regulation*, Ithaca: Cornell University Press.

Vos, H. (1997), 'Environmental taxation in the Netherlands', in Th. O'Riordan (ed.), *Ecotaxation*, London: Earthscan, pp. 246–62.

Weizsäcker, E.U. von (1994), *Earth Politics*, London and New Jersey: Zed Books.

PART III

MBIs in the policy process

5. Dialogue and economic efficiency: two antagonistic goals for environmental policy-making? Lessons from the French packaging waste management system*

Olivier Godard

ABSTRACT

Contemporary public environmental policies appear to be affected by a 'double bind' imposed by two requirements: to be cost-effective, and to be based on dialogue and partnership between public bodies, industry and local authorities in order to be acceptable. If policies are designed to be economically efficient, for example through the use of incentive taxes, they are either rejected as unacceptable by industry or poorly implemented. If they are based on dialogue and negotiation, their designs suffer from important incentive weaknesses. The present interpretation of this 'double bind' makes a connection between the two phases of policy design and policy implementation. To cooperate in the building of a framework for common action, competitors adopt rules which prevent their respective pre-existing economic positions (market shares, relative costs) from being destabilized, although economic efficiency would result from changing them on the basis of treatment and external costs. Meanwhile, once the new cooperative system has been set up, a process of collective learning may take place and leave room for the progressive incorporation of more appropriate incentives.

These points are well illustrated by the main features of the current system of packaging waste management in France. A description of the institutional organization is followed by an analysis of the incentive content of this organization. It is shown how initial incentives do not respond to the requirements of economic efficiency, and that they do not drive the system towards the targets initially defined by public authorities regarding materials recycling. Meanwhile, the new organization has demonstrated a capacity for collective learning. Two critical features are gaining new information on costs and revising operational rules. Some adjustments have already been introduced since the system was initiated in 1992 and more are expected in future. The extent to which they are actually going to increase the incentive compatibility of the system remains unknown.

INTRODUCTION

According to a standard economic viewpoint, the economic efficiency of most environmental policy instruments used by the Organization for Economic Co-operation and Development (OECD) governments since the late 1960s is questionable. The usual administrative, regulatory and 'command-and-control' approaches have been strongly criticized for their implementation weaknesses and lack of economic efficiency. They still constitute the basis of environmental policies, although other tools (financial) supplement them.

Economists frequently advocate economic instruments (taxes, tradable permits) on grounds of efficiency. They are supposed to best address contexts of imperfect and asymmetrical information about technical opportunities and abatement costs between governments and industry. Economists have not been much listened to until now: for instance, most uses of taxation have only retained the financial dimension by earmarking resources. It has been argued that this type of financial approach has certain efficiency advantages compared to a pure 'command-and-control' approach (Andersen, 1994). Surely, significant potentials of improvement still remain untapped. Unhappily, the use of economic incentives generally faces strong hostility from industry, except if they include a distribution of new rents and protection against competitors, grandfathered tradable permits being a case in point.

So, even before economic instruments are given the full opportunity to match up with reality, some scholars think the time has come to develop a 'third generation' of policy instruments (Dente, 1995), one based on information, persuasion, dialogue, cooperation and voluntary agreements. If taken as substitutes for and not supplements to economic instruments, these approaches have not definitely proved their capability to achieve efficient allocations of efforts in pollution control, in spite of the advocacy efforts of some analysts (Glachant, 1994). They are deemed to be more palatable because they have been negotiated with the stakeholders. Nevertheless, it may be contended that the happy result of an efficient allocation will come about only if policy-makers prescribe strong commitments and offer credible threats, and if appropriate incentives are implemented to induce a real shift in the motivations and interests of industry. Basically, such 'third generation' instruments may facilitate the elaboration of environmental policies rather than become substitutes for 'older' types of incentive instruments (Godard and Beaumais, 1994).

In the beginning of the 1990s, new European initiatives were taken in the field of waste management in order to develop various forms of materials and energy recovery. More specifically, organizations were set up to stimulate packaging waste valorization, and in response to quantified targets and timetables, new organizations were established. Based on the rationale of private firms receiving fees paid by packing firms in order to finance waste collection and sorting, such organizations were adopted in Germany as well as in France. They provide interesting cases to test how dialogue, cooperation and voluntary approaches do perform in combining various instruments.

This study is devoted to an examination of the French system for valorizing packaging waste. The main direction of analysis is to consider the incentive dimensions of this system. It will first show the gap between initial targets of reference and the physical recycling performance that can be achieved, and secondly, the lack of appropriate incentives in the initial design for a full integration of the environmental costs (treatment and residual external costs) generated by the use of packaging throughout the economy. Why is this so? It is suggested that such weaknesses may be linked to the conditions under which this packaging waste system has been devised and negotiated, first among firms and then between industry and government. Asking industry to elaborate the rules of the game may have been politically clever, but it should be acknowledged that this approach is responsible for the initial weaknesses in incentives. Dark pessimism is nevertheless not inevitable. There is a way out of the initial 'double bind': the new organization is able to develop collective learning and adapt to changing contexts through the provision of a regular revision of targets and incentives. A progressive trajectory of adjustments may improve the overall economic efficiency of the system. If economic efficiency cannot be achieved when the system is first instituted, it may be approached in a dynamical fashion on the basis of experience.

The first section presents some theoretical views about the formation of management systems and the issue of economic performance at the implementation stage. The second section describes the institutional organization of French packaging waste management. In the third section the consistence and the incentive content delivered by the main components of the system are considered. The last section describes two mechanisms which allow for a collective learning: the use of an experimental approach and provisions for adapting the rules.

ON INSTITUTIONAL TRAJECTORIES, AND THE DOUBLE BIND AROUND ECONOMIC EFFICIENCY

Two Opposite Viewpoints on Public Policies

Many differences in assessments of policies originate in the theoretical bases from which insights on regulatory changes are gained. Two opposite viewpoints can be extracted from the contributions of economics and political science, respectively. Normative economic theory assumes that the choice of a new policy instrument is guided by the search for economic efficiency. In this framework, determining which is the most cost-efficient instrument depends on specific features of implementation contexts: number of agents to be regulated, information asymmetries, cost heterogeneity, relative slopes of damage and abatement cost curves under uncertainty, scope of practical options to which agents have access, impact on technological development and so on (Godard and Beaumais, 1994). Regarding actual, empirical choices, policy-making leaves an open field for lobbying and the capture of policies by some stakeholders. Instruments which were presumed to be efficient on paper are thus perverted. According to some scholars (Glachant, 1994; Lévêque, 1996), it would be better to acknowledge these facts and try to improve the process of negotiation on environmental regulations.

Taking the opposite view to normative economics, positive comparative analyses supplied by political science focus on the fact that policy choices are more dependent on specific features of the institutional framework than on the objective characteristics of the problems to be solved, while economic efficiency is not at the core of the policy process. Several variants of this idea can be found. For some analysts, new policies are not constructed as the best response to an objective problem, but as a reaction to the consequences of previous policies dealing with the same category of problem; and they are thus framed by national policy styles (Merrien, 1993). Others think public decisions result mainly from rhetorical practices and logic (Majone, 1989) or that they are derived from specific compromises between several orders of legitimacy ('industrial', 'market', 'civic', 'tradition' and so on) (Boltanski and Thévenot, 1991). Institutional rules and organizational cultures express such compromises. Economic efficiency is then merely an additional element of the current modern rhetoric. Despite a pervasive presence in discourses, most political scientists deny that policy choices are made directly on the basis of economic arguments.

Institutional Trajectories

Is there some way to bridge the gap between these two viewpoints? One approach is provided by the concept of 'institutional trajectories' (Godard, 1995). It links the margin for change with the inherited features of the previous regulatory system. Due to the costly 'investment in forms' which has been made in the existing regulatory system, changing it all is not an easy endeavour. Social actors should perceive this change as a strong necessity or as a way to capture very significant benefits. Innovation will mainly be achieved at the margin of existing rules and devices, making compatibility with the existing framework a critical condition.

A rather simple – but radical to economists – conclusion results: the main issue of real-world policy changes is not economic efficiency but problem-solving. The very definition of the problem to be solved is an issue of arbitration and compromise between alternative ways of shaping a problem for public action in a controversial universe (Godard, 1997). In that process, problem-shaping is directly related to the concerns of social actors, not some objective, scientific, extra-social definition of environmental issues and economic efficiency.

For the choice of policy instruments, this means that economic efficiency as such does not matter in most cases[1] to most actors, even if some of them use this rhetoric strategically in order to achieve their aims (for instance, budget reductions aimed at by the Ministry of Finance).[2] To be incorporated as policy instruments in a changing system, economically efficient instruments have to have other features besides their economic efficiency, features that will be appreciated by social actors in a problem-solving context. Economists interested in the development of such instruments have to demonstrate that these instruments can fit well into the existing institutional context and solve the problems at stake.

A 'Double Bind' on Environmental Public Policies

Environmental public policies are subject to a 'double bind':[3] on the one hand, they must be based on dialogue, consultation, partnership and so on, with firms and other decentralized agents, while, on the other hand, they must be cost-effective and efficient. The choice of the concept of 'double bind' means that these two requirements inherently are opponents. Two explanations can be given for this opposition:

1. Conditions of dialogue and cooperation in the construction phase of a system have a key influence on the effectiveness and economic efficiency of the system in the implementation stage; upstream and downstream parts of the policy process cannot be separated. It is upstream that trust or distrust, basic expectations about the legitimate distribution of rights, and the credibility of the system are generated. Quite obviously, it is upstream

that acceptance of policy change or innovation is gained or denied. The behaviour of downstream decentralized agents will reflect what was achieved upstream: are agents going to play the game or are they going to behave in a way that would ruin the new system? In this respect a new, purely top-down policy instrument imposed on firms or various users may remain poorly implemented or unintentionally generate undesirable side-effects expressing legitimacy troubles. In any case, economic efficiency would be badly affected.

2. To associate some industrial stakeholders with the construction of a new system, or to delegate this task to them in order to make the new system acceptable, will lead to a set of rules which will fall short of the appropriate incentives needed to achieve a cost-efficient equilibrium in resource allocation. This weakness originates in three features of the process of consultation: (1) the possible gap between the stakeholders being selected for dialogue and the various groups affected by the system; (2) the initial imperfection of information related to technology and costs; and (3) the specific constraints deriving from the voluntary setting up of a new framework for common action between economic competitors. These three points are now looked at in detail.

First, dialogue and cooperation are always partial and selective regarding the type of stakeholders associated. Practical, but also political reasons are involved: policy-making is an issue of finding adequate majorities and avoiding blocking minorities. So, choosing who is going to be associated with the design of a new system is a critical variable in the hands of policy-makers (Dente, 1995). Only those organized stakeholders who globally accept the policy aims may be associated with the process, while neither the unorganized nor absolute opponents may be so. To that end, agreed rules will tend to fix a compromise acceptable to direct participants, even at the expense of other groups. Those who participate may easily come to an agreement around the idea of transferring a significant part of the financial burden onto silent, unrepresented groups. For instance, the new concept of 'shared responsibility' in waste management is a way for industry to transfer part of the burden of environmental costs onto other agents (local communities and taxpayers).[4]

Second, dialogue and cooperation are initially developed in contexts where information is insufficient for calculating first best optima. Information on costs is not commonly available. Ignorance is common to all agents on some aspects, while asymmetric information characterizes other areas. Proposals and counter-proposals during the negotiation phase do provide means for exchanging information (Glachant, 1994), but generally, cost assessments remain controversial and strategic. This is far from the ideal context of perfect information on external and internal costs and negligible transaction costs, while such an ideal context is required in order to make direct negotiation an economically efficient procedure (Coase, 1960). This nexus of information and negotiation issues cannot be resolved without developing a social framework for common action.

Third, and most importantly, in order to convince competing firms and industries to develop sustained cooperative links for constructing and managing a new system, a common interest and a common will to pursue cooperation have to be generated, in spite of basic uncertainties about the future contexts for individual action. To achieve this result, the first aim of competitors will be to neutralize their current rivalry. Protecting the pre-existing conditions of competition (relative prices, market shares) quite often does this. The justification offered is that environmental policy should not interfere (they say distort) with current conditions of competition. In the case of packaging waste management, the main competition is between rivalling materials (plastics, glass, aluminium, steel, cardboard).[5] If neutralization is not achieved, some stakeholders will neither take part in the process of dialogue, nor join the agreement, because they see themselves as potential net losers.

Meanwhile, internalizing treatment and external costs of waste would generally require a change of previous conditions of competition and a differentiation of requirements, since not all materials, technologies and commodities impose the same rate of environmental costs. So, the setting up of a new framework of common action between competitors cannot incorporate appropriate incentives for economic efficiency right from the beginning. A sort of cross-sector community must first be constituted, stabilized and equipped (constitutive rules, monitoring and enforcement procedures, arbitration and sanctions and so on) among various types of actor with conflicting interests, due to the setting up of a new framework of common action. Then, after several years of shared experience, participants may be able to envisage various types of uncompensated differentiation of individual treatments and change the rules ordering the previous state of affairs.

This means that, given time, running a framework for common action generates the possibility of collective learning. Therein lies an opportunity to progressively improve the incentive content of the system. If this happy result is to be reached, learning should take place in two directions: on the one side an improvement of economic information regarding the costs of treatment technologies and external costs generated by each type of competing product (packaging materials in this case); and on the other side an institutional reinforcement of the common framework (routines, rules, predictability of respective behaviours, trust and commitments). A critical question is the respective pace of progress in these two directions of learning. If transparent information about costs and burden-sharing comes too early, a reactivation of rivalry may ruin the framework for common action and halt the learning process. Trust and common will between the participants should be sustained, and the common framework must be made strong enough to resist the increasing tensions generated by improved information, for instance information revealing an unfair distribution of costs between participants, and to allow for a revision of rules and commitments in accordance with this. At the same time, improving information about internal and external costs of competing products is a condition for adjusting the rules so as to approach economic efficiency.[6]

The evolution of the European Union (EU) decision rules, or the development of the Long Range Transboundary Air Pollution Convention of Geneva with its successive protocols of Helsinki and Oslo, give empirical evidence of the possibility of this type of adaptive progress towards showing greater consideration towards economic efficiency within a common framework of action. The French system for packaging waste management will provide another illustration of the main general points made above.

KEY FEATURES OF THE FRENCH SYSTEM FOR PACKAGING WASTE MANAGEMENT

A new organization of packaging waste management was adopted in France in 1992 (Whiston and Glachant, 1996; Buclet *et al.*, 1997; Defeuilley and Godard, 1997). The corner-stone of this system, set up by Decree of April 1992, is a new obligation imposed on packing firms to ensure proper management of the waste they generate through their packaging decisions. They are given three options: implementing a returnable system, recovering the products, or joining and financing an authorized consortium to take care of this obligation on their behalf. Most firms have chosen the latter solution and become associated with the consortium Eco-Emballages. Moreover, the public authorities have set a general objective: packaging waste flows must be valorized at a rate of 75 per cent in mass by 2002 and beyond. The text of the agreement on Eco-Emballages also refers to an assumption of a three-quarter objective for materials recycling, leaving the remaining quarter to be incinerated or composted.

A New Consortium: Eco-Emballages

In accordance with an option noted in the Decree a new private consortium, Eco-Emballages was created by the industries concerned,[7] and officially agreed to by the public authorities. A 1975 Law assigned the responsibility for municipal waste management to local communities ('communes' in French) and their groupings (intercommunal syndicates), where they exist. This was not changed by the new system. So the role of Eco-Emballages is to contract with municipalities[8] in order to develop a valorization of packaging waste, mainly through selective collection and sorting of materials intended for recycling.

These contracts define the subsidies given by Eco-Emballages for each type of technical option according to materials (glass, aluminium, plastics and so on). The basic rule is that subsidies should cover the extra costs of these operations, compared to the treatment costs resulting from incineration with energy recovery technologies that meet the most recent legal standards.

To be able to finance subsidies, Eco-Emballages must raise resources. So, adherent packing firms have to pay fees to Eco-Emballages on the basis of the number of packages sold. In return, they have the right to affix a 'green dot' to their products, certifying that they are exempt from retaking obligations. The initial rates have been fixed at an average of 1 centime per package (Table 5.1), and it is expected to reach cF3[9] in a few years' time, when the system is fully operational. Contributions paid do not vary according to materials or types of packaging, but by volume only: all packages are subject to the same rates whatever their composition.

Table 5.1   Contributions rates to Eco-Emballages (for 'rigid empty packages')

Package volume (cm³)	Contribution (cF)
> 30 0001	10
3 001 to 30 000	2.5
201 to 3 000	1
151 to 200	0.5
101 to 150	0.25
50 to 100	0.10
< 50	0.10

Note: cF = French centime, that is FF0.01.

Source: Eco-Emballages (1992, p. 50).

Furthermore, under the aegis of public authorities, minimum guaranteed retaking prices have been negotiated between Eco-Emballages and representative associations of different materials producers in charge of recycling. These guaranteed prices provide the basis for contracts between the recycling firms and the municipalities, in accordance with the schedule

Table 5.2   Initial rates of payments to municipalities (1993) (francs per tonne)

	Direct subsidy by Eco-Emballages (F/t)	Minimum prices paid by material recyclers (F/t)	Minimal gain for a municipality (F/t)
Plastics	1500	Free retaking	1500
Aluminium			
not burnt	1500	1000–1500	2500
burnt	500	500–1000	1000
Iron/steel			
not burnt	300	50–200	350
burnt	75	0–50	75
Paper/cardboard	750	Free retaking	750
Glass	0–50	150	150

Source: Eco-Emballages (1993, pp. 10–11).

specified in Table 5.2. There is a counterpart to guaranteed prices: detailed quality standards have to be met by municipalities as regards delivered recycled materials (Minimum Technical Prescriptions (MTP)).

The aim of this system of guaranteed prices is to secure a market for recovery materials through the creation of predictable exploitation conditions for selective collection and sorting. For a long time the main economic source of weakness in the recovery sector has been the chronic price instability of recovered materials. In the past, this has resulted in a low level of investment, and thus a low technological level. Price instability was seen as an obstacle to the development of recycling.

Contextual Features

The new system is ambitious regarding the general objective stated by the authorities. Their initial expectation was that more than 4 million tonnes of packaging waste (representing 56 per cent of the total amount of packaging waste and almost 17 per cent of municipal waste) was to be recycled annually by the year 2002 and 1.3 million tonnes (19 per cent) incinerated with energy recovery.[10] In comparison, in 1990 52 per cent of all municipal waste was disposed of through dumping and 38 per cent through incineration. So, a serious effort was called for to develop recycling. At the same time, most existing incineration facilities would have to be dismantled and replaced because they do not meet current emission standards.

When compared to the approaches chosen in countries like the Netherlands and Germany, a key policy principle in France was to avoid a centralized mandatory hierarchy of valorization technologies. Production of compost, incineration with energy recovery, recycling and reuse are all considered legitimate means to limit the amounts of waste, as only 'ultimate waste' receives authorization to be disposed of in landfills by the year 2002.[11] Basically, such choices are left to decentralized agents. A tax of FF40 per tonne of waste is to be paid by users of dumping installations in order to raise the funds necessary to subsidize new valorization facilities. The 1992 Law on waste also includes what may be called a 'proximity principle': restrictions on the transportation of waste in distance and volume are a specific goal of waste management. Thus, the Law obliges counties (French *départements*) to prepare plans for waste management so as to programme adequate investments in facilities for the treatment of foreseen flows of waste. With the exception of these two constraints, the greatest autonomy is preserved when it comes to the technical choices available to actors all along the packaging 'chain': materials producers, packing firms, retailers, consumers and local communities. The goal is to achieve a good adaptation to local contexts, in the hope that such an approach will abate the costs of waste treatment as much as possible.

To a large extent, the preoccupation with decentralization of technological choices shows which industrial circles have gained influence on the French system: they clearly do not belong to the equipment sector (the latter might have been interested in developing new markets for specific technologies). Materials industries and packing firms were the ones involved in designing the system. Their aims can be assumed to be to obtain the lowest perturbation of their markets and industrial strategies possible, and the lowest possible financial charge on themselves, while providing an acceptable solution to the waste management problem in the EU context. In fact, these industries conceived of this new system in response to a request from the Ministry of Environment to make their own proposal, if they wanted to avoid a mandatory regulation based on the prescriptive approach considered by the German government at that time. So, a key feature of the process of devising the packaging waste management system in France was the combination of a horizontal dialogue between several industrial sectors, and a vertical one between certain industrial circles and government.

ON THE CONSISTENCE AND INCENTIVE CONTENT OF PACKAGING FEES, RECYCLING SUBSIDIES AND GUARANTEED RETAKING PRICES

In order to assess the efficiency of a new system, the first step is to question whether the system is organized to achieve the performance for which it was created: are means consistent with aims and targets? The second question is related to the cost-effectiveness of the system's performance. In a context of very imperfect information, it is frequently difficult to deliver unambiguous empirical answers. Nevertheless, it may be useful to look at the incentive content of the system to check the extent to which incentives are pushing in the right direction. In a decentralized system of choices such as the French packaging waste system, one main condition should be satisfied in order to exploit opportunities in an overall cost-effective way: decentralized agents must face an economic environment which provides appropriate signals.

There is some evidence that the initial rules and incentives of the French system neither permitted the achievement of the reference target initially expected, nor the development of an economically efficient way to tackle the packaging waste issue. Recycling would be undermined in the future by weak, or even counter-productive, incentives. Within this system, none of the critical actors has a vested interest in developing recycling. The municipalities are not offered sufficiently strong incentives to invest massively in selective collection and sorting. Material recyclers may not find French recovery materials sufficiently attractive because of excessive prices and insufficient quality, measured by the standards on the European market. Packing firms are interested in paying the lowest possible contribution to Eco-Emballages; this will be achieved if the rate of recycling remains low. In the following section, four main aspects are successively considered: the relationship between material and financial balances; the pattern of subsidies; the structure of fees; and retaking conditions (guaranteed prices and Minimum Technical Prescriptions).

A Gap Between Financial Flows and Material Recycling Targets

The French system can be described as a financial mechanism set up to achieve a physical performance. There is a direct link between financial flows and physical performance. If financial flows are too meagre, physical flows will be, too. What can be said of the first years of implementation?

By June 1996, nearly 6000 local communities representing 20 million inhabitants were directly or indirectly (through intercommunal syndicates) involved in contracts with Eco-Emballages. Only 8 million were involved in operations of selective collection and sorting. In 1995, amounts of recycled materials were still modest, especially of non-metal materials (Table 5.3). During the same year, energy recovery from packaging waste involved 280 000 tonnes of waste. In 1995, fees paid to Eco-Emballages amounted to FF537 million, and FF194 million worth of subsidies to local communities. The financial affluence that seemed to characterize these early years, however,

Table 5.3 Amounts of materials recycled through Eco-Emballages in 1995

Materials	Recycling (tonnes)	Total amount of packaging (tonnes)	Recycling (%)
Steel	127 000	500 000	25.4
Aluminium	1 200	30 000	4
Paper/cardboard	24 000	1 800 000	1.3
Plastic	12 000	1 200 000	1
Glass	256 000	2 300 000	11
Total	420 200	5 830 000	7.2

Source: Eco-Emballages (1996).

mainly reflected the time-lag in setting up an appropriate organization and the initial difficulties encountered while organizing selective collection and sorting. If the physical targets are really to be met in the future, the maximum level of fee, which has been agreed upon at the very beginning (maximum cF3 per package), will not be sufficient. By the year 2002, when the programme is scheduled to be fully developed, the potential amount of subsidies will be FF2.4 billion. Depending on the respective shares of recycling and energy recovery, the financial needs have been estimated to within a range of FF3.1 to FF5.2 billion on the basis of the initial 1993 rates of subsidies. This entails a mean value for required fees of cF4 to cF7 (Togia, 1996).The revision of tariffs paid to municipalities which took place in June 1996 increased the level of subsidy for non-metal materials (see Table 5.4 below). In so doing, it further expanded future financial needs. However, some Eco-Emballages' participants explicitly turned down such an expansion in advance, and it may send the system into a crisis. Another way out would be to reconsider the reference targets and recycling efforts while increasing energy recovery. This preference for incineration was the natural tendency in France, until a new consciousness arose about the huge investments required, and fears related to dioxin led to a reconsideration of the strategy.[12] In any case, this analysis leads to the same conclusion: the various components of the system are not presently coherent, and a significant adaptation of either goals or means will have to be achieved.

Subsidies to Municipalities

The main incentive used by Eco-Emballages to induce the development of selective collection and sorting is to offer direct subsidies to the municipalities to reduce the net financial burden of selective collection and sorting. The subsidy is supposed to be set at a level covering the cost difference between selective collection and sorting, and the average cost of undifferentiated collection for up-to-date waste-to-energy facilities. Is this system sufficiently attractive? At least two shortcomings must be underscored.

1. The duration of the municipal contracts offered by Eco-Emballages (a maximum of six years) is shorter than the depreciation period of the investments required from the municipalities to introduce selective collection and sorting. For a profit-making private activity, this time-scale may be considered sufficient, with a normal residual risk to be borne by the contractor. However, this is not the rationale of public local authorities: they do not have to take such entrepreneurial risks, but must manage wisely in the interest of the local population.

2. According to initial 1993 rates and rules, the financial support from Eco-Emballages could be said to be insufficient to compensate for the expenditures which municipalities would have to face. The baseline scenario, on which overcosts are estimated, does not correspond with the current situation in which the municipalities consider the opportunity to invest in the newest approach, but the situation in which they would be placed if they had invested in a brand new system for incineration. The municipalities will have to bear more net charges for waste treatment if they switch to selective collection and sorting than is currently necessary and than they can expect to go on bearing if they extend the useful life of existing waste treatment facilities. Moreover, the real costs of new options were and are still not well known. Eco-Emballages has defined its financial mechanism on the basis of estimations often described by municipal representatives as rather conservative. Therefore, for many municipalities, positive incentives to switch to recycling do not seem to be provided by the subsidies offered, which appear to be at best neutral regarding the recycling option. Admitting to this weakness of the incentive was the core issue of the revision of rates negotiated in 1996 (see below).

Fees Paid by Packing Firms

Fees paid by packing firms to Eco-Emballages have to be seen as a financial mechanism rather than an incentive instrument. Two dimensions are of concern. First, packaging industries will bear only the average overcost associated with selective collection and sorting and not the full marginal development cost of the whole set of operations needed to carry out the treatment and elimination of waste resulting from their products.[13] This is an important difference from the German system, DSD, where contributions are much higher and differentiated per material (Defeuilley and Quirion, 1995). Second, fees are not differentiated according to the downstream, treatment and external environmental costs associated with various materials. Possibly advantageous substitutions which respond to a full internalization of the social costs of packages' end of life are thus not triggered. All this can only have a limited incentive effect on the behaviour of packing firms at source, regarding either the absolute level of use of packaging or the choice of specific materials.

Retaking Conditions

The level of price paid by material producers to the municipalities for taking back sorted materials could be an important incentive. In fact, from the very beginning, retaking conditions have been an important point of tension between industry and municipalities for both price and quality reasons.

When the system was negotiated, prices were set at levels very near those of prevailing market conditions. So, incentives for the municipalities did not lie in the absolute levels of retaking prices, but in the guarantee of a minimum price which helped to avoid shocks created by market fluctuations. It means that this risk was transferred to recyclers. They were to absorb changing market conditions. This is not an easy challenge for them, since the market for materials is quite volatile. This is illustrated by the recent evolution of plastic materials. A price drop on PET (polyethylene terephthalate) made from first-hand materials, and the competitive pressure of subsidized regenerated PET coming from Germany, Italy or Austria on the European market, have made it difficult to pursue the regeneration of PVC (polyvinyl chloride), an area in which France has a high level of specialization. This resulted in partially idle capacity. The insufficient quality of materials sorted by municipalities is also directly translated into extra regeneration costs: when the quality supplied does not meet the standards of European markets, recyclers have to pay for an extra sorting in order to be able to compete. Such extra costs are not financed by the Eco-Emballages mechanism. So, the incentives that recyclers are faced with do not push in the direction of a great expansion of recycling for plastics and paper/cardboard.

In the initial bargain, the counterpart of guaranteed prices given to recyclers was the MTP for sorted materials. These standards of quality have also given rise to multiple tensions between recyclers and the municipalities, on technical as well as on institutional grounds. In the initial phase, certain municipalities which have managed pilot projects and accumulated experience in the field of selective collection, stated they could not regularly meet the MTP that the materials industry wanted to impose. Their incapacity was related to the variability of the composition of waste and the level of technological investment they could afford. This conflict has been resolved by issuing a less stringent MTP for the beginning years, with the perspective of future tightening. In the current situation, the paradox is that the MTP cannot be met regularly by municipalities, while at the same time some are not sufficiently stringent to satisfy the requirements of European markets.[14]

Beyond this technical disagreement, it is questionable to place municipalities under the supervision of private firms, a reversal of the usual pattern of relationships between public authorities and private bodies. Although the packaging firms are supposed to be constrained by the public interest to take the necessary steps to manage their waste, the system tends to submit municipalities to commercial-type requirements. This way, as with any supplier, firms may think that they have a right to dismiss their retaking obligations in case of insufficient quality! So, the step of defining quality standards appears to be a difficult operation in terms of distributing responsibilities and risks among partners with heterogeneous institutional status.

A Synthesis of the Incentive Content of the Packaging Waste System

On the whole, industry is not strongly stimulated to develop recycling by the packaging waste system. Upstream, the more recycling is developed, the more Eco-Emballages has to bear important financing, and the more the fees to be paid by packing firms increase. Downstream, the more recycling is developed, material producers have to retake increasingly large quantities of secondary raw materials, and the more they are faced with financial and technical problems of finding productive and profitable uses, of especially plastics.

The joint effect of weak incentives and technological and economic uncertainties could only lead the new system to stabilize around a sub-optimal equilibrium which implies a rather low rate of recycling for packaging waste. Several trends are mutually consistent and sustain an equilibrium which is quite disappointing regarding the initial reference targets for recycling: (1) restricted financial support from Eco-Emballages; (2) restricted investment by the municipalities (too risky, too expensive); (3) low level of fees (packing firms want to pay the smallest fees possible); (4) inability of a significant number of municipalities to satisfy the MTP for recovered materials.

With regard to this first round of analysis, it may be wondered if the new system, including Eco-Emballages as the centrepiece, was really intended as a means to promote recycling. Another motive may have been to block the dissemination of other national or European initiatives. The latter were believed by French firms to be ill-timed and to induce excessive cost. The first period of implementation may also have been conceived by industry as a useful experiment for convincing their main partners (public authorities, the municipalities) that recycling could not reasonably be a major way to tackle packaging waste. The implicit message at that time was that energy valorization was the main, economically realistic, option to consider. All these aspects may have guided the initial steps, but once set up, the system permitted collective learning. The new organization had to overcome tensions and small crises in a changing policy context. Whatever the initial motives, the self-organizational features of the system could lead to something else, for instance an improved physical and economic performance.

A SYSTEM INCORPORATING MECHANISMS FOR LEARNING

Six years after the new system was launched, packaging waste management has yet to reach a stable state. There has been movement through small crises, technological changes and progress in information. Discovering the costs and performance characteristics of selective collection, sorting and recycling technologies was a real challenge during the initial period. A 'trial-and-error' experimental approach has been adopted. Adjustment procedures incorporated in the system and the private status of Eco-Emballages also made it easier to change and adapt than if a public administration had been in charge of operating the whole system.

An Experimental Approach

From the very beginning, Eco-Emballages has adopted a strategy which incorporates an experimental dimension in order to develop collective learning with the municipalities. During the first two years, action was focused on the identification of a group of cases representative of the very diversified situations to be managed, before the domain of action was extended. The problems to be managed range from thinly populated rural areas to appartment buildings in urban neighbourhoods. After a selection of candidates 41 'pilot sites' have been chosen, covering a wide range of situations, technical combinations and organizational methods for collection and treatment. These sites are supervised and helped by Eco-Emballages, which disseminates information from these experiences to other municipalities. This approach should help identify the most suitable and efficient organizational method for each type of 'stylized problem'. The aim was to shape a limited number of reference models, the supply of which would simplify future choices for the municipalities (Eco-Emballages, 1993).

To help implement this experimental approach, special financial resources were allocated by the Fund for the Modernization of Waste Management, devoted to the development of innovative techniques and financed by the FF40 'dumping tax'. If municipal investments as a whole are sufficiently extended in time, a flow of technical innovations could result and be progressively incorporated by the municipalities, without major risks of technological 'lock-in' (Arthur, 1989). The dominance of one technology could turn out to be embarrassing if this technology is ultimately proved inferior or a source of uncontrolled environmental risks.[15]

A Regular Revision of Rates and Rules for Subsidies

The initial public agreement on Eco-Emballages was for a six-year period, with a stipulated re-examination and revision after three years. A first revision was achieved in June 1996 after a period of several months of negotiation. Significant changes were introduced to increase the level of financial support for some materials and to make recycling more attractive. During the first three years, the municipalities had demonstrated an excessive interest in incineration of plastics and paper, and insufficient interest in separate collection and sorting for recycling (see Table 5.4).

Table 5.4   Revised rates of payments to municipalities (1996) (francs per tonne)

	Direct subsidy by Eco-Emballages (F/t)	Minimum prices paid by material recyclers (F/t)	Minimal gain for a municipality (F/t)
Plastics	1500–4750	Free retaking	1500–4750
Aluminium			
not burnt	1500	1000	2500
burnt	500	750	1250
Iron/steel			
not burnt	300	50–200	350
burnt	75	0–50	75
Paper/cardboard	750–1650	Free retaking	750–1650
Glass	20–50	150	170–200

Sources: Perrier (1996); Guellec (1997).

The revision introduced non-proportional incentives for paper/cardboard, plastics and glass. The rate of subsidy became much higher for municipalities with superior yield in selective collection per inhabitant. For instance, for plastics the subsidy is only FF1500 per tonne if the yield is less than 2.5 kilograms/year/inhabitant and FF4750 per tonne if the yield is above 5 kilograms/year/inhabitant.

At the same time, incineration with energy recovery is only subsidized if a minimum rate of recycling is achieved. Thus, the number of tons of waste-to-energy subsidized depends on the amount of recycled materials: one ton of recycled plastic gives the right to a subsidy corresponding to three tons of energy valorization.

These adjustments will not be sufficient to address all current difficulties and the general gap between financial flows and physical targets, but technically the existing organization is resilient enough to achieve further adaptation. For instance, new special efforts may be required to support the recycling operations after the stage of sorting, for which local communities are responsible. But what is the political resilience of the system? There is a risk that, with better information on the costs of various materials, and with an increased schedule of fees for more diversified support, the minimum common basis agreed upon during the past years may be ruined. Revising the targets of the waste management policy has been on the political agenda in France since the 1997 Parliamentary Report on that subject (Guellec, 1997), but there is still much hesitation about the strategy.

CONCLUSION

The overall idea of this study is that two facts should be understood as linked. First, when it was introduced, the new system of packaging waste management in France was short of the incentives which could have led packaging firms and materials producers to have a clear vested interest in a broad development of recycling. With the initial rules, an implicit equilibrium of the system was to achieve a lower rate of recycling than was initially expected by public authorities, and having no significant impact on packaging choices at the source. Second, one important characteristic of this new organization was the delegation of the design of the new system to certain industrial circles. The initial constraints of generating cross-sector common interests and constructing a framework for common action led to a neutralization of the incentives which were required to achieve economic efficiency.

Fee rates were undifferentiated according to the type of material and set at a rather low level, and did not represent the full internalization of treatment and external costs of packaging waste. It looks as though the system was initially conceived to achieve two implicit aims: not to affect the economy of packaging and materials industries; and not to change previous conditions of competition between competing packaging materials.

This system has nevertheless constructed a framework for common action which incorporates both mechanisms for learning about technological opportunities and costs, and mechanisms for deepening and adapting cooperation between the parties associated with the running of the system. Taken together, the learning capacity and the reinforcement of a framework for common action could generate an institutional trajectory which comes closer to economic efficiency. However, there is a serious risk that the conditions for maintaining a common cross-sector interest among industry will not persist. The path of viability for an institutional trajectory towards economic efficiency is not that broad.

A more general lesson can, therefore, be gained from this case study. For research on environmental policy instruments, the greatest challenge is no longer to identify efficient states of allocation of resources, nor the best instruments leading to efficiency in rather abstract contexts. The priority is to elicit social procedures of cooperation between government and industry which could set up a framework of common action between competitors that is capable of sustaining a collective learning and that will ultimately open the way to economic efficiency.

NOTES

*   This study benefits from the results of a research programme of the Centre International de Recherche sur l'Environnnement et le Developpement (CIRED) about systems of domestic waste management in Europe. The financial support of the Agence de l'Environnement et de la Maîtrise de l'Energie (ADEME) and the Programme Interdisciplinaire de Recherche 'Environnement, Vie et Société' du Centre National de la Recherche Scientifique (PIREVS-CNRS) in France for the period from 1994 to 1996, and later of the DG XII of the European Commission (project SUSTAINWASTE) for the period from 1996 to 1999 is gratefully acknowledged.

1.   It may happen that improving the economic efficiency of public policies is put on the public agenda as the problem to be solved. This is a particular case. Like any other problem, it must be shaped by some social actors in such a way as to achieve specific ends: cutting public budgets, stopping a major project, destabilizing specific public agencies and so on.

2.   Whiston and Glachant (1996, p. 169) assume that a common goal is shared by government and industry as to the choice of means for achieving given targets, namely to minimize the total social cost of policy implementation. This should be understood as a postulate, something that has an axiomatic value for them, and not a statement about facts, since we can find numerous cases demonstrating the absence of this common interest in cost-minimization. In some cases, the will of government to contain policy impacts on direct industrial costs has to be seen not as a demonstration of concern for economic efficiency, but simply of political collusion, since this containment is often obtained by imposing some less visible costs on other social groups.

3.   This concept has been elaborated by the anthropologist Gregory Bateson (1972) in order to typify communication situations in which a person is submitted to two opposite requirements without any possibility of escaping from the situation.

4.   Water management in France is a case that shows such transfers onto domestic water users. The bills for the water they consume incorporate a whole set of contributions related to water works, treatment and charges not directly connected to their own consumption, while at the

same time the municipalities benefit from various subsidies for developing their programmes. Domestic users are not directly represented on the 'water parliaments' of water agencies, but through the representation of municipalities. On these questions, see Commissariat général du Plan (1997).

5. This requirement is quite the opposite of the famous polluter-pays-principle that was adopted by the OECD and the EU a long time ago (in the early 1970s).
6. Improvements may nevertheless include just those beneficial to the stakeholders actively involved in the system. A 'community' could presumably target an overall efficiency goal if all relevant stakeholders are adequately represented.
7. The capital of Eco-Emballages is primarily held by packing firms, and also by distributors and materials producers.
8. Municipalities are the executive bodies of local communities.
9. 1 cF = FFR0.01.
10. The respective share of 25 per cent energy recovery and 75 per cent materials recycling is only an indicative goal stated by Eco-Emballages and publicly acknowledged in response to the expectations of the authorities. This reference is not legally binding.
11. According to the 1992 Law on waste, 'ultimate waste' is waste which, under existing technological and economic conditions, cannot be valorized or further treated so as to achieve a more complete neutralization of its pollutant content (Law no. 92–646 of 13 July 1992).
12. An analysis of county plans for domestic waste management has shown that investing in incineration was the main option considered by local authorities until 1996. According to first drafts of county plans, this solution represented 78 per cent of the total amount of investments planned for the period 1995–2002. This bias in favour of incineration led a 1997 parliamentary report to criticize this technological fix as being too costly – an annual investment amounting to FF10 billion would be required to meet the 2002 objective – and ill-adapted to numerous local contexts. This report suggested that recycling be developed, and that the concept of 'ultimate waste' be reconsidered, so as to upgrade landfilling as an appropriate solution in many cases, mainly in rural areas (Guellec, 1997). Since the government swung left in 1997, a new priority has been announced in favour of materials recycling and reductions at source.
13. To give a sense of the order of magnitude, traditional treatments (undifferentiated collection and incineration) of waste costs an average of FF750 per tonne and the new approach (selective collection and sorting of materials) amounts to a rather underestimated FF1650 per tonne.
14. For example, the MTP for PET is a maximum of 2 per cent impurities, while the private Petcore standard on the European market is 0.5 per cent.
15. For instance, choosing incineration as the main technology for waste management could expose France to some major legitimacy crises related to the presumed residual noxious effects of burning emissions (the dioxin controversy).

REFERENCES

Andersen, M.S. (1994), *Governance by Green Taxes: Making Pollution Prevention Pay*, Manchester: Manchester University Press.

Arthur, B. (1989), 'Competing technologies, increasing returns and lock-in by historical events', *Economic Journal*, **99**, 116–31.

Bateson, G. (1972), *Steps to an Ecology of Mind*, New York: Chandler Publishers.

Boltanski, L. and L. Thévenot (1991), *De la justification. Les économies de la grandeur*, Paris: Gallimard (Coll. 'Les Essais-NRF').

Buclet, N., C. Defeuilley, O. Godard (dir.) and Y. Serret (1997), *La gestion des déchets ménagers en France et en Europe. Régimes nationaux, besoins de coordination européenne et enjeux de compétitivité pour l'industrie française*, final report to ADEME, PIREVS-CNRS, January, Paris: CIRED.

Coase, R. (1960), 'The problem of social cost', *Journal of Law and Economics*, **3**, October, 1–44.

Commissariat général du Plan (1997), *Evaluation du dispositif des Agences de l'Eau, Rapport au gouvernement 1997*, Paris: La documentation française.

Defeuilley, C. and O. Godard (1997), 'The economics of packaging waste recycling in France: institutional framework and technological adoption', *International Journal of Environment and Pollution*, **7** (3), 538–46.

Defeuilley, C. and P. Quirion (1995), 'Les déchets d'emballages ménagers: une analyse économique des politiques française et allemande', *Economie et statistique*, (290), 69–79.

Dente, B. (ed.) (1995), *Environmental Policy in Search of New Instruments*, Dordrecht: Kluwer Academic Publishers.

Eco-Emballages (1992), *Demande d'agrément*, Levallois-Perret: Eco-Emballages.

Eco-Emballages (1993), *Eco-Emballages et les collectivités locales*, Levallois-Perret: Eco-Emballages.

Glachant, M. (1994), 'The setting of voluntary agreements between industry and government: bargaining and efficiency', *Business Strategy and the Environment*, **3** (2).

Godard, O. (1995), 'Trajectoires institutionnelles et choix d'instruments pour les politiques d'environnement dans les économies en transition', *Revue d'études comparatives Est-Ouest*, CNRS, **26** (2), June, 39–58.

Godard, O. (1997), 'Social decision-making under scientific controversy, expertise and the precautionary principle', in C. Joerges, K.-H. Ladeur and E. Vos (eds), *Integrating Scientific Expertise into Regulatory Decision-making – National Experiences and European Innovations*, Baden-Baden: Nomos-Verlagsgesellschaft, pp. 39–73.

Godard, O. and O. Beaumais (1994), 'Economie, croissance et environnement – de nouvelles stratégies pour de nouvelles relations', *Revue économique*, **44**, 143–76.

Guellec, A. (ed.) (1997), *Déchets ménagers: pour un retour à la raison*, Information Report 3380, Paris: Commission de la production et des échanges, Assemblée Nationale.

Lévêque, F. (ed.) (1996), *Environmental Policy in Europe: Industry, Competition and the Policy Process*, Cheltenham, UK and Brookfield, US: Edward Elgar.

Majone, G. (1989), *Evidence, Argument and Persuasion in the Policy Process*, New Haven, US and London, UK: Yale University Press.

Merrien, F.-X. (1993), 'Les politiques publiques entre paradigmes et controverses', in CRESAL (ed.), *Les raisons de l'action publique. Entre expertise et débat*, Paris: Ed. L'Harmattan, (Coll. Logiques politiques), pp. 87–100.

Perrier, M.N. (1996), 'Les financements au fonctionnement des collectes sélectives', Conférence Maîtriser un programme de collecte sélective, ADEME and Eco-Emballages, Lyon, 22 October.

Togia, A. (1996), 'Une approche économique de la gestion des déchets d'emballage en France: une modélisation du système Eco-Emballages', Paris, CIRED, September.

Whiston, T. and M. Glachant (1996), 'Voluntary agreements between industry and government – the case of recycling regulations', in François Lévêque (ed.), *Environmental Policy in Europe: Industry, Competition and the Policy Process*, Cheltenham, UK and Brookfield, US: Edward Elgar, pp. 143–74.

6. Efficiency and fairness: the Norwegian experience with agri-environmental taxation*

Arild Vatn

INTRODUCTION

The negative environmental effects of modern agriculture became a political issue in most western countries during the 1970s and 1980s. Increased attention was given both to the effects of pesticide use and to losses of nutrients and soil to various water bodies. Thus, the North Sea Declaration of 1987 – an agreement developed among the countries of north-western Europe to reduce pollution of this ocean area – included a section defining goals related to nutrient losses. Combined with a poisonous algae bloom in 1988, this boosted a search for policies that could help reduce the problems.

Until the mid-1980s, policy in this field was dominated by the use of legal, administrative and informational instruments. From that time on, increased attention to the use of economic instruments has been observed. This change did not come about without serious debates, though. In Norway this was especially the case for a proposed tax on nitrogen fertilizers.

The debate is illustrative of a broad range of issues related to policy formulation in the environmental field. It illustrates the complex relationships between efficiency and fairness, and the context dependence of what may be termed 'fair solutions' (Walzer, 1983; Elster, 1992). It provides insight into the effects of uncertainty, and thus also the role of science, both in understanding the problem and in defining what is efficient and/or fair. Finally, it sheds light on the dynamics of what will be called the multi-dimensional systems of institutionalized state responsibility.

This chapter is basically divided into two sections. First, the more general merits of environmental taxes are discussed, focusing on the issue of efficiency and fairness. Second, these insights are used in an analysis of the Norwegian debate on fertilizer taxes.

FACTORS INFLUENCING THE CHOICE OF POLICY INSTRUMENTS

Efficiency and Fairness

According to Elster (1992), principles of fairness or justice[1] are applied when allocating scarce resources, necessary burdens or rights and duties to different individuals of a society. Such principles may be universal, but most typically they are 'local', implying that they are related to specific cultures, sectors or communities. This view reflects the position of social constructivism (Berger and Luckmann, 1967; Allardt, 1985), which holds that our perceptions, values and norms are socially constructed and thus context relative. This position is also supported by several institutional economists who emphasize that preferences are endogenous to the economic system (Bowles, 1998; Hodgson, 1988).

One important position concerning efficiency and fairness is the Pareto criterion, which is embraced especially by neoclassical economics. According to this criterion, an improvement is made if some become better off without others becoming worse off (Pareto improvement). There is a specific perspective of fairness embedded in this rule. First, the idea is universal. Second, Pareto improvements are viewed as the outcome of unconstrained and individually rational transfers under a given set of initial resource endowments and cost-free transactions. The focus is thus on what characterizes the move from one state to another. The initial or final distribution is either defined as a non-economic problem or circumvented by presuming the distribution to be optimal at the outset.

If ideas of fairness outside neoclassical economic theory are looked for, a wide variety of overlapping perspectives will be found. Equity – mainly related to the distribution of end states – is an important aspect (Elster, 1992). Another is the definition of fundamental rights (Rawls, 1971). In the case of pollution, the rights issue refers primarily to the definition of the reference point from where it may be judged, who is harming whom. A final important element is the procedural aspect of participation, especially in the formulation of policies pertaining to environmental risks, as Beck (1992) emphasizes in his study of the risk society.

Following neoclassical economic theory, it can be shown that Pareto efficiency is obtained under certain assumptions in competitive markets. In the economic model, problems occur only if goods exist for which individual property rights are lacking. Such goods are by definition 'external' to the market. Because of this, they may either be overused (negative externalities) or underproduced (positive externalities). It has long been asserted that, under the assumptions of the model, efficiency can be restored by attaching taxes (or subsidies) to actions causing negative (positive) externalities (Pigou, 1932; Baumol and Oates, 1988).[2]

This Pigovian policy rule has several strong properties, and economists have been puzzled by the fact that policy-makers, only to a minor degree, have based their proposals on economic insight. It has been argued that this is because strong interest groups have mobilized against extra economic burdens. The merits of this argument are fairly strong. Still, this interpretation may be incorrect in that it characterizes issues of fundamental rights and distribution as simple 'rent-seeking'. Further, there may be other important issues at stake which the standard model overlooks.

First, it can be shown that a tax on emissions is not necessarily the most efficient solution in all situations. Sometimes it may be least costly to let 'victims' undertake remedial action (Coase, 1960). Following this, Vatn and Bromley (1997) conclude that the Pigovian stand is foremost a moral position which, like the polluter-pays-principle (PPP), puts the burden of action and costs on the emitters. If so, it is confusing to couch the argument purely in terms of technical efficiency.

Second, despite its strong potential features as a moral belief or rule of fairness, the Pigovian stand also encounters several difficulties in that realm:

- Concerning pollution, rights are rarely given a priori. Typically, externalities do not become visible until long after a damaging activity has taken place. This is mainly because of huge time lags in the ecosystems involved. Since rights have to be settled in retrospect, the neat distinction between efficiency and fairness becomes blurred. Thus, the time at which an emission can be taxed in proportion to observed harm, a Pareto-improvement based on Pigovian taxes is impossible (Vatn and Bromley, 1997). Someone has to lose if compensation is not given.
- Further, if a certain practice has been accepted for a long time, a perceived 'status quo right' may develop on behalf of those who turn out to be polluters. This perception may explain some of the conflicts apparent when taxes are introduced. It should be mentioned that in Norway the national pollution act terms as legal 'ordinary pollution' from several activities, including agriculture, if it is not specifically regulated (Stortingsforhandlingene, 1981). This justifies to some extent an interpretation that 'ordinary pollution' is not pollution in the sense of bad conduct.
- Even though PPP may be accepted as the most fair rule, it may cause problems if the tax to be paid is many times the cost of the damage (Pezzey, 1988). Even more important, the distributional effect may be rather arbitrarily related to the damage level, as shall be seen. Ignoring

income effects, this observation does not influence the efficiency of the policy, but it may affect its perceived fairness.

- Finally, the use of taxes may be seen to turn basic moral issues into mere technical ones, obscuring at least some of their fundamental characteristics. Externalities reflect interdependencies between the actions of members of a society. They are basically about how we intervene in each others' lives (negatively or positively). Taxes or subsidies may be used to regulate such relationships. Following Etzioni (1988) and Sagoff (1994), it may, however, be claimed that this obscures the character of the problem by transforming what is basically a citizenry issue into mere market relations. Reducing moral issues to commodity transactions may even result in the deterioration of moral attitudes and, over time, increase the need for technical regulation. Tyler (1990) emphasizes that compliance with a rule is strongly influenced by the extent to which both the rule and the agency are considered legitimate.

The Complexity of Natural Processes

The externality theory is typically developed for point-source pollution and is simplest to operationalize for easily observable and homogenous harms. In practice, the theory must be applied to 'goods' that are very diverse and difficult to demarcate. This is the case for pollution from agriculture, where non-point-source emissions interact with complex and heterogenous natural processes.

Conclusions obtained under simplified conditions may thus be inapplicable under practical circumstances. First, if variability is large both in space and time, regulations may have to be specific for each firm, recipient and/or time period. If so, the difference in efficiency between taxes and administrative regulations may vanish (Scheele, 1997). Further, in the case of non-point-source pollution, decision-making, monitoring and taxing (that is, transaction costs) may in themselves be so costly that 'internalizing the externality' through the standard recipe of taxing emissions in accordance with their harm in most cases becomes Pareto-irrelevant[3] (Vatn, 1998). If so, taxing the input of an externality-producing substance into the economy may be an interesting alternative due to heavily reduced transaction costs. In spite of the fact that such a regulation is normally less precise, more externalities may thus become Pareto-relevant – that is worth reducing in economic terms. Concerning the aspects of rights and fairness, the problem is encountered, however, that even economic agents who use the substance in ways which produce little or no pollution have to pay the tax. This is a question of special relevance in the case studied here.

The Multi-dimensional Good and the Multi-dimensional State

The theoretical strength of the economic model is its capacity to simplify complex issues to logically tractable structures. In that respect, it undertakes to some extent the same simplification as real-life markets. Diverse value dimensions are compressed into one dimension – the price. The model also presupposes rational agents, both with respect to preference consistency and calculative capacity, as it gives no explicit room for society in the formulation of preferences. From the individualistic basis of the model, the role of the state becomes twofold: to define and secure individual property rights and to correct for external economies/public goods.

The price of even the most simple commodity captures, however, only a subset of the dimensions of its importance, worth and meaning to humans. The conditions under which it is produced may, for example, cause concern for different reasons, several of which will relate to aspects of fairness. This is, however, abstracted away in the market-clearing process, where exchange value is decisive.

In relation to this, the complex welfare state may be viewed as a way of institutionalizing some of these various other issues that markets do not handle. It is a multidimensional decision system covering a wide range of concerns. A very brief introduction to the perspective follows.

A state's ministry of finance (MF) may, due to its responsibility for integrating policy measures in the framework of a balanced budget, be considered the heart of the state administration. Further, this ministry is often found advocating market-like efficiency criteria for the distribution of state funds. The ministry of social affairs can, on the other hand, be understood as responsible for the equity dimension and the formulation of a general security net for those with insufficient market power/competitiveness. The ministry of development may be seen as responsible for parallel obligations, especially in relation to citizens of Third World countries.

In a case like ours, the ministry of agriculture (MA) and the ministry of environment (ME) are of specific interest. The MA is a sector-oriented ministry, mainly responsible for establishing institutional arrangements that handle sector-specific distributional, participatory and technical issues. Income distribution, both within agriculture and between agriculture and other sectors, has been an important question for decennia in most western countries. In Norway this is institutionalized through a corporatist structure called the Agricultural Agreement. Historically, the technical specificity and complexity of the sector and the need to create systems supporting farmers with advice seem to have been as important as income support (Vatn, 1984). Through this system of technical assistance, an attempt has been made to bridge the gap between a theory which assumes choices to be rational and fully informed, and a complex, practical world. Certainly the problem of knowledge and rational choice is extra challenging in an industry utilizing resources with high variability and uncertainty, both in time and space.

The task of the ME of formulating environmental policies has to some extent been a cross-dimensional duty parallel to that of the MF. Thus, in many countries, these two ministries have come into conflicts over whose principles of integration should dominate. In Norway the ME has come to function mostly as a sector ministry, with the same subordinate relation to the MF as other ministries, yet with cross-sectoral responsibilities. Because of these responsibilities, many conflicts have been observed between the ME and the sectoral ministries concerning the trade-off between sector-specific dimensions of responsibility and various environmental issues.

My main point – or hypothesis – is that trade-off problems in general are handled through disparate organizational channels because they cannot be taken care of in a unidimensional way. Distribution of resources and attention through these channels is, therefore, a result of societal processes that go beyond technical calculations. Certainly, many problems are related to this organizational structure. These difficulties cannot, however, be eliminated or even reduced just by asking for a single computational scheme. Efficiency and the various dimensions of fairness seem to be mingled in ways not compatible with market equilibrium and simple lump-sum transfers.

FERTILIZER TAXES AND THE AGRONOMIC SYSTEM

We shall now turn to our specific case, which will be analysed on the basis of the above understanding. As already emphasized, efficiency, fairness and uncertainty are strongly interrelated concepts. Still, what may be considered efficient or fair is heavily dependent on the models of perception that are used. In the present case strong disagreement over the potential effects of a fertilizer tax developed. The debate was especially fierce among economists and agronomists, focusing on the uncertainties related to the relationship between, on the one hand, fertilizer use and crop yields and pollution, on the other.

Taxing nitrogen emissions from agriculture is a very difficult task, because emissions are both spatially very diverse and consist of different chemical compounds. Taxing the input of nitrogen (N) in fertilizers is a much simpler policy alternative. In Norway arguments in favour of such taxes were put forward in several consecutive studies, such as Simonsen (1989), Vatn (1989), Christoffersen and Rysstad (1990) and Simonsen *et al.* (1992). The arguments were based on various types of model analyses using data about the effect of nitrogen on both yields and leaching. The conclusion of these studies was that a fertilizer tax was a much more cost-efficient measure than all other policy measures considered for reducing N losses to the North Sea. The following technical relationships were of special importance to the conclusion:

1. The marginal product of fertilizer N is smoothly decreasing, that is, the yield is a concave function of N. This implies that the optimal fertilizer level will be reduced by an increased N price.
2. A rise in fertilizer N price will simultaneously increase the value of N in other, existing N sources like animal manure. In this way, an incentive for reducing losses from these kinds of source will also be created.
3. Leaching decreases with lower fertilizer levels.

In spite of the fact that the economic analyses were built on agronomic data, the conclusions drawn were heavily disputed by agronomists. First of all, they challenged the assumption of a smooth, concave yield function (see (1) above). Their interpretation (Enge *et al.*, 1990) followed a von Liebig form of reasoning, where yields increase linearly as a function of N, up to a point where some other factor becomes limiting. If this is the case, the price of fertilizers will not influence the optimal level of fertilizer use.

Also the relationship in (3) was disputed. Vagstad (1990) argued that losses of nitrogen were more heavily related to natural processes (especially weather factors and plant growth) than to the fertilizer level. The convexity relationship found in the data was, he believed, an effect of an overrepresentation of years with low precipitation in the material. He argued that plant uptake would normally be so high up to the maximum yield level that leaching would be fairly constant up to that point. Nothing was thus gained by reducing fertilizer levels, as long as farmers were not fertilizing clearly beyond the economic optimum.

The debate over these issues showed substantial differences in what, following Kuhn (1970), may be called the 'exemplars' of the two disciplines. Economists tend to prefer smooth functional relationships, while agronomists may, as previously mentioned, have other mind-sets driving their interpretation. The complexity of the system, and thus the quality of the trial data, made it very difficult to use data to make decisive judgements over functional forms. Consequently, it was necessary to resort, at least partly, to the logical strength of the two positions. At this level agreements could not be reached. Thus, the scientific discussion cast a vast shadow of uncertainty over the case. Moreover, the technical debate among researchers gave no insight into farmers' interpretation. First of all, farmers' perceptions were undoubtedly influenced by the agronomically dominated extension service. Second, 'agronomic values' like the standing of the crop, the 'needs' of the plants and so on seem in themselves to play a role in determining the choice of practices. Besides the technical debate, it was thus also observed a debate over the character of knowledge and type of rationality driving farmers' choices (Vedeld and Krogh, 1996; Vedeld, 1998).

THE POLICY PROCESS - THE RISE AND FALL OF THE FERTILIZER TAX

From their inception in the early 1970s and up until the mid-1980s, environmental regulations in Norwegian agriculture were dominated by judicial and administrative regulations of point-sources (silage and manure storage). From the time the North Sea Declaration was signed, a much stronger emphasis was placed on the whole production system and thus also on losses from agricultural land (nonpoint-source pollution). This resulted in increased interest concerning soil preparation methods, feeding practices and fertilizer intensity. This represented a substantial change in policy orientation over a period of a few years. For example, subsidies to increase fertilizer use were given until as late as the early 1980s (Vatn, 1984).

Phase 1   The Tax as a Financial Source for Environmental Programmes

The first tax proposal is found in the proposition for the state budget for 1988. It was, however, emphasized that the aim was to raise funding for other environmental measures (Ministry of Agriculture, 1987). The idea was to collect money to support the development of farm-specific fertilizer plans, that is, to decrease leaching by reduced fertilizer use on farms fertilizing beyond the economic optimum. This was to be achieved through information measures. In some vulnerable areas, specific information campaigns were set up (*Nationen*, 1988a). The tax proposal seems to have been rather well accepted. The tax level was very low, though, only about 1 per cent of the nitrogen price.

During the summer of 1988, an extensive algae bloom in the North Sea made an impressive impact on the general perception of the nitrogen pollution problem, and the government was criticized for doing too little. In autumn 1988, the MA proposed increasing the tax to approximately 8 per cent of the nitrogen price (Ministry of Agriculture, 1988) which was supported by the Parliament (Stortingsforhandlingene, 1988). In spite of the high relative increase, the tax level was still too low to have any direct effect on fertilizer use. The idea was, as before, to use the tax as a financial basis for other measures.

Even at this stage, there were no significant opponents of the tax proposal itself, except maybe the leading fertilizer company Norsk Hydro (*Nationen*, 1988b). On the other hand, a debate about the use and control of the collected revenue emerged. The farmers' organizations – both the Farmers' Union and the Smallholders' Organization – proposed that the tax revenue should be placed in a fund under the Agricultural Agreement between the state and the farmers' organizations (*Nationen*, 1988c).

The Agreement determines yearly target prices for agricultural goods and makes detailed proposals to Parliament concerning state subsidies. The proposal would have increased farmers' influence over the fund. The proposal was, however, in line with the participatory logic of this corporatist type of agreement. The MA still opposed such a solution, arguing that it would be a totally new principle to give private organizations influence on the use of public taxes.

The minister still wanted the tax revenue to be earmarked for the agricultural sector. The MF argued, on the other hand, that environmental taxes should not be earmarked for specific tasks, but be considered normal state income to be used in accordance with what was generally of highest priority for the state.

In the final decision in the Parliament, the money remained earmarked for environmental programmes in agriculture. The farmers also got a concession, since the board for one of the existing funds under the Agricultural Agreement[4] was given a consultative role (Stortingstidende, 1988). In the same decision, Parliament asked the Government to evaluate the future potential for using environmental taxes in agriculture. This was important in bringing the scientists on stage.

Phase 2   The Tax as an Environmental Instrument

Scientists are invited into the process
On the basis of the decision in Parliament, the Department of Economics and Social Sciences at the Agricultural University of Norway was asked to evaluate the consequences of environmental taxes in agriculture. The results were presented in Simonsen (1989), and the main arguments have already been presented. Concerning the specifics of the tax proposal, it was emphasized that taxes would be a cheap way to reduce nitrate leaching, but that taxes had to be rather high (100–300 per cent) in order to have any substantial effects. If the effect on farmers' incomes was considered too large, reimbursement was an option (Simonsen, 1989). The calculations showed that in grain production, for example, more than 90 per cent of the costs for the farmer would be in the form of tax payments. Less than 10 per cent were related to the production (that is real) costs. These were mainly the effect of reduced yields.

The MA seems not to have been fully persuaded as to the correctness of the results obtained. In the MA's proposal for the budget for 1990, it is stated that 'use of taxes as a policy instrument will demand a more thorough assessment of various consequences' (Ministry of Agriculture, 1989, p. 33, author's translation). The Centre for Soil and Environmental Research, where agronomy was a core discipline, was asked to undertake such an assessment.

The tax as observed from various institutionalized decision arenas
Parallel to these developments the tax proposal became an important issue in different policy-making processes. The most important were:

- the national follow-up of the North Sea Declaration;
- the annual Agricultural Agreement;
- a committee undertaking a general evaluation of the Norwegian agricultural policy.

The understanding of the problem – the role of efficiency, fairness and uncertainty – was rather different in the three arenas. Let us look briefly at each of them.

A plan for the national follow-up of the North Sea Declaration concerning agriculture was developed by a group with representatives from the two ministries – the ME and the MA – and the Norwegian Pollution Control Authority (NPCA). The project group started its work in 1989 and evaluated a long list of measures. Concerning fertilizer taxes, the members of the group revealed very different positions. The representatives of the ME and the NPCA showed, in general, a very positive attitude, while the representatives from the MA were much more sceptical. The MA spokespersons had mainly agronomic backgrounds. They represented a section called '*Jordbruks-avdelingen*', which had been responsible for those environmental issues that concerned the Ministry (Krogh *et al*., 1998).[5] Their main arguments were based on a critique of the economists' perception of the problem. The report from the Centre for Soil and Environmental Research, which the MA had asked for in 1989, was finished in late 1990 (Vagstad, 1990). This report was, as already mentioned in the section on 'Fertilizer taxes and the agronomic system', very critical of the economists' analyses, and thus supportive of the position taken by the representatives of the MA.

From 1989 to 1991, the tax proposal went in and out of the group's list of proposed measures. It was pretty clear, however, that it would be difficult, if not impossible, to fulfil the obligations of the North Sea Declaration without applying rather tough measures.

While this group was working, the tax question entered the agenda of the Agricultural Agreement. In that context, the distributional effects and the role of the tax in the existing income system for agriculture were the important issues. As already emphasized, a central element in the Agricultural

Agreement was the interpretation and operationalization of the income goal. A special committee under the Agreement was appointed in 1990 to look at the relationship between the PPP and the structure of the Agreement.

The committee found the fertilizer tax to be in accordance with the PPP, but emphasized that it was problematic that even usages causing little environmental harm would be taxed. Regional differentiation of the tax could reduce the potential rights violation inherent in this, but such a system was found to be difficult to control (Ministry of Agriculture, 1991a).

It was observed that the tax would increase costs in agriculture. In a standard market context, this would result in increased output prices and some of the costs would be transferred to the consumers. Since output prices in agriculture were regulated, there was no such automatic effect. On the other hand, the income policy of that time included a system of compensation for increased costs through increased target prices or state subsidies. Thus, representatives for the MA and the farmers' representatives on the committee argued that compensation should be given as a mere consequence of the existing rules. They emphasized that compensation could be used in ways which increased the environmental effect. The ME supported this conclusion, while strongly emphasizing that the environmental effect should be increased by connecting the reimbursement to environmentally friendly practices. The MF maintained that the tax should be viewed as general state income (Ministry of Agriculture, 1991a).

The evaluation of the efficiency of the tax seems less a source of conflict in this committee than in the group responsible for operationalizing the North Sea Declaration. This may partly reflect that the task was not to formulate an environmental policy, but rather to study how to integrate a tax into an existing institutional system. It must be mentioned, though, that the committee was dominated by economists.

The annual Agricultural Agreement is obliged to follow general instructions given by the Parliament. Every 10–15 years, a White Paper is issued formulating basic goals and guidelines. The first step in this process is to appoint a committee responsible for evaluating the existing policy and formulating proposals for changes. In 1987 the government appointed such a committee – the Committee for the Development of a Future Agricultural Policy (CDAP). It consisted of representatives of relevant ministries, various other public bodies and private organizations.

The environmental issues became an important aspect of the committee's work. In that respect, the committee became an especially important arena for the ME. This was emphasized by its representative (*Nationen*, 1988d) and by the fact that the ministry was very active in establishing and supporting a subcommittee on environmental aspects of agricultural policy.

One of the most important proposals from the CDAP was to promote an extensification of Norwegian agriculture. This was justified both on the basis of positive environmental effects and the potential for counteracting an upcoming need for reduction in the total acreage. Keeping a fairly high total acreage was motivated by the committee's strong focus on long-term food security, regional policy and the cultural landscape. Approximately three-quarters of the committee members supported a 10 per cent reduction in average yields as a guideline (Norges offentlige utredninger, 1991). It was further indicated that this could be obtained by increasing the nitrogen fertilizer tax to 150 per cent and decreasing grain prices by about 30 per cent. It is important to note that the representative of the Smallholders' Organization was part of the majority, while the representative of the Farmers' Union joined the minority, consisting primarily of supporters of more traditional agronomic values. It should also be noted that the MA was not represented on the committee. The proposed changes were judged to have a substantial effect on losses of nitrogen to the North Sea (approximately 30 per cent). The committee left room for a compensation for the tax through the general agricultural support system, though the formulations by the majority were less binding than in the previously referred committee on the PPP.

The majority proposal was very radical, especially in comparison with what was discussed in other policy-formulating fora at the time. In the end, the group on the follow-up of the North Sea Declaration supported the idea of a tax, with explicit reference to the CDAP proposal. It did not, however, agree on any specific tax level (Statens forurensningstilsyn, 1991). When the decisions made by the Parliament are examined, it is found that the tax was increased by small increments from year to year. In the state budget for 1991 – decided on at the same time as the CDAP made its proposals – the tax reached a level of approximately 20 per cent of the nitrogen price (Stortingsforhandlingene, 1990). Simultaneously, an increased interest in the distributional effects of a tax in the public debate is observed.

Tradable quotas or a two-tier tax as a compromise
Regarding the distributional effects of the tax, it was also observed that the effect varies substantially with the way the system is formulated. Generally, the distributional effect of an input tax will be higher than that of a comparable tax on emissions (Stevens, 1988). If leaching is constant for some interval of nitrogen used, this difference is enhanced. Modelling has confirmed that this seems to be correct for lower fertilizer levels (Vatn *et al.*, 1996).[6] Furthermore, analyses done at the time showed that the effect of the tax would differ for different uses and that the costs (or 'punishment') for the farmers would, at best, be only weakly related to the external costs following from their actions. Farmers' costs would, for example, be highest for specialized grain producers, while nitrogen losses are normally much higher on farms using animal

manure. These effects not only ran counter to farmers' perception of fair treatment, but also to a standard interpretation of PPP.

The fertilizer tax is, however, a simple system to use, and the procedure of cost compensation under the Agricultural Agreement could help counteract most of the unwanted distributional effects. Still, the farmers, the MA and the ME continued to look for alternative solutions.

The ME undertook an evaluation in 1991 of a deposit/refund system, a two-tier tax system, and a system of tradable nitrogen quotas to be issued to farmers free of charge. All these solutions have lower distributional effects than a fertilizer tax as they are based on an (implicit) initial distribution of rights that is different from that of a flat tax. These measures would still be able to induce reductions in pollution levels with approximately the same efficiency as a nitrogen tax.[7] The system of two-tier tax was also proposed by the Farmers Union. In a report sent to the MA, the ME nevertheless concluded that it preferred a tradable quota system. It was emphasized, though, that some further analyses were necessary to make the system implementable (Ministry of Environment, 1991).

In a comment on this proposal, representatives of the MA (from '*Jordbruksavdelingen*') concluded that they could support neither the quota nor the two-tier tax system. The reasoning was again based on the argument that nitrogen leaching was weakly related to fertilizer intensity, while the large administrative problems related to the two systems became an extra argument (Ministry of Agriculture, 1991b).

Phase 3   The Fall of the Tax

From the beginning of 1991 – that is, around the time the committee evaluating the agricultural policy (CDAP) delivered its high tax proposal – the idea of a substantial increase in the tax level actually lost more and more momentum. The final blow seems to have come from the international arena. The trade liberalization following the Uruguay Round of the General Agreement in Tariffs and Trade (GATT) increased the need for cost reductions, especially in a country like Norway, which was among the 'leading' countries in terms of agricultural support.

There was, as previously mentioned, a small but steady increase in the N-tax from 1987 until 1990. In 1991 the Parliamentary committee responsible for agricultural affairs opposed a further increase (Stortingsforhandlingene, 1991). Both the cost arguments and the fact that the tax also hit farmers with low or no pollution were part of the argumentation. The Ministry of Environment did not wish to yield that easily, and the White Paper from the spring of 1992 on the follow-up of the North Sea Declaration still concludes that 'a comprehensive evaluation of the measures shows that an increased tax on the nitrogen content of chemical fertilizer is the most promising alternative today' (Ministry of Environment, 1992, p. 60, author's translation). No specific tax level was proposed, however. That was to be decided in the annual budgetary processes. The ministry also proposed that a system of tradable quotas should be further evaluated.

In 1992 the Norwegian government applied for European Union (EU) membership. This may be interpreted as creating extra problems for those in favour of a fertilizer tax, since the cost arguments were as pervasive in the EU context as they were in the case of the GATT agreement. Thus, in the White Paper on the new guidelines for the agricultural policy issued in the autumn of 1992, the Ministry wrote:

> The government will, while judging the development of the costs in agriculture, consider the use of environmental taxes as an integrated part of future agricultural policy. The size of the tax and possible compensation ... will be decided on in the annual budgetary processes. At the same time, the government will work for a parallel introduction of such environmental taxes in international cooperative bodies (Ministry of Agriculture, 1992, p. 25, author's translation).

This is what was left of the proposal for a 150 per cent nitrogen tax and a 10 per cent intensity reduction, which was the input from the CDAP into this White Paper process one-and-a-half-years' earlier. During the following couple of years, the issue remained part of the political agenda, kept alive mainly by the ME. No change in the tax level has occurred, though, since 1991, and the proposal for a high tax seems to be more or less dead, at least since the middle of the 1990s.

DISCUSSION AND CONCLUSION

The strongest feature of the nitrogen fertilizer tax is its simplicity. This analysis, however, reveals a wide range of problems that seem to have made it impossible to implement a high tax at a level where it could have a substantial environmental effect on its own. The reasons for this are many, and each may be sufficient as a sole explanation – a question that cannot be fully determined by studying one case only.

The economists produced strong arguments in favour of a nitrogen fertilizer tax, especially on the basis of its low societal costs compared to other measures. However, doubts about its efficiency were created by the agronomist claim that the results obtained were both very uncertain and misleading. The tax would, they believed, have no effect on the losses of nitrogen to the environment and would thus simply become a payment from farmers to the state.

The technical form of uncertainty emphasized by agronomists undoubtedly influenced the final outcome of the case. Still, the institutional 'uncertainty' – that is, the uncertainty around the political interpretation of PPP – seems to have been even more important. This was, in fact, a debate over the status of the Agricultural Agreement. Should the tax be part of the agreement and the money reimbursed or should it be considered general state income and allocated according to a unidimensional plan under the responsibility of the MF? The tax proposal seems to have become more of a game over the income goal in agriculture, rather than a solution to the nitrate pollution problem. This reasoning is also supported by the fact that when the GATT and the EU processes entered the arena, other mechanisms reducing state subsidies to agriculture were set in motion, and the nitrogen tax became less interesting.

The legitimacy of the proposal was undermined by the fact that there seemed to be no clear relationship between the level of tax paid by each farmer and the level of nitrogen lost to the environment. Following the argument that some use of fertilizer N would even reduce leaching,[8] it became a problem that the tax would also penalize farmers who did not pollute. From a rights perspective, this was a difficult issue. The effect could have been counteracted, though, by changes in the type of measure used (two-tier tax, tradable quotas and so on). Such changes were proposed, especially by the ME, in the search for a compromise with the agricultural sector. These alternatives did not, however, gain sufficient backing to be implemented.

This case seems to support the more general observation that economists hesitate to enter distributional and institutional issues. This is based on the perception that if efficiency issues are the only ones considered, the analyses can be regarded as value neutral. This position is problematic, even assuming fully compatible value dimensions (Bromley, 1989). The difficulties increase when proposals are presented in societal contexts riddled with value and distributional conflicts.

The tax was thus proposed in a setting very different from that of Pigou. It became the 'straw man' for an ongoing debate over the rationale of the agricultural sectoral policy, and there seemed little hope of finding constructive solutions. The most important lesson to be learned is that the various value conflicts apparent in a case like this must be explicitly dealt with in the policy formulating process. The existing policy system with its multiplicity of dimensions and sectors, creates a complex environment for introducing new issues. Without taking these dimensions explicitly into consideration, however, it will be very difficult to find solutions that will work. What is considered fair in the 'local' culture is of specific importance. Coercion can certainly be used to override this. In the long run, however, it is surely more reasonable to develop environmental policies that are perceived as both sensible and fair.

NOTES

* The author would like to thank Roger Salmons for comments on an earlier version of the study.
1. In parts of the literature, a distinction is made between 'fairness' and 'justice', with fairness attributed to procedures and justice to outcomes. There is by far no agreement on this (Barry, 1989), and the concepts are used synonymously here.
2. Despite its rigour and clarity, the consistency of the standard externality model is questionable (Vatn and Bromley, 1997). This issue will not be addressed here.
3. That is, aggregate costs (including transaction costs) are greater than aggregate gains.
4. 'Jordrukets Utbyggingsfond'.
5. It may be important to observe that, historically, the environmental issues were not placed in the section responsible for the sector negotiations, that is '*Landbruksavdelingen*'. This reflects, in part, the initial perception that it was a field that could be handled outside the core of the agricultural policy.
6. Actually, the modelling undertaken by Lars Bakken and Arild Vold at the Agricultural University of Norway, indicates that in an application rate up to 30–60 kg N per ha in grain production, leaching decreases with fertilizer intensity. Beyond that level it starts increasing again. Thus the analysis also supports the argument that a reduction in intensity from a normal level of about 120 kg per ha would result in reduced leaching, that is, it is in that respect contrary to the previous agronomic perception. The consequence of their analysis is that the distributional effect of an input tax could be substantially higher than that of a (hypothetical) emission-based tax.
7. In fact, precision could be increased in all the above cases. This gain could, however, be removed by increases in transaction costs.
8. See note 5.

REFERENCES

Barry, B. (1989), *Theories of Justice: A Treatise on Social Justice*, Vol. I, Berkeley, Los Angeles: University of California Press.

Baumol, W.J. and W.E. Oates (1988), *The Theory of Environmental Policy*, Cambridge: Cambridge University Press.

Beck, U. (1992), *Risk Society: Towards a New Modernity*, London, New Dehli: SAGR Publications.

Berger, P. and T. Luckman (1967), *The Social Construction of Reality*, New York: Anchor Books.

Bowles, S. (1998), 'Endogenous preferences: the cultural consequences of markets and other economic institutions', *Journal of Economic Literature*, **XXXVI** (March), 75–111.

Bromley, D.W. (1989), *Economic Interests and Institutions: The Conceptual Foundations of Public Policy*, Oxford: Basil Blackwell.

Christoffersen, K. and S. Rysstad (1990), *Foretaksøkonomiske og miljømessige effekter av virkemidler mot landbruksforurensninger*, Report no. 16, Landbruks-politikk og miljøforvaltning, Center for Contract Research and Project Management, Aas.

Coase, R.H. (1960), 'The problem of social cost', *The Journal of Law and Economics*, **3**, 1–44.

Elster, J. (1992), *Local Justice: How Institutions Allocate Scarce Goods and Necessary Burdens*, New York: Russell Sage Foundation.

Enge, R., K. Heie and S. Tveitnes (1990), 'Miljøavgift. Miljøavgifter på kunstgjødsel-N og -P og på plantevernmidler', *Landbruksøkonomisk forum*, **7**, 38–49.

Etzioni, A. (1988), *The Moral Dimension: Toward a New Economics*, New York: The Free Press.

Hodgson, G.M. (1988), *Economics and Institutions*, Cambridge: Polity Press.

Krogh, E., R. Hesjedal, F. Gundersen, A. Vatn and P. Vedeld (1998), 'Spillet om næringssaltene', report no. 19, Department for Economics and Social Sciences, Agricultural University of Norway.

Kuhn, T. (1970), *The Structure of Scientific Revolutions*, Chicago: University of Chicago Press.

Ministry of Agriculture (1987), *St.prp. 1 (1987–88), Statsbudsjettet for 1988*, Oslo: MA.

Ministry of Agriculture (1988), *St.prp. 1 (1988–89), Statsbudsjettet for 1989*, Oslo: MA.

Ministry of Agriculture (1989), *St.prp. 1 (1989–90), Statsbudsjettet for 1990*, Oslo: MA.

Ministry of Agriculture (1991a), *Forurenseren skal betale-prinsippet (FSB) i jordbruksavtalesammenheng*, Innstilling fra arbeidsgruppen som ble nedsatt av avtalepartene i 1989 og oppnevnt i 1990.

Ministry of Agriculture (1991b), *Bruk av kvoter for å regulere kunstgjødselbruken*, notat datert 23.12.91 (just 6.01.92), vedlagt sakspapirer til sak 1 1992 for kontaktutvalget for landbruk og miljø.

Ministry of Agriculture (1992), *St.prp.nr 8 (1992–93), Landbruk i utvikling. Om retningslinjer for landbrukspolitikken og opplegget for jordbruksoppgjørene m.v.*, Oslo.

Ministry of Environment (1991), *Nordsjødeklarasjonen - valg av virkemidler i landbrukssektoren*, Brev fra statssekretær B. Pettersen i MD til statssekretær T. Risholm i LD. Vedlagt notat: Kvoter på handelsgjødsel-N som alternativ til høy miljøavgift. Dated 20 December 1991.

Ministry of Environment (1992), *St.meld. nr. 64 (1991–92). Om Norges oppfølging av nordsjødeklarasjonene*, Oslo.

Nationen (1988a), *Økologi i høysetet*, article, 10 March 1988.

Nationen (1988b), *Feilslått politikk*, article, 2 July 1988.

Nationen (1988c), *Bondelaget vil ha eget miljøfond*, article, 11 October 1988.

Nationen (1988d), *Landbruket må ta miljøvern på alvor*, article, 11 July 1988.

Norges offentlige utredninger (1991), 'Norsk landbrukspolitikk. Utfordringer, mål og virkemidler', NOU 1991:2B Hovedinstilling, Oslo: Statens forvaltningstjeneste.

Pezzey, J. (1988), 'Market mechanism and pollution control', in R.K. Turner (ed.), *Sustainable Environmental Management: Principles and Practice*, London: Belhaven Press, pp. 190–242.

Pigou, A.C. (1932), *The Economics of Welfare*, London: Macmillan and Co.

Rawls, J. (1971), *A Theory of Justice*, Cambridge, Massachusetts: The Belknap Press of Harvard University Press.

Sagoff, M. (1994), 'Should preferences count?' *Land Economics*, **70** (2), 127–144.

Scheele, M. (1997), 'The decomposition approach: spatially differentiated analysis and the implementation of environmental strategies', in E. Romstad, J. Simonsen and A. Vatn (eds), *Controlling Mineral Emissions in European Agriculture: Economics, Policies and the Environment*, Wallingford: CAB International, pp. 41–58.

Simonsen, J.W. (1989), 'Miljøavgifter på kunstgjødsel-N og -P', Department of Agricultural Economics, Agricultural University of Norway.

Simonsen, J., S. Rysstad and K. Christoffersen (1992), *Avgifter eller detaljregulering? Studier av virkemidler mot nitrogenforurensninger fra landbruket*, (Taxes vs. command and control. Studies of measures for reducing nitrogen pollution from agriculture), Report no. 10, Department of Economics and Social Sciences, Agricultural University of Norway.

Statens forurensningstilsyn (1991), 'Nasjonal nordsjøplan. Tiltak innen landbruket for å redusere tilførslene av næringssalter', Rapport fra arbeidsgruppe mellom Landbruksdepartementet, Miljøverndepartementet og Statens forurensningstilsyn.

Stevens, B.K. (1988), 'Fiscal implications of effluent charges and input taxes', *Journal of Environmental Economics and Management*, **15**, 285–96.

Stortingsforhandlingene (1981), *Besl. O nr. 28 (1980-81). Vedtak til lov om vern mot forurensninger og om avfall*, Oslo.

Stortingsforhandlingene (1988), *Tidende S 1988-89. Sak 1: Innstilling fra landbrukskomiteen om bevilgninger på statsbudsjettet for 1989 vedkommende Landbruksdepartementet (Budsjettinnst. S. nr. 9)*, pp. 901–51.

Stortingsforhandlingene (1990), *Tidende S 1990-91. Sak 1: Innstilling fra landbrukskomiteen om bevilgninger på statsbudsjettet for 1989 vedkommende Landbruksdepartementet (Budsjettinnst. S. nr. 9)*, pp. 1101–44.

Stortingsforhandlingene (1991), *Budsjettinnst. S. nr 9 (1991-92). Innstilling fra landbrukskomiteen om bevilgninger på statsbudsjettet for 1989 vedkommende Landbruksdepartementet*.

Tyler, T.R. (1990), *Why People Obey the Law*, New Haven, US and London, UK: Yale University Press.

Vagstad, N. (1990), *Miljøoptimal gjødsling. Nitrogen som miljø- og produksjonsfaktor i jordbruket, spesielt i kornproduksjonen*, Report no. 5.23.8-1, Centre for Soil and Environmental Research, Ås.

Vatn, A. (1984), *Teknologi og politikk. Om framveksten av viktige styringstiltak i norsk jordbruk 1920-1980*, Oslo: Landbruksforlaget.

Vatn, A. (1989), 'Forureiningane frå jordbruket – kva bør gjerast med landbrukspolitikken?' *Landbruksøkonomisk forum*, **2**, 26–34.

Vatn, A. (1998), 'Input vs. emission taxes: environmental taxes in a mass balance and transaction costs perspective', *Land Economics*, **74** (4), 514–25.

Vatn, A., L. Bakken, M.A. Bleken, P. Botterweg, H. Lundeby, E. Romstad, P.K. Rørstad and A. Vold (1996), 'Policies for reduced nutrient losses and erosion from Norwegian agriculture', *Norwegian Journal of Agricultural Sciences*, Supplement no. 23.

Vatn, A. and D.W. Bromley (1997), 'Externality – a market model failure', *Environment and Resource Economics*, **9** (2), 135–51.

Vedeld, P. (1998), 'Farmers and fertilizers: a study of adaptations and response to price increase on nitrogen fertilizers among Norwegian farmers', D.Sci thesis, Department of Economics and Social Sciences, Agricultural University of Norway.

Vedeld, P. and E. Krogh (1996), 'Rationality in the eye of the actor: economists and agronomists and a discourse over environmental taxes in agriculture', discussion paper no. D-19/1996, Department of Economics and Social Sciences, Agricultural University of Norway.

Walzer, M. (1983), *Spheres of Justice: A Defence of Pluralism and Equality*, New York: Basic Books.

7. Explaining why the Swedes but not the Danes tax fertilizers: a comparison of policy networks and political parties*

Carsten Daugbjerg

INTRODUCTION

The idea of using taxes in pollution control was fostered by the British economist Arthur C. Pigou in 1920 (Pigou, 1932 [1920], pp. 192–3). Although green taxes are now used as environmental policy measures in many West European countries, they are rarely the major instrument in environmental policies, particularly not in the industrial and agricultural sectors, but there are, of course, important exceptions. The most famous of these is perhaps the Dutch water tax. According to many economists, green taxes have significant advantages. First, they are the most efficient and effective measures for reducing pollution (Baumol and Oates, 1988) and, second, compared to regulations the implementation of green taxes involves lower administrative costs.

Despite these advantages of green taxes, experiences in many countries have shown that it is difficult to introduce them in various economic sectors because of strong political opposition. However, there are a number of examples in which advocates of green taxes have won the battle against polluters with the result that green taxes have been introduced. Thus, the challenge for political science is to explain why green taxes have been adopted in some situations but not in others. The first step in meeting this challenge is to develop theoretical propositions which suggest the reasons for this variation in policy choices. The second step is to test these propositions by the use of comparative research methods.

The main argument in this chapter is that political structures have an important impact on environmental policy-making. In the first part of the chapter, two political structures are presented: policy networks and parliaments. The former relates to the so-called corporate bargaining channel, which consists of decision-making bodies composed of interest group representatives and state officials. The policy process in this channel is, to a large extent, based on expertise within the policy field concerned. Parliament, the other political structure focused upon here, is part of the numerical democracy channel and is composed of democratically elected bodies (Rokkan, 1966). To understand the politics of green taxes, it is necessary to analyse these political structures in a historical perspective. Environmental policy did not become an important issue on the political agenda until the late 1960s and the early 1970s. At that time, the institutions of the modern state were already well developed and environmentalists, therefore, had to manoeuvre within a set of existing political structures, be they formal or informal. These political structures provided opportunities for the introduction of green taxes in some countries but not in others. The aim of the first part of this chapter is to develop theoretical propositions about the way in which policy networks and parliaments influence the opportunities for the introduction of green taxes.

The second part tests these propositions in a comparison of green tax policy-making in Danish and Swedish agriculture. The two countries are almost ideal for a comparison because Swedish nitrate policy includes a fertilizer tax while, so far, it has not been possible to apply such a measure in Denmark, despite several attempts to do so. The comparison shows that differences in agricultural policy networks and in parliamentary support for farmers help to explain why policy choices differ in the two countries.

This article compares two nations which share a large number of important characteristics but produce different outcomes. By comparing such countries, many variables are kept constant. This means that the range of potential variables which may explain the variation in outcomes is limited considerably. Besides keeping the nature of pollution problems constant, this study also keeps other important variables constant, for instance political culture and political system. Although a number of important variables can be kept constant and can thus exclude certain explanations, there are still some which may threaten the argument that differences in agricultural policy networks and parliamentary support of farmers can explain why Danish and Swedish nitrate polices differ. Thus, they need further consideration. An alternative explanation which must be considered is that differences in the seriousness of the pollution problems can explain policy variation. However, this explanation is not relevant here. In the mid-1980s, annual nitrate leaching has been estimated at 250 000 tonnes in Denmark and 50 000 tonnes in Sweden (Eckerberg *et al.*, 1994, p. 191). Had the seriousness of nitrate pollution had an impact on the choice of policy, then the Danish nitrate policy should have been the more radical. Since this is not the case, there must be other explanations.

Some would perhaps argue that the national economic importance of agriculture explains why fertilizer taxes have not been applied in Denmark. This economic proposition suggests that in countries where agricultural production is important to the national economy, policy makers are careful not to decrease the international competitiveness of agriculture (Bennett and Baldock, 1991, pp. 221–2). Consequently, they choose solutions which do not burden farmers economically. A comparison of agri-environmental policies in Norway and Sweden demonstrates that differences in policy cannot, in general, be explained by differences in the national economic importance of an industry. In these two countries, agriculture is almost equally important to their national economies (in 1990 agriculture accounted for 1.8 per cent of the gross domestic product (GDP) in Norway and 1.5 per cent in Sweden). According to the economic proposition, the two countries would be expected to choose relatively similar policy measures, but they have not done so; the level of economic agri-environmental subsidies in Norway is much higher than in Sweden. If the economic importance of agriculture is a crucial independent variable, there should be little difference in policy outcomes (Daugbjerg, 1998a, p. 11; Eckerberg *et al.*, 1994, pp. 198–9).

Finally, it could be argued that differences in public attention can explain why environmental policies differ (Vogel, 1993). However, differences in the level of public environmental concern cannot explain why the Swedes, but not the Danes, introduced green taxes. Had this been so, Danish nitrate policy should have been the more radical in terms of using taxes. In 1986, the Danish public were very concerned about agricultural pollution (Andersen and Hansen, 1991) and in 1997, the situation was fairly similar. As regards agriculture, such situations have not occurred in Sweden.

WHY POLLUTERS OPPOSE GREEN TAXES

Before a theoretical proposition can be developed, it is necessary to consider what perceptions polluters have of green tax policy-making. It can be assumed that they perceive green taxes as more burdensome than regulatory instruments. First, in contrast to regulations, green taxes increase production costs in a very visible manner. Second, from the point of view of interest associations, green taxes create a higher degree of future uncertainty for polluters than do regulations because, in general, interest groups have limited control over the formulation of tax policies (Damgaard and Eliassen, 1978, pp. 302–11). They are, therefore, not in a position to block future increases in the tax level and this creates uncertainty. By contrast, regulatory instruments provide much better opportunities for polluters to achieve control over the future policy process and thus certainty. In order to implement such instruments, public authorities require information and knowledge possessed by interest groups (Bressers, 1995, p. 13). Further, to avoid implementation gaps it is necessary for an implementing agency to obtain support from the interest groups representing polluters. Both factors imply that polluters achieve a certain control over the policy process, a control which they cannot achieve in tax policy-making (Daugbjerg, 1998a, pp. 77–9).

POLICY NETWORKS AND GREEN TAXES

Policy networks are organizational arrangements designed to facilitate intermediation between state actors and organized interests. They emerge as a result of 'the dominance of organized actors in policy-making, the overcrowded participation, the fragmentation of the state, the blurring of boundaries between public and private' (Kenis and Schneider, 1991, p. 41; Blom-Hansen, 1997). The modern state plays a crucial role in economic and social life. To intervene in these areas, governments need resources which are not available within the state apparatus and cannot readily be developed. It must, therefore, look elsewhere. Typically, it will become dependent upon organized interests which have resources within specific policy areas. On the other hand, interest groups are dependent on governments for the access to the political decision-making process in order to influence those policy decisions which concern them (Rhodes and Marsh, 1992; Smith, 1993). This mutual dependence on resources is central to policy network analysis. Thus, a policy network can be defined as: 'a cluster or complex of organizations connected to each other by resource dependencies and distinguished from other clusters or complexes by breaks in the structure of resource dependencies' (Benson, 1982, p. 148). Normally, they occur within specific policy fields or sectors.

A crucial question which needs to be answered before proceeding further is: how do we apply the policy network concept in environmental studies? One approach is to map the participants in environmental policy-making. It is, however, questionable whether such an approach helps to explain environmental policy choices because it can easily be misleading. It may suggest that there is a distinct environmental policy network which is then classified as a loose network in which conflicting interests (polluters and environmentalists) are members. Within such a network, the policy process is characterized by conflict rather compromise. The actor constellation revealed by such an approach may, in fact, be a description of two conflicting networks (one representing polluters' interests and one representing environmental interests) rather than one loose network. The mapping approach to the study of environmental policy-making often uses a snapshot technique to describe networks and it, therefore, does not enable the understanding of policy choices because these are most often affected by structures that have historical roots. A better way to apply the policy network concept is to use a historical structuralist approach.

The starting point of the historical structuralist approach is that in many policy sectors, economic interest groups established relationships with state actors, and thus policy networks, long before environmental problems became an important issue on the political agenda. Environmentalists, therefore, have had to operate within a set of policy networks which historical actors generally did not construct with the issue of pollution control in mind; they had many other concerns. The design of these established networks has a major influence on environmental actors' opportunities for realizing their interests.

Some established networks within sectors subject to green tax proposals facilitate polluters' attempts to build up strong opposition to green taxes, whereas others prevent them from so doing. A major factor influencing the opportunities to introduce green taxes is the extent to which there is a consensus within a network on which social, political and economic objectives public policies should pursue. It is possible to achieve a consensus if network members are sympathetic to each other's interests and if they cooperate closely. Sympathy towards each other's interests 'stems from shared values and a shared view on reality' (Bressers, 1995, p. 4). Policy networks with such a consensus are cohesive (Daugbjerg, 1997, pp. 127–30, 1998a, pp. 46–52, 1998c). They put the interests of their members before those of outsider groups, and environmentalists are often among the outsiders. Confronted with demands for green taxes, network members can relatively easily agree to oppose them. They often succeed in avoiding the imposition of green taxes because a policy network which acts in unity controls the expertise within the sector subject to the use of green taxes. This gives network members a powerful position.

In a democracy, however, a majority in parliament can overrule a policy network but doing so is not without political risk because it generates problems of legitimacy within the group subject to the policy decision. This may cause political unrest and impede the implementation of policy (Smith, 1993, p. 52). Moreover, overruling the expertise of a policy network may lead to unintended policy consequences which, in turn, may lead to more political unrest. Governments and parliaments often try to prevent such situations from arising and they, therefore, tend to accommodate the members of a policy network who have formed a strong coalition opposing a certain policy measure.

It must be said, however, that unpopular policy instruments like green taxes may sometimes be applied in a sector in which a cohesive policy network does exist. In such cases the target group is more than fully compensated through various direct and indirect subsidy schemes (Bressers, 1995, p. 20).

Non-cohesive policy networks tend to prevent the formation of strong opposition to green taxes. Missing cohesion is due to a lack of consensus on which social, political and economic objectives public policies should pursue (Daugbjerg, 1997, pp. 127–30, 1998a, pp. 46–52, 1998c). Network members have not been able to develop a consensus because they have no shared values and views on reality, and because they pursue conflicting interests. This lack of consensus means that network members have difficulties in forming coalitions capable of successfully opposing demands for green taxes. Since network members tend to be unable to act in unity, environmental actors have the opportunity to introduce green taxes.

A government or a majority in parliament can overrule one or more of the actors in a non-cohesive network without risking major legitimacy problems because most often a central actor within the sector subject to green tax proposals can be persuaded to support the government's or the parliamentary majority's policy positions. To some extent, the legitimacy of policies shaped in a policy network rests on the support of actors who are believed to have technical expertise within the policy field in question. Therefore, a policy which has the support of one network member with such expertise cannot be dismissed as not being legitimate, and the likelihood of political unrest is therefore considerably diminished. There need not, however, be any guarantee that the policy will not produce unintended consequences.

So, the network proposition suggests:

● The less cohesive the established policy network in the sector subject to green taxes, the more favourable the conditions for the introduction of green taxes.

PARLIAMENTS AND GREEN TAXES

Another important factor that influences whether or not green taxes are introduced is the extent to which the group subject to green taxes has parliamentary support. This type of political support of social groups should also be analysed by using a historical structural method because current parliamentary support is often rooted in history. The influence of parliament arises from the actions of the parliamentary parties because 'party remains the basic determinant of parliamentary behaviour' (Norton, 1991, p. 80). Most political parties were founded in the 'pre-environmental era' and, therefore, the concern for the environment did not become a main issue in their manifestos. Political parties became institutionalized because once established, they tended to 'develop their own internal structure and build up long-term commitments among core supporters' (Lipset and Rokkan, 1967, p. 30). These commitments constrain, or perhaps even determine, the behaviour of party members in a way which benefits the parties' original core voters. Political parties are thus relatively conservative, but not to the same extent as policy networks because parties must respond to the electorate to a much greater degree than policy networks. Policy networks respond mainly to the interests of their members.

Increasing awareness of pollution and environmental damage within the electorate has motivated some parties to pursue environmental goals in order to attract more votes. This may involve a weakening of some parties' ties to their traditional supporters. Other parties stick to the interests of their traditional voters (Lane and Ersson, 1991, p. 112) and they are, therefore, less responsive to environmental demands. The fact that political parties tend to adhere to their original aims render many of them relatively conservative when it comes to policy innovations which come into conflict with the interests of their original core supporters. This partially explains the difficulties of introducing green taxes. Parties which are reluctant to use environmental taxes most often prefer regulatory measures and environmental subsidies as the major instruments in environmental policies. Such instruments seem more acceptable to polluters. The instances in which policy-makers have introduced green taxes in industry and agriculture can be partially explained by change in political parties' loyalty towards various groups in society in a way which favours environmental interests. In particular, changes in strategically placed parties in parliament may explain the introduction of green taxes.

In a parliamentary system, one or more of the parties represented in parliament are in government. When in government, parties have better opportunities to protect or even promote the interests of their constituencies than they do when they are in opposition. In multi-party governments, the parties will be careful not to hurt each others' constituencies in order not to split the government. This is not to say that a party never splits a government, but that it must have important reasons to do so. It must be added that in cases of minority governments, non-governmental parties which support the government may be able to place themselves in a strategic, and thus powerful, position which can be used to further the interests of their own constituencies. So, in periods with minority governments, governmental parties and parties in strategic parliamentary positions have opportunities either to facilitate the introduction of green taxes or to prevent it, depending on their policy positions.

So, the proposition concerning groups' parliamentary support suggests:

● The more the parliamentary support of a group of polluters has declined over time as a result of the growth in environmental concern, the more favourable the conditions for the introduction of green taxes.

GREEN TAXES IN DANISH AND SWEDISH AGRICULTURE

A comparison of Danish and Swedish nitrate policy reveals interesting differences. In relation to this study the most interesting difference is that the Swedes have had an environmental fertilizer tax since 1984. Although the use of such a tax was an innovation in agri-environmental policies, the fertilizer tax was a well-known measure in agricultural policy. The Swedish government introduced an agricultural fertilizer tax in 1982 to fund agricultural subsidies. When the environmental fertilizer tax was introduced in 1984 it was set at 5 per cent, doubled to 10 per cent in 1988 and increased to 27 per cent in 1994. In Denmark there have been several failed attempts to tax fertilizers. The first attempt was made in 1984 and the next one in 1986–87. In 1991 and 1994 the tax solution was discussed again but eventually rejected. Finally, there was an attempt in late 1997 to introduce a tax on over-fertilization (Daugbjerg, 1998b).

According to the theoretical propositions developed above, the differences in policy choices can be explained by differences in agricultural policy networks and in the parliamentary support of farmers. The best way to test the theoretical propositions empirically is to undertake a comparative case study analysis. The comparative case study method is based on the logic of multiple experiments. When researchers use such methods, they obtain insights into a phenomenon by replicating a series of experiments. The more times the experiment produces the results predicted by theory, the more convincing the theory. In terms of generalization the most convincing results can be obtained from multiple experiments based on theoretical replications. The essence of this method is that the researcher designs experiments which, for predictable reasons, produce different outcomes. When this logic is applied to case study research, cases which the theory predicts will produce different outcomes are selected (Yin, 1989, pp. 53, 109–10). Green tax policy-making in Danish and Swedish agriculture can be analysed by using the comparative case study method based on the logic of theoretical replication because the two countries adopted different policies. Sweden introduced fertilizer taxes, whereas Denmark did not. Applied to agri-environmental policy-making the theoretical propositions suggest that differences in agricultural policy networks and parliamentary support of farmers help to explain why policy choices differ. Therefore, the conditions which produced green taxes in Sweden should not be present in Denmark, if the empirical test is to support the propositions.

AGRICULTURAL POLICY NETWORKS AND COALITION FORMATION IN SWEDEN AND DENMARK

In this section the Danish and Swedish agricultural policy networks are compared in order to establish whether they are different in terms of cohesion and, if so, whether such differences produced the coalitions suggested by the network proposition.

Sweden

The Swedish agricultural policy network has been characterized by a low degree of cohesion. In the period from the early 1930s to the 1990s, the official goals of Swedish agricultural policy were unstable. From the 1930s until 1947, social concerns for farmers became increasingly important in agricultural policy. In 1947, they were made explicit in the policy objectives, in that the main goal of agricultural policy was to ensure that farmers' average incomes were equal to those of industrial workers. In the 1960s, the emphasis on farmers' incomes decreased and became less precise. What emerged was an emphasis that agriculture should, to a larger extent, be subject to those market forces which applied to business and industry. The pendulum swung back towards more social concerns in agricultural policy in 1977 and the income goal was once given higher priority (Steen, 1988, pp. 76–80; Micheletti, 1990, pp. 91–3, 101–3). In the mid-1980s, the priority of goals changed and the income goal was given lower priority. A major change took place in 1990. The domestic system of price regulations was removed for some products and considerably simplified for others, and market forces thus gained much more influence on price-setting (Daugbjerg, 1998a, pp. 133–41; Vail *et al.*, 1994, p. 187). This instability of agricultural policy objectives indicates that the network has not been cohesive.

This instability was closely associated with the presence of consumers in the Swedish agricultural policy network. In 1963, the Consumer Delegation[1] achieved the right to participate in price negotiations between farmers and the Swedish state. Micheletti (1990, pp. 94–7, 133) and Steen (1988, pp. 214–18) argue that since the early 1970s, the Consumer Delegation has been exercising considerable influence on agricultural policy-making. Elsewhere, that conclusion was questioned by arguing that the most important influence of the consumers in Swedish agricultural politics is that they prevented the agricultural network from developing a high degree of cohesion (Daugbjerg, 1998a, pp. 156–7; 1998c).

According to the theoretical network proposition the lack of cohesion means that Swedish farmers were unable to form a strong coalition with the agricultural authorities. The analysis of Swedish green tax formulation in agriculture undertaken below tests this statement.

In 1983, the majority of a commission set up by the Minister of Agriculture recommended the use of a fertilizer tax of 1 per cent to fund various pollution control measures in agriculture, admitting that a tax set at such a low level would not limit the use of chemical fertilizers (SOU, 1983: 10, pp. 223–4, 251–2). Not surprisingly, the commission's agricultural representatives opposed the majority's proposals (ibid., pp. 297–305). The National Board of Agriculture (*Lantbruksstyrelsen*), which administered the agricultural structural policy and provided advisory service to farmers, formed part of the commission's majority and thus left the farmers isolated in the policy process. The reason why the Board did not oppose fertilizer taxes was perhaps that it stood to benefit from the tax revenues. To improve the advisory service the commission suggested that part of the revenues should fund a staff increase in the state county agricultural boards (*Lantbruksnämnderna*), the Agricultural Board's regional implementation bodies (ibid., pp. 236–8, 251–2). In 1984, the Social Democratic government proposed a 5 per cent fertilizer tax which was accepted by the *Riksdag* (Swedish Parliament) (Daugbjerg, 1998a, pp. 99–101).

Four years later, the coalition pattern was repeated when a committee set up by the Minister of Agriculture recommended that the existing fertilizer tax be increased as a measure to motivate farmers to use less fertilizer. While the farmer representatives on the committee opposed the tax increase, the representatives of the state agricultural authorities accepted it, provided that it would be used to fund agri-environmental policy measures (Jordbruksdepartementet, 1987, pp. 68–75, 83–6; Swedish Government, 1988, Appendix 2, pp. 85–6). The government followed the recommendations of the majority of the committee and recommended that the *Riksdag* increase the fertilizer tax to 10 per cent, which it did (Daugbjerg, 1998a, pp. 101–4). The fertilizer tax was increased to 27 per cent in 1994, but this did not seem to arouse much opposition (Daugbjerg, 1998b).

Denmark

In Denmark, things developed rather differently. The Danish state became deeply involved in agriculture in the early 1930s. The Danish agricultural policy network has been, and still is, cohesive. From the early 1930s and until now, the major aim of agricultural policy has been to maintain the international competitiveness of agricultural production in order to uphold export earnings, employment and incomes in the farming and food processing sector (Daugbjerg, 1998a, pp. 147–55).

Agricultural interests have been closely tied to the national interest (Buksti, 1980, pp. 288–9), notably after Denmark's entrance into the European Community (EC) in 1973, as Denmark has a net benefit from the membership, primarily through EC agricultural subsidies (Tracy, 1993, pp. 251–2). The EC membership, therefore, has contributed to maintaining consensus within the agricultural network. Entry into the EC meant that the Community took over the costs of agricultural policy, implying that they were passed on from the Danish state to the other EC member states. As a consequence, many Danish political actors have had no incentive to question the aims of Danish agricultural policy.

The high degree of stability in agricultural policy objectives is closely associated with the agricultural policy network's membership. Since the early 1930s, the core of the network has consisted of the Ministry of Agriculture and the agricultural associations (Just, 1992, 1994, p. 39). Entrance into the EC in 1973 changed the internal organization of the network as the Ministry of Agriculture strengthened its position in relation to the agricultural organizations (Buksti, 1980, p. 288; Just, 1994, p. 44), but the main policy objectives remained unchanged. The reorganization was also an attempt to introduce a counterbalancing power into the network. The Consumer Council became a member, but never gained more than marginal influence and has not been able seriously to challenge the dominance of agricultural interests (Daugbjerg, 1998a, p. 152). The stability in agricultural policy objectives and the dominance of the agricultural associations indicate that the Danish agricultural policy network has a high degree of cohesion.

The theoretical network proposition suggests that Danish farmers would be able to form a strong coalition with the Ministry of Agriculture and thus be able successfully to avoid the introduction of green taxes because of the high degree of cohesion in the Danish agricultural policy network. The following paragraphs examine whether such a coalition actually existed in Danish agri-environmental policy-making.

In 1984, when the Danish Environmental Protection Agency (EPA) proposed the use of a fertilizer tax to help decrease nitrate leaching (Miljøstyrelsen, 1984, pp. 141–6), the Ministry of Agriculture strongly opposed the proposal, arguing that since there was no overconsumption of chemical fertilizers, there was no point in introducing a fertilizer tax which would merely be a tax on a production input with no significant environmental effect (ibid., p. 8). This view on fertilizer taxes enabled the Ministry of

Agriculture and farmers to form a strong coalition against the EPA, and it was capable of convincing a majority in the *Folketing* (the Danish parliament) that green taxes should not be applied in agriculture. A similar coalition pattern was observed in 1986 when the EPA once more put the issue of fertilizer taxes onto the agenda. The Ministry of Agriculture and the farmers opposed the use of such measures. After long and complicated discussions in the *Folketing*, it was eventually decided not to impose a fertilizer tax in June 1987 (Andersen and Hansen, 1991; Daugbjerg, 1998a, pp. 91–4). The issue of fertilizer tax appeared once more on the political agenda in 1991 and a similar coalition pattern occurred. The government had asked the Ministry of Agriculture to prepare an action plan for sustainable agriculture. To meet demands from the EPA, the Ministry of Agriculture analysed the economic and environmental effects of fertilizer taxes and quotas. It concluded that both policy instruments had negative effects on the distribution of incomes in agriculture and also on the choice of crops, and since it would be relatively complicated to avoid these negative effects, the Ministry recommended other policy measures (Landbrugsministeriet, 1991, pp. 228–42). The Ministry was thus in line with the agricultural associations. Although fertilizer taxes had considerable support in the *Folketing*, farmers once again avoided them (Daugbjerg, 1998a, pp. 94–7).

Tax solutions, however, were not definitively removed from the agenda. A committee of civil servants from various ministries discussed the issue of taxing nitrogen in the mid-1990s, but did not recommend a particular scheme. In fact, the discussion put much emphasis on the problems associated with the use of green taxes to reduce nitrate pollution. These problems were a lack of cost-efficiency, administrative complexity and the redistribution of income within the farming community (Embedmandsudvalget om grønne afgifter og erhvervene, 1994, pp. 295–311). Taxes on fertilizers were not discussed later on in the policy process, officially because the *Folketing*'s evaluation of the nitrate policy had to be awaited. This was convenient because the issue of taxing fertilizers was politically controversial: farmers strongly opposed such taxes and the Ministry of Agriculture was sceptical of them (Embedmandsudvalget om grønne afgifter og erhvervene, 1995, pp. 18, 28). In late 1997, a tax on over-fertilization was discussed. The intention was to tax the amount of nitrogen used which exceeded the quantity permitted in farmers' individual fertilizer and crop rotation plans, but the idea of imposing such a tax was eventually abandoned.

In summary, the empirical analysis above shows that the degree of cohesion of the policy network in the sector subject to the use of green taxes has an important influence on the opportunities to introduce them. Where policy networks with low degrees of cohesion exist, environmental actors tend to have the best opportunities to persuade politicians to adopt green taxes.

FARMERS' PARLIAMENTARY SUPPORT AND FERTILIZER TAXES

The theoretical part of this chapter argues that differences in farmers' parliamentary support also help to explain why policy choices vary. When applied to the agricultural sector, the theoretical proposition suggests that the more parliamentary support of farmers has declined over time as a result of growth in the level of environmental concern, the more favourable are the conditions for the introduction of green taxes. When applied to agri-environmental policy-making in Denmark and Sweden, the theoretical proposition about the relationship between the parliamentary support of farmers and the introduction of green taxes suggests that parliamentary support has declined more in Sweden than it has in Denmark. The following sections test this proposition.

Sweden

The Centre Party (*Centerpartiet*) has traditionally represented Swedish farmers in the *Riksdag*. During the 1950s, the Party tried to appeal to new groups of voters, but it was not until the late 1950s that it distanced itself from farmers' interests. The defeat in the 1956 general election and the steady depopulation of the countryside motivated a group of primarily urban and well-educated members to take the lead in the transformation from a rural and agrarian party to a party appealing to both urban and rural voters (Larsson, 1980, pp. 115–46; Steen, 1985, pp. 58–9; 1988, pp. 339–40). This change in party profile is clearly indicated by the contents of the Party programme. From 1956 to 1960, the share of the programme that dealt with agriculture fell from 37 per cent to 6 per cent (Christensen, 1994, p. 332). The emphasis on environmental protection in the mid-1970s also shows that the Party was appealing to new social groups (ibid., p. 333). Farmers' declining support within the Centre Party became evident in the 1988 decision to increase the fertilizer tax, as the party did not issue any statements supporting farmers; only the Conservatives opposed the proposal (Jordbruksutskottet, 1988, pp. 24–5, 34, 45–6).

From its early days, the Swedish Social Democratic Party pursued consumer interests in agricultural politics. However, in the 1920s, the Party gradually became more attentive to agricultural interests in order to gain electoral support from new groups, primarily smallholders and farm workers, hoping this would bring about a parliamentary majority for its social reform programme (Thullberg, 1974, pp. 130–47). It was not until the late 1950s and early 1960s that the Social Democratic Party broke with its view on agricultural policy and returned to the former consumer-friendly position. In the 1960 programme, the Party abandoned support for smallholders and began to emphasize efficiency and the benefits of large-scale farming in order to ensure reasonable food prices for consumers (Steen, 1988, p. 310). The decision to include consumers in the agricultural policy network clearly reflected the new emphasis on consumers' interests. That decision was initiated by the Social Democrats. They worried about the imbalance in favour of agricultural interests and, therefore, wanted to strengthen consumer interests (ibid., pp. 214–15). The Social Democrats 'relate[d] price increases and government subsidies to consumer interests. [The costs of agricultural policy] were defined as being a question of redistribution between farmers and consumers' (Steen, 1985, p. 52). In the 1980s, the Social Democrats' declining sympathy for the interests of farmers became very evident. The Social Democrats were in office both when the fertilizer tax was introduced in 1984 and when it was raised in 1988 and 1994.

Denmark

Danish farmers have experienced a smaller decline in their parliamentary support than their Swedish colleagues. Since the first decade of this century, two parties have represented agricultural interests. The Liberal Party (*Venstre*), has traditionally represented farmers' interests and the Radical Liberal Party (*Det radikale Venstre*) has represented smallholders. The Liberal Party is still loyal to agricultural interests, although it has recently weakened its ties to farmers in order to retain the support of urban middle-class voters. During the late 1950s and early 1960s, the Radical Liberal Party changed by moving closer to middle-class voters at the expense of smallholders' interests. Because the smallholders were becoming less important in the national economy, the Radical Liberals were no longer willing to support them with the subsidies which they required to stay in business (Daugbjerg, 1998a, p. 174).

The Liberals and the Radical Liberals have held strategic parliamentary positions during the 1980s and early 1990s, the period when pollution control in agriculture was on the agenda. During the periods of liberal conservative governments in the 1980s the Liberal Party, the staunchest defender of farmers' interests, was able to ensure that agricultural interests were not disregarded by the other government parties, primarily because it was the second largest party in these governments. From 1982 until 1988, the *Folketing* enacted two agri-environmental action plans. During that period the Radical Liberal Party (which was not one of the governmental parties) 'was pivotal in most cases of conflict' (Damgaard, 1994, p. 93). It held the balance in environmental policy-making and initially supported the use of fertilizer taxes, but eventually it had to give in to considerable pressure from members of the farming community within the party and go against the introduction of fertilizer taxes (*Press*, no. 37, 1988).

In the area of agricultural policy, the traditional concern of the Social Democrats has been employment in the food processing industry. In the 1980s, the party adopted a green profile, manifested by its support for the use of green taxes in agriculture. However, the employment and national economic concerns associated with agricultural production continued to be important to the party. For instance, the Social Democratic agricultural spokesman said in 1996 that he did not want his party to be seen as being negative towards agriculture. He then went on to say: 'I know what agriculture means to export incomes and the employment' (*Landsbladet*, 15 March 1996). This sympathy towards agricultural interests became very clear in 1997 when the Social Democratic–Social Liberal government preferred to reach a compromise on the nitrate policy with the Liberal Party, thereby giving in to farmers' interests rather than forming a majority with the left wing parties.

In summary, the comparison of farmers' parliamentary support shows that it has declined most in Sweden. The Centre Party changed from an agrarian party into one which also represented middle-class voters. Furthermore, since the late 1950s the Social Democratic Party has emphasized consumer interests over farmers' interests. This is an important reason why environmental actors were able to persuade politicians in the *Riksdag* to adopt green taxes in Swedish agriculture. The Danish Liberal Party has remained loyal to farm interests until recently, but the Radical Liberal Party has emphasized urban middle-class interests more than those of smallholders. The Social Democratic Party has been slightly more responsive to environmental and consumer interests. The fact that Danish farmers' parliamentary support has declined less than that of their Swedish counterparts helps to explain why fertilizer taxes have not been introduced in Denmark.

CONCLUSION

This comparative analysis has attempted to explain some of the reasons why green taxes have been introduced in some countries but not in others. The point of departure is that environmental policy-making must be analysed in a historical perspective. Environmentalists have to manoeuvre within political systems with well-developed structures which, in most cases, were established long before the issue of pollution control appeared on the political agenda. This study has focused on two such structures, namely policy networks and the parliamentary support of the groups subject to green taxes.

It has been argued that the less cohesive the established policy network in the sector subject to green taxes, the more favourable the conditions for the introduction of them. Realizing that the focus on policy networks is not sufficient and needs to be supplemented with an analysis of the parties represented in parliament, it has also been argued that the more parliamentary support of a group of polluters has declined over time as a result of the growth of environmentalism, the more favourable the conditions for introducing green taxes.

Sweden has introduced fertilizer taxes, while attempts to do so in Denmark have failed. The comparison of the agricultural policy networks shows that the Danish agricultural network was cohesive, whereas the Swedish network was not. This difference partially explains why green taxes were introduced in Sweden. Belonging to a non-cohesive policy network, Swedish farmers were unable to obtain support from the state agricultural authorities in their opposition to green taxes and they were, therefore, in a relatively weak political position. As a result, they had to accept green taxes. In contrast, the cohesive Danish agricultural policy network was a major political resource for farmers because they could mobilize the support of the Ministry of Agriculture in their battle against fertilizer taxes. The existence of this strong opposition meant that the farmers won the battle.

The comparison of farmers' parliamentary support shows that since the 1950s, the parliamentary support of Swedish farmers has declined more than that of Danish farmers. In Sweden, the Centre Party, which traditionally supported farmers, changed from an agrarian party into one which also represented middle-class voters, and the Social Democrats upgraded consumer interests at the expense of smallholders' interests. In Denmark, the Radical Liberal Party has emphasized urban middle-class interests over those of smallholders and the Social Democratic Party has been more responsive to environmental interests. However, because the Liberals – the farmers' traditional party – were in government during the 1980s and early 1990s, this decline was not enough to enable the EPA to introduce fertilizer taxes. The Social Democrats' return to power in 1993 has not yet led to the use of green taxes in the nitrate policy.

The empirical results support the theoretical arguments which basically state that policy networks and political parties in parliament make a difference in environmental policy-making. Although the case study method based on the logic of theoretical replication produces robust results, an examination of more cases is needed to assess the extent to which the theoretical arguments can be generalized.

NOTES

*   I would like to thank the participants in the international workshop Institutional Aspects of Economic Instruments for Environmental Policy, 20–21 May 1997, at Eigtveds Pakhus,

Copenhagen, for valuable comments. I am particularly grateful to the discussant, Hans Bressers, and to Andrew Jordan.

1. It consists of representatives from the trade unions, from the Cooperative Union and Wholesale Society, and later on also representatives from wholesale trading companies and business associations not belonging to the farmers' movement.

REFERENCES

Andersen, Mikael Skou and Michael W. Hansen (1991), *Vandmiljøplanen: Fra forhandling til symbol*, Harlev J: Niche.

Baumol, William J. and W.E. Oates (1988), *The Theory of Environmental Policy*, 2nd edn., Cambridge: Cambridge University Press.

Bennett, Graham and David Baldock (1991), 'Conclusions', in David Baldock and Graham Bennett (eds), *Agriculture and the Polluter Pays Principle: A Study of Six EC Countries*, Arnhem, The Netherlands and London, UK: Institute for European Environmental Policy, pp. 221-31.

Benson, J.K. (1982), 'A framework for policy analysis', in D. Rogers, D. Whitten *et al.* (eds), *Interorganizational Coordination*, Ames: Iowa State University Press, pp. 137-76.

Blom-Hansen, Jens (1997) 'A "new institutionalist" perspective on policy networks', *Public Administration*, **75** (2), 669-93.

Bressers, Hans Th. A. (1995), 'Policy networks and the choice of instruments', NIG working paper 95-6, Enschede: Netherlands Institute of Government.

Buksti, Jacob A. (1980), 'Udviklingen i landbrugets organisationsforhold 1972-79', in Jacob A. Buksti (ed.), *Organisationer under forandring: Studier i organisationssystemet i Danmark*, Århus: Forlaget Politica, pp. 283-308.

Christensen, Dag Arne (1994), 'Fornyinga av bondepartia i Noreg og Sverige', in Knut Heider and Lars Svåsand (eds), *Partiene i en brytningstid*, Bergen: Alma Mater Forlag, pp. 327-54.

Damgaard, Erik (1994), 'The strong parliaments of Scandinavia: continuity and change of Scandinavian parliaments', in Gary W. Copeland and Samual C. Patterson (eds), *Parliaments in the Modern World: Changing Institutions*, Ann Arbor: The University of Michigan Press, pp. 85-103.

Damgaard, Erik and Kjell A. Eliassen (1978), 'Corporate pluralism in Danish lawmaking', *Scandinavian Political Studies*, **1** (4), 285-313.

Daugbjerg, Carsten (1997), 'Policy networks and agricultural policy reforms: explaining deregulation in Sweden and re-regulation in the European Community', *Governance*, **10** (2), 122-41.

Daugbjerg, Carsten (1998a), *Policy Networks under Pressure: Pollution Control, Policy Reforms and the Power of Farmers*, Aldershot: Ashgate Publishing.

Daugbjerg, Carsten (1998b), 'Power and policy design: a comparison of green taxation in Scandinavian agriculture', *Scandinavian Political Studies*, **21** (3), 253-84.

Daugbjerg Carsten (1998c), 'Similar problems, different solutions: policy networks and environmental policy in Danish and Swedish agriculture', in David Marsh (ed.), *Comparing Policy Networks*, Buckingham: Open University Press, pp. 75-89.

Eckerberg, K., P.K. Mydske, A. Niemi-Iilahti and K.H. Pedersen (eds) (1994), *Comparing Nordic and Baltic Countries - Environmental Problems and Policies in Agriculture and Forestry*, TemaNord 1994: 572, Copenhagen: Nordic Council of Ministers.

Embedmandsudvalget om grønne afgifter og erhvervene (1994), *Grønne afgifter og erhvervene: Midtvejsrapport*, Copenhagen: Finansministeriet.

Embedmandsudvalget om grønne afgifter og erhvervene (1995), *Grønne afgifter og erhvervene referater fra embedsmandsudvalgets drøftelser med erhvervsorganisationer*, Copenhagen: Finansministeriet.

Jordbruksdepartementet (1987), 'Intensiteten i jordbruksproduktionen. Miljöpåverkan och spannmålsöverskott. Betänkande av arbetsgruppen med uppgift att utreda vissa frågor rörande en lägre intensitet i jordbruksproduktionen', Ds Jo 1987: 3, Stockholm: Allmänna Förlaget.

Jordbruksutskottet (1988), 'Jordbruksutskottets betänkande 1987/88: 24 om miljöförbättrande åtgärder i jordbruket, m.m. (prop. 1987/88: 128)', *Riksdagstrycket* 1987/88, Stockholm.

Just, Flemming (1992), *Landbruget, staten og eksporten 1930-1950*, Esbjerg: Sydjysk Universitetsforlag.

Just, Flemming (1994), 'Agriculture and corporatism in Scandinavia', in Philip Lowe, Terry Marsden and Sarah Whatmore (eds), *Agricultural Regulations*, London: David Fulton Publishers, pp. 31-52.

Kenis, Patrick and Volker Schneider (1991), 'Policy networks and policy analysis: scrutinizing a new analytical toolbox', in Bernd Marin and Renate Mayntz (eds), *Policy Networks: Empirical Evidence and Theoretical Considerations*, Frankfurt am Main/Boulder, Colorado: Campus Verlag/Westview Press, pp. 25-59.

Landbrugsministeriet (1991), *Bæredygtigt landbrug: En teknisk redegørelse*, Copenhagen: Landbrugsministeriet.

Landsbladet, 9 October 1992, 15 March 1996.

Lane, Jan-Erik and Svante O. Ersson (1991), *Politics and Society in Western Europe*, 2nd edn, London: Sage Publications.

Larsson, Hans Albin (1980), *Partireformation - från bondeförbund till centerparti*, Lund: CWK Gleerup.

Lipset, Seymour M. and Stein Rokkan (1967), 'Cleavage structures, party systems, and voter alignments: an introduction', in Seymour M. Lipset and Stein Rokkan (eds), *Cleavage Structures, Party Systems, and Voter Alignments: Cross-national Perspectives*, New York/London: The Free Press/Collier-Macmillan, pp. 1-64.

Micheletti, Michele (1990), *The Swedish Farmers' Movement and Government Agricultural Policy*, New York: Praeger.

Miljøstyrelsen (1984), *NPO-redegørelsen*, Copenhagen: Miljøstyrelsen.

Norton, Philip (1991), 'The changing face of parliament: lobbying and its consequences', in Philip Norton (ed.), *New Directions in British Politics? Essays on the Evolving Constitution*, Aldershot, UK and Brookfield, US: Edward Elgar, pp. 58-82.

Pigou, Arthur (1932 [1920]), *The Economics of Welfare*, 4th edn, London: Macmillan and Co.

Press, no. 37, December, 1988.

Rhodes, R.A.W and David Marsh (1992), 'New directions in the study of policy networks', *European Journal of Political Research*, 21 (1-2), 181-205.

Rokkan, Stein (1966), 'Norway: numerical democracy and corporate pluralism', in Robert A. Dahl (ed.), *Political Oppositions in Western Democracies*, New Haven: Yale University Press, pp. 70-115.

Smith, Martin J. (1993), *Pressure, Power and Policy: State Autonomy and Policy Networks in Britain and the United States*, London: Harvester Wheatsheaf.

SOU (1983: 10), *Använding av växtnäring. Betänkande av udredningen om använding av kemiska medel i jord- och skogsbruket*, Stockholm: Liber/Allmänna Förlaget.

Steen, Anton (1985), 'The farmers, the state and the Social Democrats', *Scandinavian Political Studies*, **8** (1-2), pp. 45-63.

Steen, Anton (1988), *Landbruket, staten og sosialdemokratene: En komparativ studie av interessekonflikterne i landbrukspolitikken i Norge, Sverige og England 1945-1985*, Oslo: Universitetsforlaget.

Swedish Government (1988), 'Regeringens proposition 1987/88: 128 om miljöförbättrande åtgärder i jordbruket, m.m.', *Riksdagstrycket 1987/88*, Stockholm.

Thullberg, Per (1974), 'SAP och Jordbruksnärngen 1920-1940: Från klassekamp til folkhem', *Arbetarrörelsens årsbok 1974*, Stockholm: Bokförlaget Prisma.

Tracy, Michael (1993), *Food and Agriculture in a Market Economy: An Introduction to Theory, Practice and Policy*, La Hutte: Agricultural Policy Studies.

Vail, David, Knut Per Hasund and Lars Drake (1994), *The Greening of Agricultural Policy in Industrial Societies: Swedish Reforms in Comparative Perspective*, Ithaca: Cornell University Press.

Vogel, David (1993), 'Representing diffuse interests in environmental policymaking', in R.K. Weaver and B.A. Rockman (eds), *Do Institutions Matter? Government Capabilities in the United States and Abroad*, Washington, DC: The Brookings Institution, pp. 237-71.

Yin, Robert K. (1989), *Case Study Research: Design and Methods*, Newbury Park and London: Sage Publications.

8.   Considering feasibility and efficiency: the Danish mix of CO_2 taxes and agreements

Martin Enevoldsen and Stefan Brendstrup

1.   INTRODUCTION

In 1992 Denmark became one of the first European Union (EU) countries to introduce an eco-tax on CO_2 emissions. The Bill was pushed through by the alternative green majority in the Danish Parliament against the will of the Liberal–Conservative government. It was the first time in Danish history that energy taxes were not avoided by the business sectors. Nevertheless, the business community retained considerable tax exemptions, and when some of the parties from the alternative green majority formed a government headed by the Social Democrats in 1993, plans were introduced to go even further with CO_2 taxes.

A committee headed by the Ministry of Finance – the Dithmer committee – was to prepare a proposal for eco-taxes in accordance with economic textbook standards in a number of business sectors. The political leaders and the committee believed that a Pigouvian tax on CO_2 emissions constituted the most cost-effective means of regulation, and they were willing to push very hard for such measures in their negotiations with the business organizations (Finansministeriet, 1994). However, the Danish government never considered – at least not explicitly – how the assumptions underlying the recommendations of economic experts might be circumvented by institutional factors during decision-making and implementation. Feasibility was never considered.

In analysing the choice of Danish CO_2 policy instruments it is argued that institutional factors during decision-making made it impossible to uphold the Pigouvian tax solution put forward by the government. Due to formal institutions of governance and the institutions shaping public–private interaction, the government had to give up the theoretically efficient solution. Instead, a policy instrument mix of earmarked CO_2 taxes supplemented by binding agreements committing the enterprises to make specific energy-savings was introduced.

This study focuses on the way institutional factors affect the design and performance of policy instruments. The institutional influences appear in two stages: during decision-making where the policy instruments are given a particular design and during implementation where the existence of transaction costs play an independent role for the eventual efficiency of the policy instruments. The main conclusion is that institutional factors contribute to a separation of the choice and implementation of policy instruments, each process becoming subject to its own logic. In consequence neoclassical recommendations specifying a straightforward relationship between instrument design and efficiency must be criticized. However, trying to bridge the two processes ought to be a matter of utmost concern. This conclusion is not, that any attempt to design an efficient policy instrument is futile. But theoretical efficiency should not be the overriding criterion for instrument design. Feasibility is equally important. By designing policy instruments with a view to the institutional conditions that shape public–private interactions it will be possible to achieve a better integration of feasibility and efficiency.

The chapter is structured as follows: in sections 2 and 3 our theoretical arguments are presented and a model describing institutional influences on the design and efficiency of policy instruments is proposed. In section 4 the actual choice of Danish CO_2 policy instruments is briefly presented and in section 5 an institutional analysis of the choice leading to the mixing of CO_2 taxes and other policy instruments is discussed. Commenting on selected *ex-post* aspects of efficiency, in section 6, on the one hand, the transaction costs associated with administering and enforcing the Danish CO_2 instrument mix are considered and, on the other, how the institutional framing of informational transaction costs affect the chances of achieving dynamically efficient solutions by means of those instruments. A conclusion follows in section 7.

2. INSTRUMENTS, INSTITUTIONS AND TRANSACTION COSTS

In political science, policy design theory deals with the following questions: 'how do governments choose goals, how do they select means for reaching goals, and how do those means conform to evaluative standards appropriate for assessing public policy?' (Linder and Peters, 1989, p. 38). While largely ignoring the third question, the policy instrument literature has investigated how governments choose policy instruments. The more advanced contributions convincingly show that the mechanistic resource approach – according to which governments choose the instrument with the best technical virtues in view of the problem they face and the resources at their disposal – is naive. To a very large extent, the government's choice of policy instruments is determined by the political institutional context which may predispose decision-makers for certain instruments, regardless of their objective (in)efficiency. In particular, the following institutional factors have been proposed as determinants of instrument choice: national policy styles and political culture (Linder and Peters, 1989; Howlett, 1991; Crepaz, 1995); organizational features of the government and target groups (Dahl and Lindblom, 1953; Hood, 1986); and political ideologies (Doern and Phidd, 1983).

In contrast to the political science literature, economic theory has shown more interest in the third question posed by Linder and Peters concerning the effects of policy instruments. In particular, economic theory has focused on the possible contribution of policy instruments to Pareto-efficiency. In analysing this relationship, standard neoclassical economics largely ignores the autonomous influence of institutions. However, a major branch of the new institutional economics has recognized that economic transactions of any kind involve significant transaction costs (Rutherford, 1994). Transaction costs are rooted in the costliness of information (North, 1990b, p. 27). As real world economic agents have only limited information, and as property rights are not perfectly specified, resources must be spent on measuring the valuable attributes of what is being exchanged and on enforcing economic contracts. Moving from simple economic exchange to complex policy instruments, which are designed by policy-makers to influence the behaviour of economic agents, the significance of measurement, enforcement and other information-related transaction costs increases.

When it is costly to transact, institutions become important (Coase, 1937, 1960). However, whereas some institutional economists merely view institutions as constraints to rational behaviour, Douglass North demonstrates that institutions are complexity-reducing mechanisms which enable cooperation – including economic contracting and political action – in an uncertain world (North, 1990a). North makes a crucial distinction between organizations and institutions. Metaphorically, he portrays the former as the players (groups of individuals with certain skills, strategies and structures of coordination), whereas the latter are seen as the rules of the game (self-imposed institutional constraints). Organizations as well as institutions are created and modified with a view to reducing transaction costs: 'Organizations and their entrepreneurs engage in purposive activity and in that role are the agents of, and shape the direction of, institutional change' (North, 1990a, p. 73). On the other hand, North observes that institutions may be designed to serve the narrow purpose of an élite, rather than what would be optimal for the society according to the Pareto-criteria (North, 1981). Moreover, institutions emerging from 'thousands of individual decisions by organizations and their entrepreneurs' may have unintended long-term consequences which actually increase the transaction costs of political and economic systems (North, 1990b). Thus, on balance, institutions are not necessarily efficient: 'institutions everywhere are a mixed bag of those that lower costs and those that raise them' (North, 1990a, p. 63).

The common denominator of political theories focusing on policy instrument design and economic theories focusing on instrument efficiency is that institutions matter. In fact, the institutional theories of both disciplines define institutions in a similar manner. Their agreement goes at least this far: *ex-ante* and *ex-post* choices with respect to policy instruments are conditioned by, on the one hand, informal institutional factors such as norms, conventions, codes of conduct and unwritten standard operating procedures and, on the other hand, formal institutional factors such as constitutions, rules and contracts.

North's suggestion to apply a transaction cost theory to the study of politics (North, 1990b) implies that the gap could be further bridged by also analysing the *ex-ante*, political choice of policy instrument in terms of transaction cost. However, on that point we disagree. Instead it is argued that the striking differences between the focus of political scientists and economists is a reflection of the different logic which dominates decision-making and implementation of policy instruments respectively. Policy instruments are neither chosen with a view to minimizing the transaction costs of decision-making, nor to maximize subsequent efficiency during implementation. They are chosen because they fit certain political interests and institutional requirements. As Majone has noted:

> In practically any field of public policy one can find examples where optimal or satisfactory solutions are known to exist but cannot be implemented because they presuppose a level of knowledge and an institutional flexibility that are not to be found in the real world (Majone, 1989, p. 72).

On the other hand, it is far from certain that the chosen policy instruments are efficient just because they are politically feasible.

3.   ASSUMPTIONS AND A BASIC MODEL

This section starts by clarifying the theoretical assumptions which are common to the respective institutional analyses that will be carried out regarding design aspects and efficiency aspects of Danish CO₂ policy instruments.

These assumptions begin with the bounded rationality of the actors responsible for choosing instruments and overseeing implementation (governmental decision-makers), and the agents who actually implement environmental policy instruments (industrial companies). Bounded rationality involves two basic assumptions: (1) the actors have limited information about the state of the world and the behaviour of other actors; and (2) the actors have limited computational abilities, that is, the capacity of the mind to process, organize and utilize information is limited (Simon, 1957; North, 1990a; Hammond, 1996, pp. 116–23). However, despite the limited reach of the actors' rationality due to imperfect information and subjective fallibility, it is maintained that they are 'intendedly rational', that is, their behaviour is mainly based on utility-oriented motivations.[1] However, the nature of motivations differs between governmental decision-makers and private enterprises. Whereas it is argued that the main purpose and motivation of enterprises is to economize on transaction costs (Williamson, 1985), it is not believed that this motivation is valid for governmental decision-makers. In the absence of economic competition, transaction costs have a different meaning, and sometimes no meaning at all, to governmental decision-makers. Instead, it is assumed that their utility considerations are based on heterogeneous political motives and movable preferences (Dunleavy, 1991).

Our second set of assumptions specifies which kinds of institution influence instrument design and efficiency. It is assumed that the following institutional factors are the primary determinants: first, design of policy instruments is determined by formal 'institutions of governance' (Hammond, 1996), that is, legal constitutional rules defining the competencies and powers of governmental institutions. Second, design is also influenced by the formal and informal institutions shaping public–private interaction, including the institutional set-up of public administration and private interest groups and their informal style of interaction. The institutions shaping public–private interaction can be separated into at least three sub-categories:

1.   Interest mediation institutions, for example, corporatist, neo-corporatist and pluralist arrangements;
2.   Policy styles, for example, active versus reactive, consensual versus adversarial, legalistic versus pragmatic policy styles;
3.   Policy culture, for example, interactions based on trust versus mistrust.

These types of institution influence not only the design of policy instruments but also the way they are implemented, and thus their relative efficiency. Third, to the extent that implementation of policy instruments requires investments in new technologies, the institutional setting of technology know-how transfer influences efficiency.

Figure 8.1 is a simplified model of the determination of instrument choice

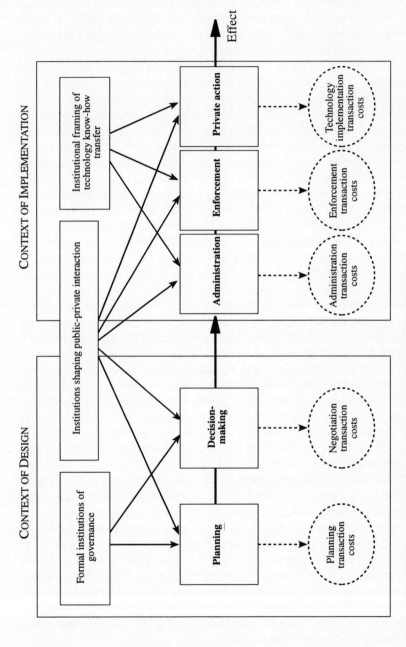

Figure 8.1   The process of designing and implementing policy instruments

and efficiency. Any policy instrument undergoes certain phases, which can also be conceived of as distinct types of transaction. The respective phases take place either in the institutional context of instrument choice or in the context of implementation. The transactions occurring in each phase are influenced by certain institutional factors.

As the illustration shows, the formal institutions of governance and the institutions shaping public–private interaction influence the planning and decision phases, which together form the stage of instrument choice.

The transactions occurring in the three implementation phases – administration, private action and enforcement – are also influenced by the institutions shaping public–private interaction. Thus, it is postulated that this factor exercises overlapping institutional influences on both design and efficiency (cf. the stretch of the box into both contexts). Another determinant is the institutional framing of technology know-how transfer. For example, being a major source of transaction costs, the conditions for obtaining information on new pollution abatement technologies influence the extent to which enterprises are willing to invest in environmental improvements. Thus, it is asserted that transaction costs related to search for and exchange of information influence decisions during the implementation stage.

The disconnection between the choice and implementation stages indicates that efficiency considerations are lacking in the former stage. Our model thus differs from the model of rational decision-making. The crucial question is whether there is an inherent contradiction between feasibility and efficiency concerns, or if it is possible to find a means to bridge the logic of design and the logic of implementation in order to achieve both ends. Our central thesis is that the institutions shaping public–private interaction have an impact on the decision process as well as the implementation process. When the designers of policy instruments realize this particular continuity, and take advantage of it, the policy will not only be feasible, but also reasonably efficient as it will generate fewer transaction costs.

On the other hand, failure to address the institutional context, especially the institutions that impact both stages, will prevent success in this dual sense. One general case of failure is where the design of policy instruments only considers narrow political interests in the decision-making process and not the institutional mechanisms that determine the course of implementation. In these cases the policy instruments may be quite feasible, and yet fail on any criterion of efficiency. Another general case of failure is where the policy design rests on abstract theoretical promises of efficiency. Very often these policy proposals do not survive the decision-making process and, when they occasionally do, their efficiency is likely to be undermined by unforeseen institutional frictions during the implementation process.

4.   DANISH CO$_2$ POLICY INSTRUMENTS TOWARDS THE BUSINESS SECTORS

Danish enterprises are faced with the following mix of policy instruments aimed towards CO$_2$ pollution abatement:

- a tax per ton CO$_2$ emitted;
- an option to enter into an agreement which entitles deductions in the CO$_2$ tax;
- an option to obtain subsidies for investments in energy savings.

Even though the CO$_2$ tax is the most important instrument in the package it is not a Pigouvian tax by the book. Instead of a general tax on the companies' energy consumption, it is broken down into three categories subject to different tax rates. The categories are space heating, light processes and heavy processes. The heavy process category is defined by a list consisting of about 35 very energy-intensive types of process. Any energy consumption other than space heating and heavy processes is defined as a light process. An enterprise wanting to pay the lower tax rates on processes must have separate energy meters installed. The tax rates are illustrated below in Table 8.1.[2]

As shown in Table 8.1 the tax rates are not only divided according to the category of consumption, but are further differentiated if the enterprises enter into an agreement. The option to enter into an agreement is given to enterprises when they (a) carry out energy-intensive, individual production processes included in the above-mentioned list, or (b) when the overall energy taxes exceed 3 per cent of the company's turnover. An agreement can be

Table 8.1   The CO$_2$ tax rates

CO$_2$	Ecu per ton CO$_2$ emitted				
	1996	1997	1998	1999	2000
Space heating	26.6	53.1	79.7	79.7	79.7
Light processes:					
without agreement	6.6	8.0	9.3	10.6	12.0
with agreement	6.6	6.6	6.6	7.7	9.0
Heavy processes:					
without agreement	0.7	1.3	2.0	2.7	3.3
with agreement	0.4	0.4	0.4	0.4	0.4

concluded with the Energy Agency after a survey of possible improvements in the company's energy efficiency has been carried out by an 'energy survey consultant'. The energy survey contains details of actual energy consumption and possible energy-saving measures. Based on the energy survey the enterprise draws up an action plan which also contains considerations on how to organize a system of energy management within the enterprise. The action plan carries obligations for the enterprise in three respects:

1. energy-saving measures with a pay-back time of less than 4–6 years;
2. special investigations of energy projects with large but so far uncertain savings potential;
3. specified targets for energy management.

A statutory order constitutes the legal framework for the agreements.[3] If the agreement is not fulfilled the enterprise will automatically be fully taxed and, therefore, the term 'binding agreements' is the most appropriate.

The third element of the instrument package consists of subsidies for energy-saving measures. The CO_2 tax reform is intended to be fiscally neutral (Ministry of Finance, 1995, p. 16). The recycling of the revenue includes three elements:

1. earmarked subsidies for investments in energy savings;
2. a reduction of the employers' labour market contributions;
3. funds to be recycled to small businesses.

The investment subsidies support the system of agreements with industry. The energy-savings measures, which are identified through the energy survey, are qualified for subsidies of up to 30 per cent of the investment.[4]

5. INSTITUTIONAL CONDITIONS FOR THE CHOICE OF DANISH CO_2 INSTRUMENTS

Why did the decision-making process end up with this untraditional mix of taxes and agreements that lacked theoretical support and, therefore, could not (on theoretical grounds) be expected to be efficient? Of course, it was neither the first time in history that environmental regulations were designed as a mix of instruments, nor the first time that efficiency was not the primary criterion for the choice of instruments. In fact, both incidents seem to be the rule rather than the exception, as some authors have already pointed out (Bressers and Huitema this volume, Chapter 4; Larrue, 1995). Especially economists have been disappointed with what they consider a lack of political will to follow their prescriptions, and pose the question, why politicians are not rational. We pose the question, why it is not possible to maintain the efficient solution, even when it is actually aimed for?

The Danish case of CO_2 abatement instruments is interesting in this respect, as the agenda was clearly formulated in terms of a lack of efficiency in the overall Danish CO_2 strategy (Energiministeriet, 1990; Udvalget om Personbeskatning, 1992; Det Økonomiske Råd, 1993). Moreover, the basis for the decision (Finansministeriet, 1994) was intended as a guide for the decision-makers, directing them towards an efficient solution in economic theoretical terms. The Danish case can thereby shed light on a process where efficiency was actually aimed for by the government, but was subverted by other criteria and other types of rationality. The question then is, why was it not possible to implement CO_2 taxes by the book? Which institutional conditions affected the decision?

5.1   The Background to the Decision-making Process

New environmental regulation has to build on the foundation of already existing regulations. Some would describe this by using the term 'path dependency', but in a broader sense than that put forward by North (1990a). In the case of the Danish CO_2 taxes on the business sector, the path of former regulation is of great importance.

Denmark introduced energy taxes back in 1977 to help solve the economic problems of the time, when primarily the balance of payments was in political focus. For that reason business was totally exempted from taxes; only households were taxed. In 1979 these taxes were raised and the tax base broadened to include almost every type of fuel, but still for households only. The next step was taken in 1986 when reduced energy prices, caused by the drastic fall in world market prices for oil and the reduced dollar rate, were countervailed by an increase in energy taxes by 300 per cent to 500 per cent, but still for households only. During this process Denmark 'muddled through' with a system of high taxes raised step by step but without coordination or an overall political goal. For example, there were no reflections about the design in relation to the environmental problems, which were put on the political agenda in the late 1980s.[5]

Thus, in relation to the political strategy for the regulation of business, the starting point was a gap in energy consumption prices between households and industry of more than 100 per cent due to the one-sided taxation of the households. Such a difference was hard to defend in terms of economic efficiency and made it obvious that the coming regulation of industry had to include an increase in energy prices in order to narrow the gap and thereby improve overall economic efficiency.

Thus, the new regulation of industry was not developed on the background of a *tabula rasa*. On the contrary, a set of arguments and positions were already defined and had to be taken into account. In addition certain political ideas prevailed at the time and inspired the proposal. At least three different, though mutually related, ideas could be identified; the concept of ecological modernization, the idea of ecological tax reforms and the argument of taxes as the most efficient environmental instrument.

This is not the place for a thorough analysis of the dominating discourses within which new proposals for environmental regulation came to be formulated and legitimized. However, it is relevant to emphasize the fact that Denmark in general seems to have adopted an understanding of the economic prescriptions put forward by the Organization for Economic Co-operation and Development (OECD) and the EU Commission, among others, to a greater extent than most other European countries, which is reflected in the fact that Denmark is at the top of the list ranging countries by number of green taxes introduced (OECD, 1997).

It is necessary to point out circumstances like those above in order to understand the framework within which the actual decision was to be taken. Differences in these kinds of background variables often constitute an important part of the explanation of why national strategies aimed at the same environmental problems diverge. However, on the other hand, they are insufficient to explain why a specific result emerged in a certain situation. With this explanatory ambition, a more detailed institutional analysis is needed.

5.2   The Informal Institutional Conditions for Decision-making

The informal institutional conditions for decision-making mainly include the tradition of public–private interaction. As illustrated in Figure 8.2, the period of negotiations at the administrative level was very long in comparison to the duration of the process at the political level. The high priority of informal negotiations reflects the Danish tradition of involving interest organizations in policy-making. Moreover, the existence of multiple veto points in the government made it even more attractive to seek a compromise at the informal level.

It has been discussed whether Denmark could be labelled as a corporatist society (Johansen and Kristensen, 1982), a negotiated economy (Nielsen and Pedersen, 1991), or if the term 'corporate pluralism' would be the more appropriate description of the character of the public–private interaction (Damgaard and Eliassen, 1978; Enevoldsen, 1998b). It is not intended to contribute to that particular discussion here. However, it is worth while to note that the long tradition of involving interest organizations, developed on the labour market since the turn of the century, has accompanied the organizations

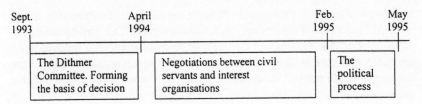

Sept. 1993	April 1994	Feb. 1995	May 1995
The Dithmer Committee. Forming the basis of decision	Negotiations between civil servants and interest organisations	The political process	

Figure 8.2   The decision-making process

as they have become involved in new policy areas such as pollution control. The tradition could be described as a strategy of making the private actors responsible for social aims through involvement in policy formulation and implementation.

This tradition has spread to environmental policy where the dominant strategy of business organizations is to try to optimize their influence through cooperation with the government, instead of trying to fight off any proposal from the political level. In the case of the CO_2 tax, the Chamber of Danish Trades and Crafts, the Chamber of Commerce and the Chamber of Danish Commerce and Service were, in principle, open to discussions about the conditions for implementing the instrument. Only the Federation of Danish Industry seriously opposed the new tax. The differences in attitude within the business community did, of course, to some degree reflect the distributional effects of the proposed tax, but it also demonstrated the more general lack of a comprehensive, centralized organization of business interests, which, in turn, is an important element in explaining why a CO_2 tax was not avoided in Denmark in contrast to most other countries. Regulation in general and taxes, in particular, do not face as much opposition in Denmark as in most other industrial countries.

The answer to the question of why CO_2 taxes emerged in Denmark is primarily to be found in the historical path of tax regulation in combination with the strong influence of the welfare economic paradigm, and the institutionalization of public–private interactions. However, the question of why a combination of taxes and agreements was reached still cannot be answered.

5.3   Formal Institutions of Governance

Changing an existing policy involves playing by a set of rules concerning the distribution of power and competence amongst the political parties and between the politicians and the bureaucracy. Hammond uses the term veto points, which he defines as 'some individuals or set of individuals whose agreement is necessary, under the policy-making rules, for the status quo policy to be replaced by some other policy', as an important variable when new political proposals are to pass through the parliament (Hammond, 1996, p. 133). Two kinds of veto point can be distinguished. The 'institutional veto point' implies that one or more institutional actor must agree in order to upset the status quo policy. The 'partisan veto point' implies that the votes of the members of each party in the coalition are decisive when it comes to changing the status quo. Another focus is the legal rules of distribution of competence between the politicians/parliament and the bureaucracy. At least since Weber it has been discussed whether the bureaucracy is neutral or tends to affect policy-making in a more or less systematic way.

For the analysis of the emergence of a policy instrument mix lacking clear theoretical support, like the Danish combination of taxes and agreements, both the existence of veto points and the role of the bureaucracy seem to be relevant. An electoral system based on proportionality and a low 2 per cent entrance threshold for seats in the Danish Parliament combined with ideological diversity has created a multi-party system. Thus, in 1994/95 the government was a three-party minority coalition consisting of the Social Democrats, the small Social Liberal Party *(Radikale Venstre)* and the small bourgeois party, the Centre Democrats. The existence of veto points were quite obvious, and as the Social Liberal Party advocated a strong environmental policy, in general, and the use of green taxes, in particular, while the Centre Democrats saw themselves as the defenders of industrial interests in the government, it was difficult to overcome the veto points. Furthermore, the government was dependent upon support from either the left-wing or the right-wing opposition.

In order to weaken the importance of the veto points, the Social Democrats, which included both the Minister of Finance and the Minister for Environment and Energy, tried to move the differences of opinion from the political level to the level of bureaucracy, which in their turn bargained with business interest organizations. Furthermore, the bureaucracy, and especially the Ministry of Finance which headed the Dithmer Committee and the negotiations, was in favour of an economically efficient solution using taxes without modifications, an attitude that perfectly matched the Social Democratic point of view. This strategy called for a sequence in the decision-making process which entailed a relatively short period of entirely political negotiations, as illustrated in Figure 8.2.

Looking at this decision-making process, it would be expected that a consensus was to be reached among the negotiating parties, leaving only minor adjustments to be handled at the political level. Nevertheless, the formal institutions of governance made it impossible to separate these two processes, and the political process, in fact, added considerable changes to the choice of instruments.

The final mix of taxes and agreements was remarkable because such a solution had been forced off the agenda during negotiations at the bureaucratic level. The civil servants were not accorded political competence to abandon the idea of attaining an economically efficient solution by the use of taxes. They even refused an industrial proposal about integrating agreements into the package of instruments. A delegation was sent to the Netherlands to enquire about the Dutch approach, but were certainly not convinced of its merits, or able to understand the philosophy behind it: 'we had difficulties in understanding that it should be possible to realise so many behavioural changes just because of a piece of paper, when at the same time the competition argument was upheld'.[6] Consequently, a general tax solution was continuously aimed for. The business interest organizations, on the other hand, tried to demonstrate how unreasonable a general solution would be in specific cases of energy-intensive industries. The result of the negotiation process was the breakdown of energy consumption into three categories, a general though somewhat adaptive solution.

At the political level the bourgeois party, the Centre Democrats, made their political support for the proposal contingent upon the support of the business community to the final proposal. They made use of an institutional veto point. The Social Democrats and the Social Liberal Party were thereby forced to modify the use of taxes by providing for exemptions via binding agreements. A general solution was no longer attainable. The Social Democrats did not succeed in their attempt to disconnect the political process from the informal search for consensus at the bureaucratic level. Even though various technical solutions were in focus during 10 months of negotiations, the political disagreement persisted and a consensus was never reached. This may to some degree be explained by the fact that the business organizations were aware that they could expect support from the Centre Democrats during the final political process. Some of the political aspects of the process were thus put aside until very late in the process, resulting in the political compromise of mixing 'efficient taxes' with 'adaptive agreements'.

To conclude, neither efficiency nor feasibility was reached in a systematic way. On the one hand, efficiency was aimed for, but was overrun by the coalition of the business sector and the Centre Democrats, and on the other hand, design and implementation was never taken into common consideration in order to find the most feasible solution. The result was something in between. Nevertheless, the actual performance of the mix of instruments could give us important information about the conditions decisive for efficiency of instruments in general.

6. INSTITUTIONS CONDITIONING THE EFFICIENCY OF DANISH CO₂ POLICY INSTRUMENTS

We now turn to the question of efficiency. When analysing the Danish CO₂ policy instruments, however, only a few selected aspects of this question are dealt with. In the first section the transaction costs incurred by the public and private parties for administration and enforcement during the implementation of the CO_2 policy instrument mix are discussed. An institutional explanation is given for the moderate level of these costs. In the second section there is a discussion on how the institutionally framed transaction costs of information and technology transfer influence the energy-saving and conversion measures undertaken by enterprises in response to the CO_2 policy instruments. It is argued that – in combination with the bounded rationality of the actors – such transaction costs form a barrier to the realization of the theoretical efficiency of Danish CO_2 taxes.

6.1   Administration and Enforcement Costs of the CO_2 Instrument Mix

This evidence on the administration and enforcement costs of the CO_2 tax package stems from two sources: (1) Personal interviews with representatives from public authorities and private industry (Enevoldsen, 1998a); and (2) a recent mid-term evaluation of the green tax package carried out by the government (Finansministeriet, 1999) in which the cost-efficiency of the policy is estimated.

With regard to public administrative costs, it was originally planned that 43 extra staff would be needed in the Energy Agency to administer the tax-related agreements and subsidy schemes for energy investments. Currently, a representative from the Agency estimates the annual workload as follows: 26 man-years are consumed in the fourth and the sixteenth offices, which are responsible for implementation. Of the 26 man-years, 7–9 are consumed solely in the administration of agreements. However, in view of the fact that more than 100 energy agreements were concluded during the last two and a half years, the negotiation costs are much lower than expected by the government and other commentators. The Danish Court of Auditors have estimated the annual costs of administering the green tax package to DKK29.5 million for the Energy Agency. For the Ministry of Taxation the annual costs relating to energy tax assessment and collection is estimated to DKK15.1 million. Thus, the total annual public administration costs amount to approximately DKK45 million.

The private administration costs paid by the industrial companies can be estimated for each of the three instruments in the CO_2 tax package (taxes, agreements, subsidies). With regard to the CO_2 taxes, the companies face extra administrative costs because of the difficulties in measuring the precise amounts of fuels and electricity consumed for space heating purposes and process purposes, respectively. Accurate measurements are necessary in order to compute the amount of deductions each company is entitled to. For the 5000 companies using fuels for both space heating and process purposes, it has the consequence that separate energy meters must be installed and readings must be made periodically. The government estimates the annual costs of these extra activities to DKK7–40 million (Finansministeriet, 1999, p. 71). It is argued, however, that the government overlooks that extra benefits are associated with the installation of energy meters. Thus, most of the companies interviewed were happy about the advantages gained in terms of better energy husbandry that was achieved with more specialized monitoring. Moreover, many of the companies would have had to meet these costs anyway as a natural consequence of the implementation of energy management systems. Although the government seems to have overlooked some extra costs relating to the companies' tax auditing as a consequence of the increased complexity of the energy tax system, it is still suggested that the tax-related private administration costs are lower than estimated by the government; probably as low as DKK7–15 million annually.

Whereas this estimate of the tax-related administration costs is lower than the government estimate, the opposite is the case with regard to the agreement-related administration costs. The government evaluation explicitly states that it has only considered parts of the administrative costs, that is, the costs relating to the preparation and reporting of agreements (Finansministeriet, 1999, p. 79). However, in our interviews, a question was asked about the companies' total extra workload that was a consequence of the energy agreements. In interviews with 10 heavy energy-consuming enterprises from the paper, glass and stone sectors enquiries were made about their costs relating to energy agreements. As part of the agreement process, all the enterprises were required to contract with an external energy consultant who was to carry out an energy survey of the savings potentials. The enterprises themselves had to bear the full consultancy costs. In all cases but two these costs varied between DKK100 000–300 000 per plant (DKK50 000 and 2 000 000 constituting minimum and maximum). In a few cases the companies also had to pay for a verification of their energy survey (DKK20 000–50 000).

However, besides the consultancy costs the enterprises used only few administration-related resources with respect to the agreements. The usual estimate of the workload expended on negotiation and monitoring activities within each enterprise varied between one half and one man-year for the entire three-year agreement period, that is, 300–700 hours annually. Setting the cost of an hour to DKK250, and multiplying the above figures with the number of agreements, a conclusion was reached that annual private administration costs relating to agreements lies somewhere between DKK12–25 million (compared to the DKK7–15 million estimated by the government).

The companies also face administrative costs incurred during the preparation of applications for investment subsidies and for making final accounts of the implemented project in order to receive the subsidy. The government has estimated these costs at DKK5–15 million annually (ibid., pp. 77–9).

On top of public and private administration expenditures, there are enforcement costs in cases of dispute or non-compliance. In a number of cases, time and resources were spent in solving disputes between the tax authorities and enterprises as to whether single industrial energy processes constitute heavy or light processes (which are subject to different CO_2 tax rates). Thus, the Court of Audit estimates that the Energy Board of Complaints consumes DKK5 million annually. Other than that, however, there have been no major problems in enforcing the CO_2 taxes. With regard to the energy agreements, enforcement problems arise when companies do not fulfil the obligations to which they agreed. So far, however, there has been only one case in which the Energy Agency took steps to apply the sanction of higher tax rates. It is, therefore, estimated that the total public and private enforcement costs amount to DKK5–10 million annually.

Summing up these individual estimates, it is concluded that total public and private administration and enforcement costs range between DKK69–105 million annually. Assuming that the CO_2 tax package results in the projected annual reduction of 1.5 million tons CO_2 emissions, the total costs of reducing 1 ton CO_2 amount to DKK45–70. All the above suggests that – contrary to these first expectations (Enevoldsen and Brendstrup, 1997) – the transaction costs generated during the implementation phase of the CO_2 policy instrument mix have been relatively low. How may this be explained? Part of the reason for the well-functioning implementation can be attributed to the design of the policy instrument mix. For instance, by legally specifying that energy surveys form the basis when negotiating energy agreements with individual enterprises, and by legally specifying that all energy projects with an expected pay-back time of 4–6 years shall be part of such agreements, the procedure for entering into binding agreements gives preference to formal approval of technical proposals, rather than open political negotiations between enterprises and the Energy Agency. Furthermore, the legally specified sanction of higher CO_2 taxes in cases of non-compliance certainly deters enterprises from neglecting their obligations.

Concurrently, however, smooth negotiations, monitoring and enforcement of agreements is reinforced by a favourable institutional structure of public–private relations. Based on interviews with the public and private parties, it is concluded that consensus emerged very quickly during the negotiations and there have been almost no tensions in the subsequent monitoring of progress. Both parties ascribe this partly to the high degree of trust which exists between the industries and the civil servants in the Energy Agency, and the local branches of the Ministry of Taxation. This trust and credibility is rooted in the corporatist Danish tradition, touched upon as one of the main institutional factors in the preceding section (section 5.2). In continuation of this explanation, the broader hypothesis, that a strong institutionalization of public–private interaction has a disciplining effect on administrative transaction costs, could be formulated (Crepaz, 1995, p. 398). In order to verify this hypothesis one could imagine a situation (or country) characterized by more adversarial relations between private business and environmental authorities due to the absence of historical corporatist relations. In such a case it would be quite likely that the negotiation of energy agreements and the implementation of taxes would be much more protracted, that careful and costly monitoring would be necessary and that enforcement issues would arise more frequently.

6.2   Information and Technology Transfer Costs as Barriers to Environmental Effectiveness

In the preceding section it was argued that the administrative transaction costs of the CO_2 policy package are, in fact, quite low. However, due to the bounded rationality of enterprises there are additional transaction costs; the enterprises have only limited information about new energy-saving technologies and they are not always capable of, or interested in, making the optimal energy choices from the viewpoint of long-term survival (DeCanio, 1993). These imperfections give rise to information transaction costs, which make it more costly for the enterprises to implement environment-friendly energy solutions. The question is the extent to which the presence of such transaction costs challenges the efficiency that the Danish CO_2 tax strategy is claimed to possess.

Reduction of CO_2 pollution from production activities can be achieved in various ways; shift to more energy-efficient production technologies, introduction of energy recovery and co-generation systems, conversion to fuels with lower carbon content and so on. In Denmark most of the well-known, profitable energy solutions are already incorporated into industrial production. Further development, therefore, depends upon innovation and transfer of new energy technologies. In that respect the Danish government justifies the use of CO_2 taxes by referring to 'dynamic efficiency', that is, the taxes offer a permanent incentive for developing new technologies which reduce pollution and thereby the tax burden (Finansministeriet, 1993, p. 301).

Nevertheless, evidence suggests that market-oriented incentives – that is, economic gains from lower CO_2 taxes and reduced energy consumption – are not sufficient to stimulate Danish enterprises to realize potential energy-saving projects with even very short pay-back times (Ingerslev, 1996; Shopley and Brasseur, 1996). One of the main reasons is that the relevant information is not readily available. Often the enterprises – especially small and medium-sized enterprises (SMEs) - lack thorough information about the availability and potentials of new energy technologies. Of course, the information is, in principle, available through the market channels, but as enterprises are highly motivated to economize on transaction costs they are reluctant to engage in a costly and troublesome search for new energy information with uncertain pay-offs.

In the theoretical section it was argued that the types and numbers of informational transaction costs are influenced by the rules of the technology transfer game. Looking at the Danish CO_2 case, two institutional arrangements were found which exercise a strong influence on the transaction costs of obtaining new energy technology information:

● a non-cooperative organization of energy-related expertise;
● internal benchmarking systems in heavy energy-consuming Danish enterprises.

In contrast to many other countries, no Danish expert organization has been formed at the public or semi-public level for the purpose of accumulating and communicating knowledge on energy-efficient production technologies and other means of reducing CO_2 pollution. Moreover, private joint organizations of energy expertise are limited to *ad-hoc* information-sharing through committees in the Federation of Danish Industries. Due to the strong internal competition within most heavy energy-consuming sectors in Denmark, the branch organizations are not given the responsibility of acting as information centres on new technologies. In fact, the organization of energy expertise is highly fragmented: it rests within the individual enterprise and with the multitude of energy consultancy firms scattered across the country. The absence of cooperative arrangements on energy-related knowledge means that enterprises must obtain most of the relevant information through the market. Here the transaction cost of information search is much higher than in cooperative forums of information exchange. Moreover, our interviews have shown that the level of expertise in the Danish energy consultancy firms used in the preparation of binding energy agreements is moderate. Due to information asymmetries the enterprises themselves play the leading role in drawing up the energy surveys and there is seldom any real innovative input from the energy consultants.

The widespread existence of internal benchmarking systems in large heavy energy-consuming enterprises is, however, an institutional factor which serves to reduce informational transaction costs. All the Danish enterprises that were interviewed made heavy use of internal benchmarking with foreign associated companies with a view to know-how transfer on energy efficiency improvements. Fortunately, for the process of bench marking, all 10 enterprises were part of multinational companies – sometimes Danish-owned, but more often foreign – with a number of European subsidiary companies working with similar production technologies. Internal benchmarking involves setting up work groups, holding seminars and other activities between associated companies for the purpose of discussing the newest technology information and exchanging experiences relating to production processes. The internal benchmarking systems ensures that technological innovations are spread much faster among associated companies. In contrast, the benchmarking system does not leave room to learn from competing companies. Moreover, internal benchmarking systems usually do not exist in small- and medium-sized enterprises. It can be concluded that internal bench-marking systems are important institutional mechanisms that help relieve transaction costs in large enterprises, but that even here major transaction costs remain because it is difficult to gain access to energy technology know-how between competing companies.

In view of the institutional framework of energy know-how transfer there are reasons to note some critical points with regard to the cost-effectiveness claimed for the Danish CO_2 tax strategy. First of all, the enterprises face considerable information transaction costs in their efforts to introduce new environment-friendly energy technologies in response to the CO_2 taxes (Glachant, 1996). Although internal benchmarking systems sometimes do help to reduce such transaction costs, the enterprises can basically only turn to the market in their search for new information. Here transaction costs appear to be so high as to form a barrier against the realization of the dynamic efficiency, which is supposed to be a result of the tax solution.

The Danish mixing of taxes with agreements and subsidies, however, can be viewed as an attempt to overcome some of the above-mentioned transaction cost barriers. By obliging the enterprises to contract with an energy consultant for the purpose of drawing up an energy survey, the agreements are supposed to focus the former on providing new energy information that may form the basis of innovations. The subsidies are intended to help the enterprises overcome the financial barriers. None of these instruments imply, however, a cooperative organization of information exchange. The agreements are individualistic in nature, with the negotiations taking place only between a civil servant and a single enterprise, and the information search is restricted to a cooperative relation between the enterprise and a small energy consultancy firm. Thus, in the Danish CO_2 policy package, there is a deficit of instrumental arrangements that may potentially facilitate the transfer of energy-related know-how within and across industrial sectors.

However, contrary to the expectation of the economic experts, it is doubtful whether the originally proposed Pigouvian tax would have been more efficient than the Danish CO_2 policy instrument mix of taxes, subsidies and binding agreements. First, the transaction costs of the administrative efforts have been very moderate. Second, although the Danish policy instrument mix faces transaction cost barriers against the realization of dynamic efficiency, such problem would be even more prevalent if a pure tax solution had been instituted.

7.   CONCLUSION

Although Denmark is one of the only countries where eco-taxes on CO_2 emissions survived opposition from the business community, Denmark never got the pure Pigouvian tax. The plans to introduce theoretically efficient CO_2 taxes were precluded by institutional veto points within the government and in the Danish Parliament. Instead, a policy instrument mix of taxes, agreements and subsidies was adopted. The Danish CO_2 case is just one example of how institutional factors can impede the prevalence of efficiency considerations in the choice of environmental policy instruments. A principal explanation is that the formal institutions of governance that formulate the rules for decision-making leave little room for rational technocratic instrument design.

It is a paradox, however, that this evidence indicates that although the actual CO_2 policy instrument mix lacked theoretical support, it is probably no less efficient than a Pigouvian tax solution. The analysis both indicates that the theoretical merits of the Pigouvian tax were somewhat overestimated, and that the potential gains of playing in accordance with the institutions shaping public–private interaction in the actual case were underestimated.

Due to the particular institutional conditions of energy technology know-how transfer in Denmark, environmental improvements are not sufficiently stimulated by a Pigouvian tax alone. This is because the latter is a non-cooperative market-based instrument, which does not address the transaction cost barriers against obtaining the relevant energy technology information. The better than expected performance of the Danish CO_2 instrument mix, on the other hand, indicates that institutional bridging between design and implementation may, in fact, influence the overall efficiency of the chosen instruments in a positive direction.

This conclusion is not, however, that any attempt to design an efficient policy instrument is futile. While the aforementioned institutional factors work to separate design and implementation considerations, the institutions shaping public–private interactions exercise overlapping influences. By playing on the institutional strings of public–private interaction, these can be recruited to assist in achieving better integration of design and efficiency. To some extent such options were – against the will of the Danish government –

exploited in the actual case of designing the instrument mix, in view of the corporatist relations to industry. It thus succeeded in keeping administration and enforcement costs at a moderate level.

NOTES

1. For the empirical testing of the enterprises' reactions on the imposed means, a set of enterprises have been chosen, which are most likely to act according to these assumptions. These enterprises are characterized by an energy-intensive production and a situation of price competition due to homogeneous products such as concrete, steel and so on which is impossible to differentiate from the products of the competitors. These enterprises are of certain interest, since they represent the optimal case and by that the best basis for a test of the enterprises' optimal response to the imposition of economic instruments. Other types of enterprise characterized by an energy-extensive production and differentiation as strategy of competition are more likely to act according to less economic rationality concerning their energy behaviour, since it is less important in economic terms.
2. Exchange rate used: ECU1 = 7.53DKK.
3. *Energistyrelsens bekendtgørelse nr. 863, 17 November 1995.*
4. This amount has in the spring of 1998 been raised by another 10 per cent as the recycling was too slow, which meant that the goal of revenue neutrality was not attained. However, as a maximum the subsidy may bring the pay-back time down to a level of three years (two years if the enterprise does not have an agreement).
5. The first initiative to evaluate the system was taken in 1988 where it was analysed in relation to the possibilities of attaining the new political goal of CO₂ reductions (Energiministeriet, 1990). This report constitutes the beginning of the process leading five years later to the introduction of the mix of taxes and agreements analysed in this study.
6. Interview 13 February 1998, Ministry of Environment.

REFERENCES

Coase, Ronald (1937), 'On the nature of the firm', *Economica*, **4**, November, 386–405.
Coase, Ronald (1960), 'The problem of social cost', *Journal of Law and Economics*, **3**, 1–44.
Crepaz, Markus M.L. (1995), 'Explaining national variations of air pollution levels: political institutions and their impact on environmental policy-making', *Environmental Politics*, **4** (3), 391–415.
Dahl, Robert and Charles Lindblom (1953), *Politics, Economics and Welfare*, New York: Harper and Row.
Damgaard, Erik and K. Eliassen (1978), 'Corporate pluralism in Danish law-making', *Scandinavian Political Studies*, **1** (new series), 285–313.
DeCanio, Stephen (1993), 'Barriers within firms to energy-efficient investments', *Energy Policy*, **21** (9), 906–14.
Det Økonomiske Råd (1993), *Dansk Økonomi maj 1993*, Copenhagen: Economic Council.
Doern, G.B. and R.W. Phidd (1983), *Canadian Public Policy: Ideas, Structure, Process*, Toronto: Methuen.
Dunleavy, Patrick (1991), *Democracy, Bureaucracy and Public Choice*, London: Harvester Wheatsheaf.

Energiministeriet (1990), *Redegørelse om energiafgifter*, Copenhagen: Ministry of Energy.

Enevoldsen, Martin (1998a), *Joint Environmental Policy-making and Other New Abatement Strategies for Industrial CO₂ Pollution*, Environmental Sociology Publication, the Netherlands: Wageningen Agricultural University.

Enevoldsen, Martin (1998b), 'Review studies: Austria, Denmark and the Netherlands', final report, annex A, in J*oint Environmental Policy-making: New Interactive Approaches in the EU and Selected Member States*, Research Project under the European Union's Environment and Climate Research Programme (1994–1998), Contract no, ENV4-CT96-0227.

Enevoldsen, Martin and Stefan Brendstrup (1997), 'Mixing green taxes and agreements: considerations over Danish CO₂ policy instruments', paper presented at the workshop on The Institutional Aspects of Economic Instruments for Environmental Policy, Copenhagen, 20–21 May.

Finansministeriet (1993), *Finansredegørelse 93*, Budgetdepartementet, Copenhagen: Ministry of Finance.

Finansministeriet (1994), *Grønne afgifter og erhvervene: midtvejsrapport fra embedsmands-udvalget om grønne afgifter og erhvervene*, April, Copenhagen: Ministry of Finance.

Finansministeriet (1999), *Evaluering af grønne afgifter og erhvervene*, Copenhagen: Ministry of Finance.

Glachant, Matthieu (1996), 'The cost-efficiency of voluntary agreements: a Coasean approach', paper presented at the conference on The Economy and Law of Voluntary Approaches in Environmental Policy, Venice, 18–19 November.

Hammond, Thomas H. (1996), 'Formal theory and the institutions of governance', *Governance: An International Journal of Policy and Administration*, **9** (2), April, 107–85.

Hood, Christopher (1986), *The Tools of Government*, Chatham: Chatham House Publishers.

Howlett, Michael (1991), 'Policy instruments, policy styles and policy implementation: national approaches to theories of instrument choice', *Policy Studies Journal*, **19** (2), Spring, 1–21.

Ingerslev, Christina (1996), 'Reduktion af industriens CO₂ emission: en analyze af rationalitet og regulering på energiområdet', Ph.D. thesis, Roskilde University.

Johansen, Lars Nørby and Ole P. Kristensen (1982), 'Corporatist traits in Denmark 1946–76', in G. Lembruch and P. Schmitter (eds), *Patterns of Corporatist Policy-making*, London: Sage Publications, pp. 189–219.

Larrue, Corinne (1995), 'The political (un)feasibility of environmental economic instruments', in Bruno Dente (ed.), *Environmental Policy in Search of New Instruments*, Dordrecht: Kluwer Academic Publishers, pp. 37–54.

Linder, Stephen and Guy Peters (1989), 'Instruments of government: perceptions and contexts', *Journal of Public Policy*, **9** (1), 35–58.

Majone, Giandomenico (1989), *Evidence, Argument and Persuasion in the Policy Process*, New Haven: Yale University Press.

Ministry of Finance (1995), *Energy Tax on Industry in Denmark*, Copenhagen: Ministry of Finance.

Nielsen, Klaus and Ove K. Pedersen (1991), 'From the mixed economy to the negotiated economy in Scandinavian countries', in R. Coughlin (ed.), *Morality, Rationality and Efficiency: Perspectives in Socio-Economics*, New York: M.E. Sharpe.

North, Douglass (1981), *Structure and Change in Economic History*, New York: Norton.

North, Douglass (1990a), *Institutions, Institutional Change and Economic Performance*, Cambridge: Cambridge University Press.

North, Douglass (1990b), 'A transaction cost theory of politics', *Journal of Theoretical Politics*, **2** (4), 355–67.

OECD (1997), *Evaluating Economic Instruments for Environmental Policy*, Paris: OECD.

Rutherford, Malcolm (1994), *Institutions in Economics: The Old and New Institutionalism*, Cambridge: Cambridge University Press.

Shopley, Jonathan and Delphine Brasseur (1996), 'Summary report on two micro-economic case studies in the field of business and the environment', paper presented at the Conference on Environmental Economic Policies: Competitiveness and Employment, Dublin, 17 October.

Simon, Herbert (1957), *Administrative Behaviour: A Study of Decision Making Processes in Administrative Organizations*, 2nd edn., New York: Macmillan.

Udvalget om Personbeskatning (1992), *Rapport fra udvalget om personbeskatning*, Copenhagen: Statens Information.

Williamson, Oscar (1985), *The Economic Institutions of Capitalism: Firms, Markets, Relational Contracting*, New York: The Free Press.

PART IV

Implementation problems of MBIs

9. The limitations of economic instruments as stimuli for technical change, technological change and innovation

Dominic Hogg

INTRODUCTION

There is a pervasive sense of frustration among many who believe that an environmental crisis is ahead. This is borne not out of this belief alone, but also out of a feeling that even where matters are improving, the pace of improvement is laboured. In particular, production techniques and technologies are being adopted and adapted relatively slowly even in cases where environmental problems have already reached critical levels, and despite the fact that in a number of cases there would appear to be private benefits to be gained from adoption of these technologies.

Traditionally, environmental policy has consisted, in the main, of regulations designed to improve environmental standards. More recently, policy-makers, at the prompting of economists, have been seduced by the prospect of solving environmental problems through the market mechanism. Economists have pointed out the existence of failure after failure, either of markets, governments or institutions, and their responsibility for perpetuating environmental problems. It is believed that the remedy is to be found in correcting for each of these failures, so allowing the market to convey the correct signals to all actors in the economy. Yet the criteria against which the standard of failure is applied dooms markets to continuing failure, the question being one of degrees of deviation from the unfailing ideal model.

This chapter seeks to question the assumption that environmental taxes work effectively through the assumed ability of the price mechanism to induce technical and technological changes and innovation.[1] It suggests that as a representation of how such changes occur, this picture is likely to lead to overestimates of the beneficial impact of environmental taxes.

Modern theories of technological and technical change, and innovation in the firm stress disequilibria as a permanent feature of the economy, the role of uncertainty and the fact that information is not costless to obtain. Learning and path-dependence are given heightened significance. An attempt is made to understand the significance of this perspective on technological change for the claims made for environmental taxes, particularly those regarding dynamic efficiency.

It is important to note that the terms 'technical change', 'technological change', and 'innovation' are often left undefined, and consequently are sometimes used interchangeably. Here, it is understood that 'technique' is a way of doing things. A technique is characterized by a particular way of combining inputs, or technology (including both tools and knowledge). Technological change will usually imply technical change because different combinations of inputs need to be integrated using different knowledge.[2] Innovation, on the other hand, is defined as the first use of a particular technology or technique.[3]

ENVIRONMENTAL EFFECTIVENESS AND TECHNOLOGICAL CHANGE

The critical importance of elasticities in determining the environmental effectiveness of economic instruments is noted by Opschoor *et al.* (1994, p. 36); it must be realized that financial and economic instruments provide an incentive, the significance of which depends on the elasticities that operate on behaviour (price elasticities, substitution elasticities, income elasticities), on the strength of the signal given (for example, the level of the charge), and on the availability of substitutes or alternative actions.

The significance of both short- and long-term impacts of economic instruments is also widely recognized in the evaluation of their environmental effectiveness. Environmental effectiveness, therefore, depends on the elasticity of response of the relevant actors.

The response of actors to an environmental tax can be categorized, broadly, in the following way:

1. The actor makes no response to the tax, simply paying the higher price for the taxable substance.
2. The actor reduces use or emissions at the margin, with no significant change in technology or technique.
3. The actor seeks to find a substitute where the tax is in the form of an input tax, or to install end-of-pipe technologies in the case of a pollution tax, reducing exposure to the tax without major changes in the production technique.
4. The actor responds by seeking to make use of existing cleaner production

techniques employing different technologies and reducing exposure to the tax either by reduced input use or reduced emissions from the production process.

5. The actor, having made use of existing technology, invests in new research and development aimed at uncovering innovative technologies and techniques for use in production.[4]
6. Last, but by no means least, the actor seeks to reduce exposure to the tax by acting illegally, or acting to exploit loopholes which it becomes financially profitable to exploit once the incentive structure it is faced with has been altered by the tax.

With the exception of the last of these, the responses indicate progressively more sustainable approaches to the problem posed by the environmental tax.

Issues of inelastic behaviour in response to price are noted in the literature with respect to pesticides in Sweden, Denmark and the Netherlands (Reus *et al.*, 1994, p. 75; Oskam *et al.*, 1992), the UK (ECOTEC, 1997), nitrogenous fertilizer in the UK (England, 1986), West Germany (De Haan, 1982) and Denmark (Dubgaard, 1989; Hanley, 1990), fuel taxes (Convery *et al.*, 1996, p. 23), and surface minerals taxes (ECOTEC, 1991).[5] Only on relatively few occasions are the reasons for this explored in any detail.[6]

Regarding the longer-term dynamic situation, economic instruments are favoured since supposedly they provide incentives for continuous technological change and innovation. The fact that each unit of pollution, for example, costs the firm money will lead to attempts to reduce the intensity of pollution on a continuous basis. Regulatory instruments are perceived, at least in theory, as having an impact on technological change only insofar as such change helps the given standard to be met. Yet the limited responsiveness characterized by the small elasticities mentioned above must cast doubt over the ability of environmental taxes to further dynamic efficiency in the way that is often claimed.

ENVIRONMENTAL TAXES AND TECHNICAL CHANGE / INNOVATION

Wallace (1995, p. 21) suggests that theoretical work undertaken regarding the impact of economic instruments on innovation, technical and technological change has been flawed by virtue of its being largely the result of simple deductive reasoning with little connection to the real world (Kemp, 1997). Furthermore, when technological change and innovation are being discussed, the only thing that is not explored in any detail are the processes by which these actually occur. In following this 'black box' inducement approach, environmental economists have followed the majority of twentieth century economists in their apparent unwillingness to explore the process in depth, despite technical change and innovation being key determinants of economic growth, as well as chronic features of twentieth-century life (Rosenberg, 1982).

All major attempts to understand the influence of economic instruments on technical change suffer from similar limitations regarding the implied model of how technical change, technological change and innovation occur. Essentially, in the treatments of Zerbe (1970), Downing and White (1986) and Milliman and Prince (1989), what is at issue is the strength of any economic incentive to change technique or innovate as though the firm acted with complete autonomy, and in such a way as it always acts as a strictly profit-maximizing entity, even in some cases where investments in research and development (R&D) are posited. The actual processes involved in the search for, and utilization of existing techniques and technologies, and the far more complex processes involved in innovation are simply not addressed. There is little room in these models for:

1. the discreteness of techniques which may be available to the firm (for example, demand for plant protection products or pesticides might more closely resemble a step-function owing to the fact that agricultural inputs tend to be integrated, more or less well depending on the skill of the farmer, within a given technique);

2. the uncertainties which accompany any attempt to innovate (how can it be known with certainty what will be discovered in the research and development process? Applying the concept of profit maximization to this activity implies knowing in advance the very thing one is seeking to discover); and

3. the institutionally governed, and path-dependent nature of the processes through which research and development are carried out in various sectors of the economy. Especially in the context of environmentally oriented research, it is often the case that a major shift in perception is required to move 'alternative' research paths into the mainstream. The financial incentive provided by a tax may help in this regard, but the change in attitudes and perceptions, often developed through years of training, may be resilient to change, especially where powerful interests rely on things remaining more or less as they currently stand (see Hogg, 1997).

Opschoor *et al.* (1994, p. 36) note that such empirical evidence as exists casts doubt on the dynamic efficiency argument, though citing only one study on effluent charges. This should not necessarily cause any surprise. There are a number of studies which suggest that firms should, whatever the decision rule applied (be it payback period, rate of return on investment or another form of cost-benefit analysis), already be investing in activities to reduce pollution and waste. What is it about the application of an environmental tax that would suddenly make firms behave as profit-maximizers when they were not doing so before?

(ENVIRONMENTAL) ECONOMISTS' VIEW OF THE FIRM

Clearly, there are reasons to believe that environmental taxes may play a signalling role which persuade firms to take a new look at things which they had neglected, or glanced at only cursorily, in the past (Hogg, 1999). However, this study suggests that firm behaviour is far more complex than economic theory tends to suggest, and that a number of factors are likely to play a role in shaping a company's response to an economic instrument. These are not given much appreciation in the environmental economics literature (where the algorithm employed by actors is uniform across them all).

Economic instruments are deemed to have particular advantages where marginal abatement costs are heterogeneous across actors. The flexibility in response (relative to regulation) that economic instruments allow means that if actors respond in a rational manner, most abatement will be undertaken by those for whom it is least costly to do so. A disadvantage of environmental taxes, however, may lie in the fact that firms may not be very flexible at all, and that owing to their inertia (relative to the hypothesized response), firms will simply not respond at all other than by paying the tax. They may, for example, not be aware of what their abatement costs are. Alternatively, they may be aware of ways of reducing the polluting activity, but owing to downstream linkages, they may find it difficult to alter their behaviour unless downstream demands change. Agriculture provides excellent examples of the latter case, where the power exerted in commodity markets by major retailers is such that unless they take decisions to encourage reduced input use in production, the suppliers (the farmers) are unlikely to respond in the desired fashion. Contracts in agriculture sometimes specify what is to be sprayed and when, partly in an attempt to ensure cosmetic features of the produce are enhanced.

Environmental economists have made use of a theory of innovation which generally assumes that the path which technological development follows is conditioned mostly, if not entirely, by price incentives. Perhaps the most coherent exposition of what is implied in the assumptions usually found in the literature is the theory of induced innovation, as elaborated by Binswanger, and Hayami and Ruttan (Binswanger *et al.*, 1978; Hayami and Ruttan, 1985).[7] Their theory of induced innovation consists essentially of two interdependent theories, one of induced technical change, and the other, induced institutional change, which together seek to endogenize technical change within the economic system (Hayami and Ruttan, 1985, p. 3). As applied to agriculture it:

> attempts to make more explicit the process by which technical and institutional changes are induced through the responses of farmers, agribusiness entrepreneurs, scientists and public administrators to resource endowments and to changes in the supply and demand of factors and products (ibid., p. 4).

Induced technical change hypothesizes that technical change occurs in such a way as to economize on factors which are becoming relatively more scarce and thus more expensive. In their view, research administrators and research scientists can be viewed as responsive to economic indicators in the same way as can a profit-maximizing firm (ibid., p. 88). Induced institutional change is postulated to occur in response to similar signals as induced technical change, though the two are seen as connected.

There are a number of major problems with this conception of technological change.[8] However, only three will be examined here, the aim being to understand why it might be that a firm's response in terms of technological and technical change, and innovation, may be rather more muted than some of the literature indicates.

Influence of Prices on Research Possibilities

If markets can influence the direction of technical and institutional change, might they not influence the direction of science itself? Marx saw the possibilities for this when he wrote: 'Invention then becomes a business, and the application of science to direct production itself becomes a prospect which determines and solicits it' (Marx, [1857–8] 1973, p. 704). Hayami and Ruttan's theory holds that science leads technological development. It is quite possible that the path which R&D follows may be difficult to change because of institutional factors. The tools and concepts which researchers employ are shaped by their education and their learning processes. These cannot be changed overnight, and nor can the culture of the organizations for which they work. The growth of knowledge is path-dependent, reflecting the development of a particular view not only of the way in which certain problems might be solved, but also, of the world itself.

The Influence of Prices on Processes of Technical Change

Companies are not profit maximizers in the strict sense. For them to be so would require knowledge and information about technologies which few can even aspire to. Most fall far short of this ideal, and for a number of reasons. Thus, even before an environmental tax is put in place, few companies will be employing techniques and technologies which enable them to maximize profits.

It is important here to distinguish between technical and technological change (use of processes and things that already exist) and innovation. Techniques and technologies may already exist that allow enterprises to adapt to the tax in the manner suggested by induced innovation theory. Whether, in fact, they do so is another matter. The following issues appear to be relevant in this context:

1. availability of information concerning the technologies concerned;
2. ability/willingness of companies to access this information;
3. ability/willingness of companies to assess its significance (quality investment appraisal and so on);
4. the extent to which useful technologies require new skills of management and the workforce, and the companies' ability/willingness to access/ provide these;
5. access to financial resources (creditworthiness of companies, strength of balance sheets);
6. the impact of the tax on the firm's costs, in particular, whether the cost element which is increased by the tax is a smaller or a larger part of the company's total costs (in which case, for a tax of a given magnitude, the perceived impact of the tax will be larger or smaller respectively);
7. the seniority of management dealing with the cost element which is affected by the tax.

Most of these clearly allude to the capability of the firm to respond to the instrument. The size of the tax is not under the firm's control, but as the last two points make clear, there may be variations from company to company which affect the perceived magnitude of any stimulus provided by the tax.

It is intellectually dishonest to suggest that all firms will act as profit-maximizers. Any theory that does so is bound to overstate any potential gains from the changes it purports to examine. Furthermore, such assumptions make light of the obvious need, in the case of fiscal instruments, for complementary instruments which loosen up the responsiveness of targeted actors through the provision of information and advice, and demonstration projects.

The Impossibility of Applying Cost-benefit Analysis to R&D Programmes

The third important criticism of induced innovation theory is that it assumes not only that technical and technological change are influenced by relative factor prices, but also that innovation is influenced by relative factor prices as well. The ability to skew innovation in the manner suggested implies a prescience which researchers are not blessed with. If innovation is by definition a process with an uncertain outcome, the relative factor intensity embodied in that outcome cannot be known in advance with great certainty.[9]

Several models of how economic instruments affect the extent of use of pollution control technologies make utterly implausible assumptions concerning the amount of resources which companies will devote to R&D in the pursuit of new techniques and technologies. The assumption that such decisions can be made on the basis of a profit-maximizing calculus deserves to be expunged from any meaningful analysis. In addition, innovation in new directions may require new skills, different personnel, and different ways of approaching particular problems. How quickly such changes can be made depends on the extent to which innovation as practised in advance of the tax is locked into a particular trajectory.

LOCK-IN AND ITS RELEVANCE FOR THE EFFECTIVENESS OF ENVIRONMENTAL TAXES

It will be appreciated from the above that the view in which prices are the only drivers of innovation, technical and technological change is very much a partial one. The OECD (1984, p. 29) recognized more than a decade ago that as a firm matures, it can become locked into a production sequence reducing the ability and managerial propensity to introduce major changes in products and processes: 'as a firm matures, it becomes increasingly "locked in" to a rigid production sequence which greatly reduces its ability, and its managerial propensity, to introduce major product or process changes'. Opschoor *et. al.* (1994) comment that innovation is:

> more often than not the result of firms' market based interactions with others (clients, suppliers etc.). These interactions produce multiple influences on the products' and processes' environmental performance 'upstream'. Pure efficiency considerations can, in such circumstances, only play a limited role. [...]

> [I]nnovation must then be seen as the outcome of a complex process within a 'structure of co-operation'. Depending on, for example, the level and type of innovation (process or product) and the actors involved, different policy instruments may provide different stimuli resulting in different environmental impacts (ibid., p. 36).

Industry case studies confirm the possibility of lock-in occurring, though this seems not to affect all industries. Appreciation of this possibility has not been matched by appreciation of its potential significance, yet, what in some cases appears to be an inelastic response to environmental taxes, might suggest that the problem is not so narrowly confined. While it is accepted that the inelastic nature of response will not always prevail, there is a suggestion that the potential effects of environmental taxes may be being overstated, possibly leading to disillusion when their implementation creates somewhat muted responses.

In the following section, some of the elements of theories of innovation and technological change are explored in order to shed some light on why responses to economic instruments might be more muted than had been hoped.

TECHNOLOGICAL TRAJECTORIES

Modern theories of technological change treat the subject within an evolutionary framework. At the heart of these theories are notions of path-dependence, the relevance of uncertainty and the irrelevance of equilibrium considerations. A number of scholars of technological change, not all starting from the same perspective, have come to the conclusion that technological development appears to follow a particular path or trajectory (Dosi, 1982; Nelson and Winter, 1982; Perez, 1983; Dosi and Orsenigo, 1988; Freeman and Perez, 1988; Orsenigo, 1989). These scholars have developed their views on the basis that:

1. innovation is an inherently uncertain process;
2. the process is founded upon learning;
3. innovation within industry is channelled in accordance with existing institutional and organizational forms. New technologies may necessitate the evolution of new institutional forms;
4. related to the first point above, the use of (profit) maximization procedures in addressing the problem of selecting and screening R&D projects is implausible.

There is some consensus on the view that technological change occurs with an apparent inner logic, reflecting the fact that once a particular technology has matured, the heuristics associated with it enable pay-offs to be realized by continuing development along trajectories which are carved out over time. Trajectories are linked to technological regimes, or paradigms, which relate to technicians' beliefs about what is feasible or at least worth attempting. The attention of innovators is focused by those opportunities not yet exploited, but which appear feasible on the basis of past learning. At the same time, the way the problem is framed essentially excludes consideration of alternative approaches.

The importance of the social and institutional framework is well recognized. This becomes not just a 'selection environment', but equally, an environment that is itself selected by the possibilities contained within new combinations of technologies and institutions. As has been noted elsewhere, 'the assumption of a selection environment that is truly independent of a particular technological trajectory is hard to justify' (van den Belt and Rip, 1987, p. 141). It is the fit of the two that becomes important, not the fitness of a technology in a given environment. This underlines the plausibility of the notion that technology and the social and institutional framework coevolve (see Norgaard, 1994 on coevolutionary approaches to the theory of technological change).

Common to all these approaches is the idea that the innovation process is in some way channelled by a degree of consensus about how something should be done, and the possibilities for further development. The exclusion effect implied by these ideas appears to suggest that changing the behaviour of those who are involved in the innovation process may be far from straight-forward. There is at least a hint within these theories of the possibility for lock-in to occur through the exclusion effect implied by following a particular path.

THE ROLE OF HISTORY, PATH-DEPENDENCE AND LOCK-IN

The idea of technological lock-in is closely related to the relevance of path-dependence for the evolution of technological (and economic) systems. Path-dependence, or non-ergodicity, implies not simply that history matters, but that history plays a crucial role both in shaping the existing state of affairs, and determining the menu of futures which can become the present. The very notion of a trajectory, as discussed above, implies a form of path-dependence, the path, in those cases, being determined by technicians' beliefs about what can be done within a particular regime, or paradigm. Typically, within a given trajectory, innovations are incremental ones. They are improvements on existing designs, the need for which may become apparent either during testing, or through its performance in a market, or even owing to complementary innovations elsewhere in the economy. In sectors where patents are an important source of competitive advantage, much innovation may arise from competitors' desire to innovate around a patent, thus being at the same time both incremental, yet sufficiently 'radical' to entail patentability in its own right.

The concept of path-dependence has been most closely associated with the work of Arthur (1988a, b, 1989) and David (1972, 1985, 1987). Arthur's work is closely related to the existence in economic processes of phenomena exhibiting increasing returns, or self-reinforcing mechanisms. Arthur (1988b, p. 591) cites five sources:

1. learning by using;
2. network externalities;
3. scale economies in production;
4. informational increasing returns;
5. technological interrelatedness.

Path-dependence is one of four properties of such mechanisms in economics noted by Arthur (1988a, p. 10), the others being the existence of multiple equilibria, possible inefficiency and lock-in.

An initial choice on the basis of a discounted cash flow comparison can lock the R&D department into its initial choice, regardless of the nature of what the pay-offs of alternatives might be as more is learned about them. Uncertainty as a cause for regret must surely be prevalent when discussing alternative research projects whose outcome is, by definition, unknown. Thus, where lock-in has a chance of occurring, there exist possibilities for regret, even where there is no conventional economic inefficiency (Arthur, 1988a, p. 13). The possibility of choosing 'the wrong technology' would appear to be very real indeed (Cowan, 1987).

Arthur also shows that lock-in can occur through a stochastic process in which, under conditions of increasing returns, the random order of arrival of agents with differing 'natural' preferences for the technologies available in the market can determine the way in which the market is ultimately shared. In some cases, monopoly becomes inevitable, but exactly which technology achieves monopoly cannot be predicted in advance. Relatively innocuous events can determine the outcome (Arthur, 1989, p. 122). Even the simple elimination of uncertainty regarding the relative performance of competing technologies in their early stages of development can act as a source of lock-in (Agliardi, 1991, 52–71).

Arthur's work clearly shows the need for a historically informed approach to the understanding of how things have become as they are. David's work starts from exactly this view of the importance of history (David, 1972: 1, 1985, p. 332). Using the example of the standardization of the QWERTY keyboard, he raises the possibility of 'lock-in' occurring. He suggests that the decision of typists to learn one or other keyboard is like Arthur's problem of technological choice, adding that there may also be an element of self-fulfilling expectations at work. He suggests that expectations about the outcome of competition between the QWERTY keyboard and that of its Remington competitor were sufficient to guarantee that the industry eventually would lock in to a *de-facto* QWERTY standard (David, 1985, p. 335). Over time, the cost of the typewriter came down but the costs of retraining typists remained high. As a result, the short-run decision was made to adapt the machines to people rather than the other way round. The QWERTY keyboard became the standard to which those to be trained were trained. With new hardware technology, the QWERTY arrangement has been proved to be slower than alternatives which led to mechanical problems on earlier typewriters. Yet the early standardization, and the costs of retraining means that QWERTY survives.

In a later paper dealing with the setting of standards, David makes some important observations relating to the possibility of lock-in occurring. First, there may be only brief 'windows in time' in which policy-makers have scope to act before lock-in sets in. Second, this period is likely to coincide with the time at which policy-makers have least relevant information – they act as 'blind giants'. Third, whatever decision is made, some investors will have sunk resources into paths to be no longer pursued – they become 'angry orphans' (David, 1987, p. 210).

ECONOMIC WEBS AND TECHNOLOGICAL INTERRELATEDNESS

One of the factors which Arthur cites as being likely to lead to lock-in is technological interrelatedness. This concept has been explored by David, as well as by Kauffman (1988) and Bijker (Pinch and Bijker, 1987; Bijker, 1995). In evolutionary approaches to technological change, fitness, both in biological, but even more so, in social systems must be understood as internally referential. This highlights the difficulty of talking in terms of 'evolutionary progress'.

The fitness of technologies and institutions to fulfil a given purpose is conditioned by those technologies and institutions already in place. Indeed, these may provide the rationale for the development of new innovations as new needs arise out of the use of a new technology. Thus, as technological systems mature, they tend to assume the character of interrelated webs of technologies. These webs can be responsible for considerable inertia in the face of apparent possibilities, or needs (perhaps on the basis of feelings of regret), for change. The relationship of producers of intermediate goods to up- and downstream suppliers and buyers is an obvious case in point, especially where these are, respectively, monopolistic and monopsonistic in character.

Pinch and Bijker (1987) follow through the concerns of sociologists of science (particularly their empirical programme of relativism) and apply them to the social construction of technology. Bijker (1995, p. 273) suggests 'the technical is socially constructed and the social is technically constructed' (again, the idea of coevolution seems applicable). He prefers to speak in terms of the study of sociotechnology. For Bijker, technical artefacts rarely exist in isolation, but are usually part of a seamless web – a 'sociotechnical ensemble'. He suggests also that many artefacts display an 'obduracy' which makes it difficult, if not impossible, to entertain significant flexibility. In such instances, social groups have invested so much in a given exemplar that its meaning becomes fixed.

Environmental Effectiveness and Lock-in

Few authors have attempted to bring the lessons of evolutionary theories into the economic instruments debate, and the environmental debate more generally (exceptions are Freeman, 1992; Ashford, 1996; Faucheux, 1997; Kemp, 1997). The relevance of such theories appears to be considerable if what is being sought is a dynamic process of technological change and innovation within a trajectory that reflects environmental concerns.

Considerations regarding lock-in are clearly important if it subsequently becomes clear that technologies in use are creating problems which were not foreseen (raising questions as to the ability of institutions to foresee such problems). Those technologies responsible for environmental damage would appear to be good examples, and it is only necessary to consider the length of time which typically elapses between recognition of a technology as environmentally problematic, and its substitution/removal, to understand the relevance of the concept under discussion. The damaging effects of pesticides have been known for decades, yet total consumption, albeit of different products (not all of which are more benign than those they replace), continues to rise at a global level. Even at the time when the petroleum engine replaced steam-powered automobiles, there were comments being made to the effect that pursuit of such a path would cause serious pollution problems.

The relevance of lock-in has to be addressed at two interrelated levels, that of the situation which prevails, and that of the situation which might have prevailed. The development of technologies in interrelated webs means that they are often part of a package. Moreover, they may be part of a package which is developing along a particular path or trajectory. The evolution of supporting organizations, institutions and interests deepens and confirms the validity of the trajectory. However, unforeseen circumstances may arise that give cause for regret for using an element of what has become an interrelated system. To try to change the use of this element may imply, to a greater or lesser degree, changing the whole system. This will be made all the more difficult if:

1.   knowledge of how to do things other than in the way they are currently

done is scarce, or not available, or marginalized;

2. the user of the particular element is caught between up and downstream sectors with considerable interest in preserving the current way of doing things. They, therefore, have limited autonomy to alter their use of the element concerned; and/or

3. relatedly, the interests involved in maintaining the status quo are very powerful.

In these circumstances, lock-in may occur owing to the coevolution of techniques, organizations and institutions. Regret may surface but with limited opportunities for its easy reversal owing, not only to the possible irreversibility of the event which triggers regret, but also, to the difficulty in changing the institutional and organizational theatre in which actors function. It is interesting that in the UK, the National Farmers' Union has only moved significantly towards a more favourable view of integrated crop management now that major retailers are aware of the benefits to themselves of doing so. Farmers, typically the targets of instruments designed to alter their behaviour, may be the least influential actors in changing the system of which they are a part.[10]

That there may be limited alternatives available to facilitate a response reflects a locking in to a particular research trajectory. This forces the consideration of the possible counterfactuals that might have existed in what might be only marginally different circumstances. Technological choices are, so Arthur relates, often conditioned by historical contingencies whose impact cascades through the economic and social system. Lock-in to one research trajectory represents the locking-out of others which may, in the light of regret now surfaced, have acquired a hitherto unrecognized appeal. It can be argued powerfully that our love affair with industrial agriculture has channelled funds away from alternatives which are now despised on the basis of low yields. Yet it is rarely asked what the yield of alternative agriculture might have been had research followed a completely different trajectory.

The problem here is that while the economics of R&D may be uncertain, its direction, through education and through the awarding of research grants, can be manipulated such that only R&D that is in the interests of prevailing economic interests gets done. The division of labour between public and private sector research acquires deep significance in this regard. Unfortunately, rather than using public sector research funds to keep open alternative paths of technological development, the tendency, more recently, has been for the public sector to work ever more closely with powerful economic interests, thus bearing out Marx's prophetic words concerning the application of science to production. Typical strategies in this regard are withdrawal of the public sector from near market research (in the spirit of partnership with the private sector), or increased concern to recover the costs of research through concentrating on privately appropriable (patentable) innovations which can be sold or licensed to the private sector.

CONCLUSION

The issue of the ability of economic instruments to generate significant changes in behaviour, and to stimulate innovation in the desired direction, clearly needs to be revisited in the light of a review of theories of technological change. It is obviously not sufficient to assume that by altering relative prices of inputs to (or outputs of) production that markets will cause adjustments that are instantaneous. In some circumstances, it may not even be possible to assume this will happen to any significant degree even in the longer term. Too little is known at this stage to comment on that question.

Do environmental taxes have the capacity to deliver on their promise to encourage technical and technological change, and in the longer term, innovation? The answer to this question is that they may, but equally, they might not. This will depend on a number of issues, not the least important of which will be:

1. the magnitude of the stimulus provided by the instrument;
2. whether or not the targeted actors can reduce their exposure to the tax through illegal, or otherwise evasive activity;
3. the availability of substitute products and alternative techniques, and mechanisms available to facilitate their development (and conversely, the degree to which a particular input is essential in a given production process);
4. the extent of actors' knowledge about alternative products and techniques, and mechanisms to promote the dissemination of information;
5. the degree of discontinuity that a change in use implies for existing techniques of production;
6. the extent to which the autonomy of targeted actors is constrained by the nature of the production system (either because of up or downstream relationships, or owing to the existence of acceptable standards);
7. the timing of the tax's introduction in the context of investment cycles; and
8. the extent to which R&D investment can be channelled easily towards alternative approaches to the problems whose resolution is sought.

Some of these preceding issues will determine the extent to which enterprises are paralysed by inertia, and so forced to continue past ways of doing things. In essence, therefore, there are issues to be addressed regarding:

1.   the availability, both in terms of the universe of knowledge and that of the individual producer, of technological options; and
2.   the degree of autonomy that producers have within markets where the tax is imposed.

Market-based instruments appear ill-suited to address either of these issues. They require supplementary, or alternative policies. These will tend to be instruments aiming to increase the information-richness of the market concerning pollution control equipment, and, as regards consumers, to help inform decisions related to the characteristics of the products they purchase. Economic instruments can help in playing a role as a signposting mechanism, but beyond this, their role may be more limited than has been claimed in the literature, especially with regard to innovation.

These limits are not, in general, related to the way the instrument is applied, but inhere within the instrument, and in the nature of the firm. Without an appreciation of the limits of economic instruments in this regard, expectations will continue to be unrealistic. Policy-makers will be asked to expect what cannot be delivered because of a 'pricist' view of the influences upon firm behaviour.

NOTES

1.   Note that in most of the models of the effectiveness of economic instruments in stimulating technical change, technological change, and innovation, environmental taxes rank below tradable permits, and auctioning permits enhances the effectiveness (Milliman and Prince, 1989; Jaffe and Stavins, 1995; Kemp, 1997: 2).
2.   Some definitions seem preoccupied with 'the new', making it impossible to speak of technical or technological change when reversion to earlier ways of doing things occurs.
3.   This definition leaves it open as to whether first use is defined in an absolute sense, or whether one should consider innovation in a sector-specific or country-specific manner. A firm-specific definition reduces the distinction between diffusion of technologies and techniques, and innovation.
4.   Equally, it might seek to influence providers of technology so that they do this. In general, the possibilities for innovative techniques to be discovered by third parties is often overlooked, and for reasons alluded to later, these may be important in overcoming any existing inertia in a given system.
5.   It should be said that in many of these cases, the measurements themselves come with large health warnings.
6.   This has been assumed as the primary objective of the tax. Some taxes are used primarily to raise revenue, and it can be argued that their ability to succeed in this respect is dependent upon a muted response to the instrument, which is the subject of this study.
7.   Indeed, the theory was developed from an article written by Ruttan in 1970 on 'Technology and the environment'.
8.   For a fuller treatment, see Hogg (1997).
9.   In practice, though much is made of the 'uncertain' nature of the innovation process, the extent of uncertainty probably varies significantly with the radicalness of the innovation (and, in turn, the definition of what constitutes innovation).

10. This lays down a challenge to standard environmental economic theory where it is held that taxes are best applied closest to the problem which they are designed to address. In certain systems, policy might best focus not on actors who are the proximate cause of the problem, but on those (in this case, retailers) who are the ultimate cause.

REFERENCES

Agliardi, Elettra (1991), 'Essays on the dynamics of allocation under increasing returns to adoption and path dependence', unpublished Ph.D thesis, University of Cambridge.

Arthur, W. Brian (1988a), 'Self-reinforcing mechanisms in economics', in W. Philip Anderson, Kenneth J. Arrow and David Pines (eds), *The Economy as an Evolving Complex System*, Redwood City, California: Addison-Wesley, pp. 9-31.

Arthur, W. Brian (1988b), 'Competing technologies: an overview', in G. Dosi *et al.* (eds), *Technical Change and Economic Theory*, London: Pinter, pp. 590-607.

Arthur, W. Brian (1989), 'Competing technologies, increasing returns, and lock-in by historical events', *Economic Journal*, **99**, 116-31.

Ashford, Nicholas (1996), 'The influence of information-based initiatives and negotiated agreements on technological change', paper presented at the International Conference on the Economics and Law of Voluntary Approaches in Environmental Policy, Venice, 18-19 November.

Bijker, Wiebe (1995), *Of Bicycles, Bakelites and Bulbs: Toward a Theory of Sociotechnical Change*, Cambridge, MA and London: MIT Press.

Bijker, Wiebe E., Thomas P. Hughes and Trevor J. Pinch (eds) (1987), *The Social Construction of Technological Systems: New Directions in the Sociology and History of Technology*, London: MIT Press.

Binswanger, Hans P., Vernon W. Ruttan *et al.* (eds) (1978), *Induced Innovation: Technology, Institutions, and Development*, London and Baltimore: Johns Hopkins University Press.

Convery, Frank, Alberto Majocchi and David Pearce (1996), 'Economic incentives and disincentives for environmental protection', paper presented at the European Commission/Council Presidency Conference, Palazzo Altieri, Rome, 7-8 June.

Cowan, Robin (1987), 'Backing the wrong horse: sequential technology choice under increasing returns', D.Phil dissertation, Stanford University, July, Ann Arbor, Michigan: Xerox University Microfilms.

David, Paul A. (1972), *Technical Choice, Innovation and Economic Growth*, Cambridge: Cambridge University Press.

David, Paul A. (1985), 'Clio and the economics of QWERTY', *Economic History*, **75** (2), 332-7.

David, Paul A. (1987), 'Some new standards for the economics of standardization in the information age', in P. Dasgupta and P. Stoneman (eds), *Economic Policy and Technological Performance*, Cambridge: Cambridge University Press, pp. 206-39.

De Haan, H. (1982), 'Economic aspects of policies to control nitrate contamination resulting from agricultural production', *European Review of Agricultural Economics*, **79**, pp. 345-9.

Dosi, Giovanni (1982), 'Technological paradigms and technological trajectories: a suggested interpretation of the determinants and directions of technical change', *Research Policy*, **11**, 147-62.

Dosi, G. and L. Orsenigo (1988), 'Coordination and transformation: an overview of structures, behaviours and change in evolutionary economics', in G. Dosi *et al.* (eds), *Technical Change and Economic Theory*, London: Pinter, pp. 13–37.

Dosi, Giovanni, Christopher Freeman, Richard Nelson, Gerald Silverberg and Luc Soete (eds) (1988), *Technical Change and Economic Theory*, London: Pinter.

Downing, Paul B. and Lawrence J. White (1986), 'Innovation in pollution control', *Journal of Environmental Economics and Management*, **13**, 18–29.

Dubgaard, A. (1989), 'Input levies as a means of controlling the intensities of nitrogenous fertiliser and pesticides', in A. Dubgaard and A. Nielsen (eds), *Economics of Environmental Regulations in Agriculture*, Kiel: Wissenschaftsverlag Vauk.

ECOTEC (1991), 'Forecasting the demand for primary aggregates: a review', Stage Two Report to the Department of the Environment, Birmingham: ECOTEC.

ECOTEC (1997), 'Economic instruments for pesticide minimisation', a final report to the Department of the Environment, Birmingham: ECOTEC.

England, R. (1986) 'Reducing the nitrogen input on arable farms', *Journal of Agricultural Economics*, **37**, 13–24.

Faucheux, Sylvie (1997), 'Technological change, ecological sustainability and industrial competitiveness', in A. Dragun and K. Jacobsson, *Sustainability and Global Environmental Policy: New Horizons*, Cheltenham, UK and Lyme, US: Edward Elgar, pp. 131–49.

Freeman, Christopher (1992), *The Economics of Hope: Essays on Technical Change, Economic Growth and the Environment*, London: Pinter.

Freeman, Christopher and Carlota Perez (1988), 'Structural crises of adjustment, business cycles and investment behaviour', in G. Dosi *et al.* (eds), *Technical Change and Economic Theory*, London: Pinter, pp. 38–66.

Hanley, Nick (1990), 'The economics of nitrate pollution', *European Agricultural Economics*, **17**, 129–51.

Hayami, Yujiro and Vernon Ruttan (1985), *Agricultural Development: An International Perspective* (revised and expanded edition), Baltimore, US and London, UK: Johns Hopkins University Press.

Hogg, Dominic (1997), 'The determinants of the path of technological change in agriculture', Ph.D. thesis, Cambridge University (to be published in full by Macmillan).

Hogg, Dominic (1999), 'The effectiveness of the UK landfill tax – early indications', in Thomas Sterner (ed.), *The Market and the Environment: The Effectiveness of Market-based Policy Instruments for Environmental Reform*, Cheltenham, UK and Northampton, US: Edward Elgar.

Jaffe, Adam B. and Robert N. Stavins (1995), 'Dynamic incentives of environmental regulations: the effects of alternative policy instruments on technology diffusion', *Journal of Environmental Economics and Management*, **29** (3), S-43–S-63.

Kauffman, Stuart A. (1988), 'The evolution of economic webs', in Philip W. Anderson, Kenneth J. Arrow and David Pines (eds), *The Economy as an Evolving Complex System*, Redwood City, CA: Addison-Wesley, pp. 125–46.

Kemp, René (1997), *Environmental Policy and Technical Change: A Comparison of the Technological Impact of Policy Instruments*, Cheltenham, UK and Brookfield, US: Edward Elgar.

Marx, Karl (1973), *Grundrisse: The Foundations of Political Economy* (rough draft) (first published in German in 1939, drafted in 1857–8), translated with a foreword by Martin Nicolaus, London: Allen Lane with New Left Review.

Milliman, S.R. and R.J. Prince (1989), 'Firm incentives to promote technological change in pollution control', *Journal of Environmental Economics and Management*, **17**, 245-65.

Nelson, Richard R. and Sidney G. Winter (1982), *An Evolutionary Theory of Economic Change*, Cambridge, MA: Harvard University Press.

Norgaard, Richard B. (1994), *Development Betrayed: The End of Progress and a Coevolutionary Revisioning of the Future*, London: Routledge.

OECD (1984), *Environment and Economics. Background Papers for an International Conference*, Vol. II, 18-21 June, Paris: OECD.

Opschoor, J.B., A.F. de Savornin Lohman and H.B. Vos (1994), *Managing the Environment: The Role of Economic Instruments*, Paris: OECD.

Orsenigo, Luigi (1989), *The Emergence of Biotechnology*, London: Pinter.

Oskam, A.J., H. van Zeijts, G.J. Thijssen, G.A.A. Wossink and R. Vijftigschild (1992), 'Pesticide use and pesticide policy in the Netherlands: an economic analysis of regulatory levies in agriculture', *WES Study 26*, Agricultural University, Wageningen.

Perez, Carlota (1983), 'Structural change and assimilation of new technologies in the economic and social systems', *Futures*, **15** (5), 357-75.

Pinch, T. and W. Bijker (1987), 'The social construction of facts and artefacts: or how the sociology of science and the sociology of technology might benefit each other', in Bijker *et al.* (eds), *The Social Construction of Technological Systems: New Directions in the Sociology and History of Technology*, London: MIT Press, pp. 17-50.

Reus, J.A.W.A., H.J. Weckseler and G.A. Pak (1994), *Towards a Future EC Pesticide Policy: An Inventory of Risks of Pesticide Use, Possible Solutions and Policy Instruments*, Utrecht: CLM.

Rosenberg, Nathan (1982), *Inside the Black Box: Technology and Economics*, Cambridge: Cambridge University Press.

van den Belt, Henk and Arie Rip (1987), 'The Nelson-Winter-Dosi model and synthetic dye chemistry', in Wiebe E. Bijker, Thomas P. Hughes and Trevor J. Pinch (eds) (1987), *The Social Construction of Technological Systems: New Directions in the Sociology and History of Technology*, London: MIT Press, pp. 135-58.

Wallace, David (1995), *Environmental Policy and Industrial Innovation: Strategies in Europe, the US and Japan*, London: RIIA and Earthscan.

Zerbe, Richard O. (1970), 'Theoretical efficiency in pollution control', *Western Economic Journal*, **8**, pp. 364-76.

10. A socio-economic evaluation of the SOₓ charge in Japan*

Yu Matsuno and Kazuhiro Ueta

1. THE POLLUTION LOAD LEVY AND POLLUTION REDUCTION INCENTIVES

Pollution control policy for the reduction of sulphur oxides (SO_x) emissions from stationary sources in Japan has been cited as a case of successful environmental policy worthy of international scrutiny (Weidner, 1995). A fundamental component of this policy is the Compensation Law for Pollution-Related Health Damage, which was passed in September 1973 in order to provide redress for pollution victims, and came into effect in September 1974. The Compensation Law imposed a system of pollution load levies (referred to hereafter simply as the CL levy) on stationary sources, and, although the system was not originally established as an economic incentive system to reduce emissions, this structure was akin to a system of emission charges in the sense that 'taxes' were assessed on polluters. However, whether or not this system of levies provided an incentive effect leading to the actual reduction of pollution is the subject of debate.

Some investigators maintain that the CL levy system did not confer a pollution reduction effect. Horiuchi (1995, pp. 39–40), for example, shows that the average cost of SO_x reduction at three thermal power plants exceeded the CL levy rate (fiscal 1979), suggesting that the installation of desulphurization equipment was due not to the Compensation Law but instead to direct controls. Tsukatani (1983, p. 20) also finds that the increase in production costs attributable to the CL levy was so small as to be hidden by price fluctuations, concluding that the levy had little inductive power, and that its pollution reduction effect was negligible.

Others assert that the CL levy did, in fact, deliver an incentive effect for pollution reduction. Imura (1988, pp. 115–18) compares the reduction rates of SO_x emission between Compensation Law designated areas and other (non-designated) areas from the year that regulatory standards for total pollution load control were enforced (1978), finding that reduction rates were greater in those areas with relatively higher levy rates, and suggesting that differences in levy rates were a major factor. Weizsäker (1994, p. 126) holds that direct controls were rendered meaningless by the CL levy, stating that, 'Japan also has emission standards for power stations, which, however, were rendered meaningless by the SO$_2$ charge. It simply would not have occurred to a power station operator to exhaust the potential allowed by the standards, because of the expense'.

The question arises, then, as to how such radically different evaluations can be produced. In fact, the aforementioned studies all contain methodological shortcomings that cannot be overlooked. The Horiuchi approach considers only desulphurization stack-scrubbers from among the various options for SO$_x$ reduction, while the greater portion of Tsukatani's 'increase in production costs attributable to the CL levy' has no direct relation to the reduction of SO$_x$ emissions. A more appropriate comparison would be marginal abatement cost of SO$_x$ emissions versus the level of levy rates. Meanwhile, even if changes in industrial structure are ignored, Imura's comparison of SO$_x$ reduction rates from the year that regulatory standards for total pollution load control were enforced cannot be viewed as complete without empirical, quantitative consideration of the effects stemming from administrative guidance on the part of the national and various local governments and individually negotiated pollution control agreements. Furthermore, the study (Jesinghaus, 1988), which serves as the basis for Weizsäker's analysis, neither appropriately compares levy amounts against SO$_x$ abatement costs nor recognizes the existence of pollution control agreements.

Given these sorts of limitations, it is difficult, if not impossible, to use existing research to definitively judge whether or not the CL levy provided a real incentive towards pollution reduction. Here, the structure of the CL levy system from the standpoint of economics is clarified, and an empirical consideration of the effectiveness of the system in reducing pollution is presented.

2. THE FRAMEWORK OF JAPAN'S SO$_x$ REDUCTION EFFORTS

Since the early 1970s, SO$_x$ emissions have decreased nationwide. Reasons for this trend include the implementation of direct controls such as total pollutant load controls, higher prices for petroleum products caused by the two oil crises, and the CL levy (here it is considered whether the CL levy actually deserves to be included in this list), which have resulted in a shift in Japan's industrial structure towards less energy-intensive, cleaner industries, the installation of desulphurization stack-scrubbers, and the use of low-sulphur fuels.¹ Accordingly, even in those areas of Japan most severely affected by air pollution, SO_x concentration levels fell to within prescribed environmental quality standards (Figure 10.1). Because it is generally held that the primary factor responsible for the accomplishment of these reductions was direct controls, first consider the basis for this view.

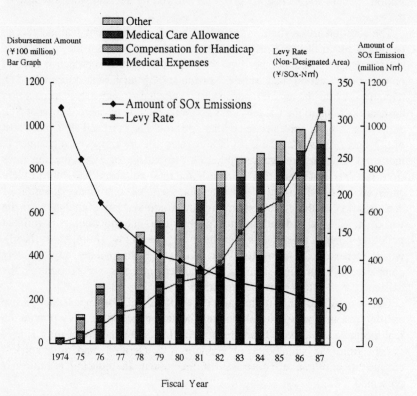

Note: The average levy rate in designated areas is simply nine times that in non-designated areas, and the shape of the graph is analogous.

Figure 10.1 SO_x emission, levy rates and disbursements

2.1 National Government-imposed Legislative Regulations

The 1962 Law Concerning Controls on the Emission of Smoke and Soot stipulated concentration standards for smokestack outlet emissions, but, because human health is affected by air pollution levels near the ground, K-value controls were implemented from 1968. The calculation of K-values is performed as follows:

$$q = K \times 10^{-3} \times He^2,$$

where q[Nm³/h] represents tolerable limits of pollution per hour among facilities generating smoke and dust, and $He[m]$ is effective chimney height. For each area, K-values were decided as a part of overall policy, and amounts of SO_x emissions were regulated for each individual stack. Gradually tightened revisions of K-values were carried out seven times through 1976. However, because it was difficult to meet environmental quality standards in concentrated industrial zones using K-values alone, total pollutant load controls were introduced in 1974 (although not completely enforced until 1978). By means of these regulations, the national government specified designated areas, with prefectural governments responsible for drawing up plans in order to meet environmental standards, giving consideration to local conditions, and establishing the following 'a' and 'b' values:

$$Q = a \times W^b,$$

where Q is the tolerable amount of SO_x emissions [Nm³/h], W is the amount of fuel used converted to heavy oil equivalent [kl/h], and $0.8 \leqslant b < 1$.

Unlike K-values, which are calculated for individual stacks, regulatory standards for total pollutant load control are applied to entire plants, and are actuated for relatively large-scale installations (as defined by comparison of W-values) that generate roughly 80 per cent or more of total SO_x emissions in a designated area. For smaller and medium-scale facilities, fuel usage regulations are employed which mandate the use of low-sulphur fuel. Further, for newly established emissions-generating installations, a stricter Q figure than in the foregoing formula is implemented. Despite being known as 'total' pollutant load controls, however, permitted emissions are actually defined in terms of hourly flows, meaning that emissions foregone in one period or season cannot be 'made up for' in another. A total of 24 areas were officially designated from 1974 to 1976, with controls enforced in all of them by May 1978.

2.2 Local Government-enacted Ordinances and Pollution Control Agreements

Local governments in Japan have generally preceded the national government in adopting pollution countermeasures. Local governments have often adopted more stringent emissions standards than the national government, leading the way by imposing their own total pollutant load controls. Additionally, local governments have negotiated pollution control agreements with large-scale facilities, and, even though these agreements are not legally compulsory and specify tighter limits than legislated standards, enterprises that have accepted such agreements have subsequently abided by them. Administrative guidance is also thought to have been useful in achieving SO_x emissions reductions.

2.3   Other Factors

Subsidies for the purchase of pollution control equipment were also made available, but these did not make a noticeable direct contribution to the reduction of SO_x emissions. On the other hand, nationally administrated energy conservation policies and energy source diversification (that is, away from oil) following the two oil crises, while not specifically designed to promote SO_x reduction, are thought to have made a real contribution. Additionally, through such legislation as the Industry Relocation Promotion Law, it is possible that contributions to SO_x emissions reduction have been brought about in severely affected areas (for example, those areas designated by the Compensation Law for Pollution-related Health Damage) by the consequent dispersion of polluting facilities to comparatively more rural sites.

3.   THE BASIC STRUCTURE OF THE CL LEVY SYSTEM

Apart from the above-mentioned control measures, and independently of the Air Pollution Control Law and other similar legislation, the Compensation Law imposed a levy on SO_x emissions, naturally leading to assertions that it provided an incentive effect with regard to SO_x reduction. Here, the structure of the CL levy system is briefly considered.

3.1   Overview of the CL Framework

First, the overall framework established by the Compensation Law as the CL framework is examined. In addition, since all new certification of air pollution health victims was halted in 1988, the present research focuses primarily on the period prior to this extensive legislative revision.[2]

The structure of the CL framework is illustrated in Figure 10.2; air pollution problems are relevant to Class 1 areas.[3] The CL framework essentially provided for the collection of levies from SO_x-emitting installations (accounting for 80 per cent of CL-related disbursements) and a certain supplementary amount from motor vehicle tonnage taxes (furnishing the remaining 20 per cent of disbursements), utilizing this pool of funds to compensate certified sufferers. In designating certified sufferers, the CL specified regions ('designated areas') where frequent occurrences of illness

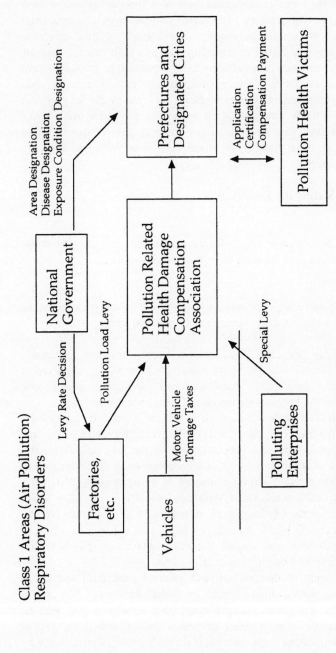

Class 1 Areas (Air Pollution)
Respiratory Disorders

Class 2 Areas (Water Pollution)
Minamata Disease, etc.

Note: In class 2 areas, compensation has generally been arranged through direct agreements between enterprises and victims or groups of victims.

Figure 10.2   Compensation Law framework

resulting from significant air pollution had occurred. When a person exposed to air pollution in the home or workplace beyond a specified period of time ('minimum exposure requirements') contracted chronic bronchitis, bronchial asthma, asthmatic bronchitis, pulmonary emphysema, or their sequelae ('designated diseases'), a causal relationship between such diseases and air pollution was systematically established. Compensation amounts were decided in advance, and the levies were collected in order to provide the funds necessitated by compensation payments. Here, the case of the levy system with regard to pollutants from stationary sources is presented. Such levies were imposed on those facilities releasing maximum gas emissions over a certain threshold, and the number of installations from which levies were collected was between 8000 and 9000 annually.

3.2 Method of Setting the Levy Rate

Basic structure

The levy rate is defined as amount of levy paid versus unit SO_x emissions (yen/Nm^3). The conceptual formula for setting the levy rate is:

> levy rate =
> anticipated compensation disbursements in t fiscal year/amount of nationwide SO_x emissions in $(t-1)$ calendar year

During $(t-1)$ fiscal year, the Environment Agency projects anticipated disbursements in t fiscal year from past data, had major SO_x emitters report their emissions records for the $(t-1)$ calendar year, estimated total emissions accordingly and set the levy rate by the end of $(t-1)$ fiscal year.

The foremost feature of this framework is that the express purpose of the levy is to secure the level of funding dictated by compensation requirements, that is, levy receipts are decided first, followed by the levy rate. Next, SO_x emitters do not know at the actual time of emission exactly what the rate will be. Third, levies are not imposed on emissions of nitrogen oxides (NO_x) and other presumably health-deteriorative pollutants. Finally, because the health damage identified by the CL framework is stipulated to be cumulative and irreversible, even though health damage in t fiscal year is partly the result of emissions in $(t-2)$ year and earlier, the entire burden of compensation disbursements is imposed on emitters in $(t-1)$ year.

Viewed in the light of the polluter-pays principle, the third and fourth factors cited above place an unfair burden on current emitters of SO_x and, at the same time, the amount of compensation (that is, levies) may well be virtually unresponsive to even major decreases in SO_x emissions. This is accentuated by the fact that compensation is driven by total requests made by applicants, which, as the programme becomes better known over time, is likely to expand. Thus, the amount of stipulated compensation is both independent of current SO$_x$ emissions, and, as suggested by the above-noted first feature of the framework, tends to induce expansion of the levy rate (see Figure 10.1).[4]

The converse, however, is that excessive burdens placed on current emitters of SO$_x$ may serve as a deterrent to current SO$_x$ emissions. In general, if the amount of compensation for damage is averaged over polluting emissions, the levy rate becomes lower than the marginal damage cost caused by such emissions (the rate of a Pigouvian tax), thereby inviting a greater than optimal level of pollution (Hamada, 1977, pp. 93–101). However, in case the damage is cumulative and irreversible and the pollution in the past was serious, where total compensation is covered by a levy on current emissions, the levy rate could exceed the Pigouvian tax rate. The fact that at almost 100 per cent of observation points SO$_x$ concentration fell below the national ambient standard by 1980, 93.8 per cent in 1978 FY, 98.9 per cent in 1981 FY, suggests that this is the case for the CL levy. That is, the resulting anti-pollution incentive would function even more strongly than a Pigouvian tax (Figure 10.3). The foregoing line of reasoning is pursued from the standpoint of a Pigouvian tax which takes into account only the damage effected by current emissions in the current period of analysis, but even if a Pigouvian tax oriented towards future damage is considered, in the case of large past emissions, it is possible for the levy rate of a damage compensation system imposed only on current pollutant emissions to be higher than the Pigouvian tax.

Regional differences among levy rates

According to the principle that 'liability for compensation' was incorporated into regulatory reasoning (that is, according to a report by the Central Environmental Pollution Control Council), it was contended that enterprises located in areas designated as having a high incidence of pollution-related health damage should pay at least half of total costs. Levy rates in designated areas were consequently averaged and set at nine times the rate in non-designated areas. However, because reduction rates of SO$_x$ emissions in designated areas were actually higher than in other areas, and because the 'nine times' figure was not adjusted, the share of the total burden borne by enterprises in designated areas fell below 50 per cent from fiscal 1979. When the law was subsequently revised, the share paid by enterprises in designated areas fell to about one third.

Differences in levy rates were established not only between designated and non-designated areas, but among designated areas as well. This was because, following implementation of the regulatory framework, sharp differentials appeared among designated areas in terms of the ratio between SO$_x$ emission

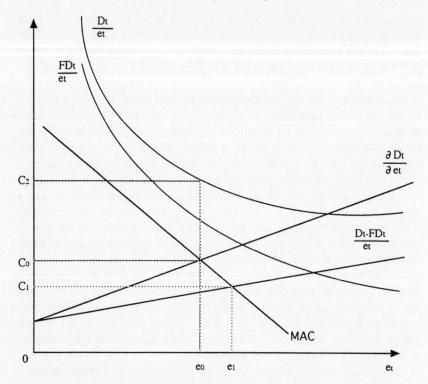

e_t : amount of SOx emissions during period t

D_t : monetary amount of damage inflicted during period t

FD_t : monetary amount of damage inflicted during period t, caused by SOx emissions in the past and current/past other pollutions emissions, that is $FD_t=D_t$ ($e_t=0$). The value is exogenous to Figure 10.3

MAC : marginal abatement cost of SOx emissions

e_0 : efficient amount of SOx emissions

C_0 : Pigouvian tax rate

C_1 : damage compensation levy rate in effect for damage inflicted during period t, that is D_t-FD_t additionally caused by et.

C_2 : damage compensation levy rate in effect for D_t

Note: Pigouvian tax rate C_0 attains efficient amount of SO_x emissions e_0. When the damage is caused only by current SO_x emissions, if the amount of compensation for damage is averaged over current SO_x emissions, the damage compensation levy rate C_1 becomes lower than C_0 which entails more amount of SO_x emissions e_1 than e_0. But if the damage is not caused only by current SO_x emissions but also SO_x emissions in the past and current/past other pollutant emissions, and if damage compensation levy was imposed only on current SO_x emissions, the levy rate for emission level e_0, C_2, can become higher than C_0. In Figure 10.3, FDt is assumed very large and Dt/et curve does not intersect and always comes over MAC curve. This means that the levy system always lacks in revenue to meet what is needed for compensation at any level of the levy rate. But the Japanese CL levy system actually imposes levy not on e_t but on e_{t-1}, which cannot be changed during *t* period, so it cannot happen theoretically aside from the problem of disbursements projection and it has not happened empirically. Nonetheless the shape of Dt/et curve suggests that if SO_x emissions are reduced for any reason, the CL levy rate inevitably becomes higher.

Figure 10.3   Damage compensation levy rate versus Pigouvian tax

levels and compensation amounts and differing rates were required in order to rectify inter-area inequities.

As can be seen from the foregoing, levy rates were basically decided according to the need for funds, with adjustments made to allocate the burden between stationary and mobile sources of emissions and among various areas. It is theoretically possible for levy rates to be higher than the corresponding Pigouvian tax, but solving the question of whether or not the implemented levy rates provided an anti-pollution incentive to enterprises requires independent empirical analysis.

4.   THE POLLUTION REDUCTION EFFECT OF THE CL LEVY

In determining if the CL levy system did, in fact, create an incentive effect, it is necessary to compare the levy rates and marginal abatement costs of SO$_x$ emissions. Cost schedules that evaluate each SO$_x$ reduction method are required in order to do so, but this kind of data is extremely difficult to obtain. Thus, as a practical measure, our consideration is limited to thermal power plants in Osaka Prefecture, one of the most densely populated areas of Japan.

4.1   A Case Study of Thermal Power Plants in Osaka Prefecture

Reasoning supporting case selection

Viewed by industry, electric power generation is the largest producer of SO$_x$, accounting for over 30 per cent of emissions. Even within designated areas, where the steel industry is the leading emitter, electric power ranks second with about 20 per cent of emissions. Thus, consideration of reductions in SO$_x$ emissions achieved by the electric power industry provides a reasonable picture of the overall situation. Also, given the nature of the participating enterprises as public utilities, and specifically because the Osaka Prefectural Government and Kansai Electric Power Corporation (the regional electric utility) have concluded a pollution control agreement, required data on estimated costs is more readily available than for other industries and areas, thereby allowing a more detailed analysis.

The relationship between pollution control agreements and total pollutant load controls

The pollution control agreement between Osaka Prefecture and Kansai Electric Power was concluded in May 1974, and it originally specified annual SO$_x$, annual NO$_x$, and daily SO$_x$ emissions limitations, as well as sulphur content of fuel, amount of fuel used and the utilization rate of generating plants. The thermal efficiency of the power plants did not change to a significant degree, but, because the agreement did take efficiency into account, limitations on fuel use and plant utilization rates served as a proxy from the standpoint of emissions. Additionally, since maximum permitted SO_x emission is the product of maximum permitted fuel use and maximum permitted sulphur content, the specified emissions targets are automatically achieved so long as fuel use and sulphur content limits are carefully adhered to. The agreement was modified in March 1980, eliminating fuel use (and, practically speaking, utilization rate) limits for plants equipped with denitration stack-scrubbers. However, other control values specified by the agreement, even at their weakest in fiscal 1975 (the first year of implementation), were stricter than subsequently adopted total pollutant load controls, and were actually tightened over time.

The SO_x emissions reduction record at thermal plants in Osaka prefecture
Kansai Electric Power consistently adhered to the agreement, and has since reduced its SO_x emissions. Such reductions are generally considered to be achieved at thermal power plants by reducing the amount of electricity generated, improving thermal efficiency (that is, energy savings), using low-sulphur content fuel, and/or installing desulphurization stack-scrubbers. Total power generated by Kansai Electric increased over the period under consideration, but most of the increase can be attributed to nuclear power plants. Although nuclear plants raise issues apart from air pollution, it cannot be denied that their use holds down increases in SO_x emissions. However, the decision to move towards nuclear power generation is preferentially influenced by energy policy independent of strategies for air pollution reduction. For the purposes of simplification, therefore, SO_x reduction measures are considered by taking the volume of electricity generated at each thermal plant as given.[5] The period of analysis is for the years after 1975, for which data is available.

Of the above-noted SO_x-cutting methods, energy savings at individual existing plants (improvement of thermal efficiency) is technically difficult, leaving low-sulphur content fuel and desulphurization stack-scrubbers as realistic options. The respective costs of SO_x reduction for these two methods are then weighed. Figure 10.4 shows the relationship between SO_x emissions and cost (converted to cost per kl of heavy oil) faced in fiscal 1975 by the area's largest thermal generating plant, Sakaikou Power Station.[6] It can readily be seen that SO_x reductions bring about increased costs, and, as a profit-motivated enterprise, Kansai Electric could be expected to implement the least expensive method of reaching targeted emissions levels. According to Figure 10.4, if desulphurization stack-scrubbers are not installed, C heavy oil only can be used for a level of SO_x between 10.8 and 18.9 [Nm^3/kl], a mixture of

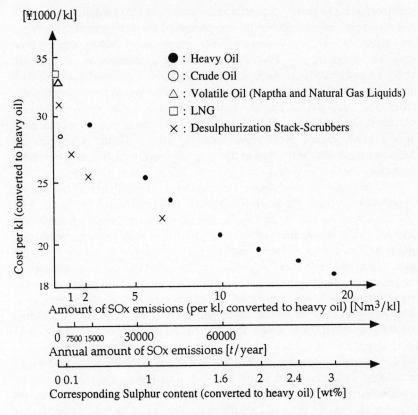

[¥1000/kl]

● : Heavy Oil
○ : Crude Oil
△ : Volatile Oil (Naptha and Natural Gas Liquids)
□ : LNG
✕ : Desulphurization Stack-Scrubbers

Amount of SOx emissions (per kl, converted to heavy oil) [Nm³/kl]

Annual amount of SOx emissions [*t*/year]

Corresponding Sulphur content (converted to heavy oil) [wt%]

Notes
1. Heavy oil is for July–September 1975 (Nippon Oil, prices for electric power companies), taken from the 1984 edition of *Oil Price Statistics*.
2. Crude oil, volatile oil and LNG represent the average FY1975 purchase price paid by Kansai Electric Power, taken from the 1980 edition of *The Current State of KEP*.
3. Efficiency of 90 per cent is assumed for desulphurization stack-scrubbers. Cost schedule of desulphurization stack-scrubbers was estimated based on FY1985 *Report on Smoke and Soot Control Technology* prepared by the Japan Industrial Equipment Association.

Figure 10.4   SO$_x$ emissions and costs at Sakaikou power station (FY1975)

C heavy oil and crude oil for between 0.63 and 10.08 [Nm³/kl], and a mixture of LNG and crude oil for between 0 and 0.63 [Nm³/kl]. When the option of desulphurization stack scrubbers is considered, C heavy oil alone (without scrubbers) can be used to achieve emissions of between 12.6 and 18.9 [Nm³/kl], C heavy oil with partial installation of scrubbers for 1.89 to 12.6 [Nm³/kl], and low-sulphur fuel with full installation of scrubbers for 0.63 to

1.89 [Nm^3/kl]. The pollution control agreement called for a sulphur (S) content of 0.16 wt per cent (1.0 [Nm^3/kl]), and an annual average level of 0.15 wt per cent (0.95 [Nm^3/kl], or total annual SO$_x$ emissions of 5440t) was, in fact, achieved.[7] It can be seen from Figure 10.4 that a combination of crude oil, heavy oil and volatile oil (such as naptha and natural gas liquids – not LNG) in the ratio of 97:3:0 (heat generation comparison) would be the least costly alternative, and this is roughly matched by the actual ratio of 77:17:7 (rounded) that was adopted. Desulphurization stack-scrubbers would have been a viable choice given these levels of emissions, but it appears the decision had already been taken at this point to convert to LNG, thus obviating the future need for scrubbers.

Constructing a marginal abatement cost curve according to Figure 10.4, we arrive at Figure 10.5; the level of SO$_x$ emissions determined by the CL levy rate (the following year's rate versus relevant emissions) was 15 [Nm^3/kl], as opposed to the achievement of actual emissions of 0.95 [Nm^3/kl] between r_2 and r_4 in Figure 10.5, showing that the CL levy played no role at all in the reduction of SO$_x$ emissions.[8] Accordingly, the reductions must be attributed to the pollution control agreement. Given certain periods of full plant utilization, the maximum daily emissions level (10-day average) set by the agreement is more stringent than the annual level, and the achieved level of 21.1 [t/day] (or 0.63 [Nm^3/kl]) was under the agreed level of 22.6 [t/day] (or 0.67 [Nm^3/kl]).

CL levy rates subsequently rose, but the analysis for the same (Sakaikou) installation yields the same result in 1980, with Figure 10.6 illustrating the relationship between the amount of SO$_x$ emissions and costs. As can be gleaned from Figure 10.6, the price of virtually non-sulphur LNG is below that of other fuels.[9] The use of LNG alone allows cost-minimization, and also leads to minimization of SO$_x$ emissions (this state of affairs has persisted up to the present). In this case, neither total pollutant load controls nor the pollution control agreement have any bearing on the reduction of SO$_x$ emissions. In fact, however, a mix of about 70 per cent LNG with the remainder made up of crude and heavy oil was used; because of the nature of long-term LNG contracts, there are limits on the amounts that can be used. Without such limits, similar curves could be constructed for other plants, all of which would be using 100 per cent LNG. However, this is not the case, as dictated by energy source diversification policy and difficulties in locating LNG storage facilities.

Thus, let us examine the case of oil-fired thermal plants which are both located in the same designated area and which do not use LNG. None of the three such plants found use crude oil, which contains relatively little sulphur and is comparatively inexpensive. Instead, all three exclusively rely on heavy oil, meaning that the marginal abatement costs of SO$_x$ emissions are high and

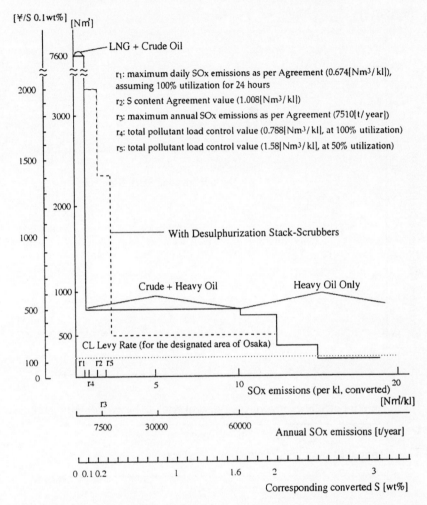

Note: Total pollutant load control values for r$_4$ and r$_5$ were not yet in force. The FY1975 utilization rate was 48.7 per cent.

Figure 10.5   SO$_x$ marginal abatement cost at Sakaikou power station (FY1975)

that the CL levy should not have had any effect as of 1980. Conditions changed in 1983, however, in that price differentials shrank among heavy oils with differing sulphur content. Figure 10.7 represents the marginal abatement cost curve for one of these plants, known as the Sanpou Generating Station. The annual average sulphur content of fuel was specified in the pollution

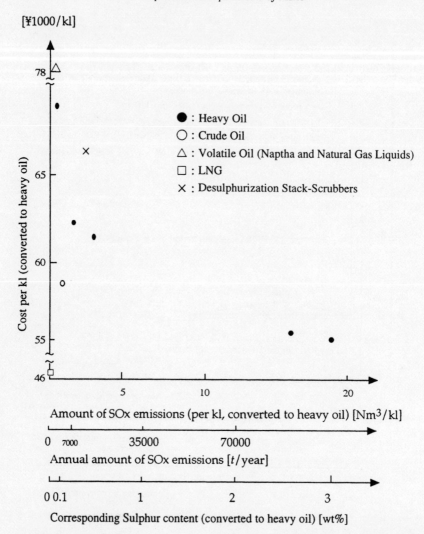

[¥1000/kl]

Figure 10.6   SO$_x$ emissions and costs at Sakaikou power station (FY1980)

Notes
1. Heavy oil is for July–September 1980 (Nippon Oil, power generation basis), taken from the 1984 edition of *Oil Price Statistics*.
2. Crude oil, volatile oil and LNG represent the average FY1980 purchase price paid by Kansai Electric Power, taken from the 1985 edition of *The Current State of KEP*.
3. Same assumption for desulphurization stack-scrubbers as in Figure 10.4.

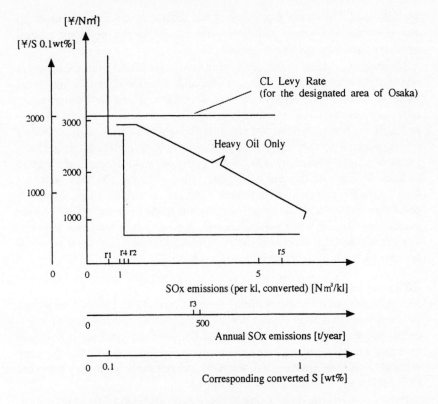

r$_1$: maximum daily SOx emissions as per Agreement (0.63[Nm³/ kl]),
     assuming 100% utilization for 24 hours

r$_2$: S content Agreement value (1.26[Nm³/ kl])

r$_3$: maximum annual SOx emissions as per Agreement (470[t/ year])

r$_4$: total pollutant load control value (1.17[Nm³/ kl], at 100% utilization)

r$_5$: total pollutant load control value (5.83[Nm³/ kl], at 20% utilization)

Note: The FY1983 utilization rate at the Sanpo Power Station was 15.1 per cent. The price of C heavy oil for power generation is for April–December 1983, taken from the 1989 edition of *Oil Price Statistics*.

Figure 10.7   SO$_x$ marginal abatement cost at Sanpou power station (FY1983)

control agreement as 0.2 wt per cent (1.3 [Nm³/kl]), while a level of 0.12 wt per cent (0.76 [Nm³/kl], or SO$_x$ emissions of 110 t/year) was actually achieved between r_1 and 1 in Figure 10.7. There is a possibility, then, that the CL levy did provide a reduction incentive effect, although one reason for this is that the plant is small-scale (only 8 per cent of the generating capacity of Sakaikou) and is subject to looser standards with regard to the pollution control agreement and total pollutant load controls.

Meanwhile, a plant located in a more rural part of the prefecture, where regulatory standards on total pollutant load control are loose, control agreement values are strict, and, because the area is non-designated for Compensation Law purposes, the CL levy rate is low, there is no indication that the CL levy provided any pollution reduction effect. In the end, consideration of individual power generating plants suggests that SO_x reductions at thermal plants in Osaka Prefecture were essentially due to the pollution control agreement and to relative declines in the price of LNG. Basically, the CL levy was not responsible for a significant pollution reduction effect, although there is a possibility that the levy did come into play due to the narrowing of price gaps among fuels with differing sulphur content, in a case where both total pollutant load control and the effected pollution control agreement had weak influence because the scale of the plant in question was small.

Effects on small and medium enterprises

Assuming the same features resulting from the formula deciding CL levy rates as noted in section 3, and given that large-scale producers reduced their SO_x emissions, there is a possibility that the CL levy did generate a pollution reduction incentive among small and medium enterprises located in the same areas as large-scale emitters and, therefore, subject to the same levy rates, but facing relatively less stringent direct controls.

Before concluding, then, a case in the vicinity of Osaka City is examined. The minimum scale for application of regulatory standards for total pollutant load control in this area is defined as a rated fuel consumption of 0.8 [kl/h] (or about 2 per cent of that of the Sanpo Power Station), equivalent to an approximate gas emissions level of 9400 [Nm³/h]. This level is well above the 5,000 [Nm³/h] maximum gas emissions threshold for required payment of the CL levy and is, therefore, within the range of consideration of the CL levy rate incentive effect. The minimum scale for application of the regulatory standards for total pollutant load control is 1.65 [Nm³/h] (or 2.06 [Nm³/h]) for Osaka City and Sakai City, and 2.48 [Nm³/h] (or 3.1 [Nm³/h]) for other municipalities in the prefecture. Desulphurization stack-scrubbers are comparatively expensive for operations on this scale, and the main anti-SO_x measure consists of fuel choice (C heavy oil, A heavy oil or kerosene). Constructing a SO_x abatement cost curve as with large-scale power plants (Figure 10.8), it appears that the levy did not play a role in 1975, but that a SO_x emissions reduction incentive became manifest in 1980 as a result of narrowing price gaps among fuels with differing sulphur content and of higher levy rates. The situation appears to be the same after 1980 as well.

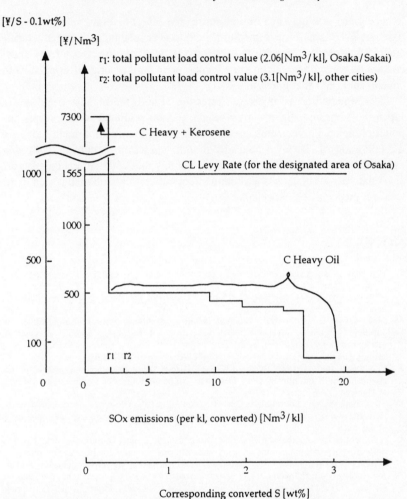

Figure 10.8   SO$_x$ marginal abatement cost for small/medium-sized enterprises (FY1980)

5.   CONCLUSION

For electric power generating plants in Osaka Prefecture, the main factor inducing reductions in SO$_x$ emissions was not the CL levy but direct controls, especially those controls stemming from the pollution control agreement concluded with the regional electric utility. However, the anti-pollution incentive effect of the CL levy cannot be completely ignored, as it does appear to have come into play in a limited sense. The effect is found to increase over time *vis-à-vis* small- and medium-scale power plants and manufacturing enterprises which are subject to relatively weaker direct controls, under conditions where there are ongoing narrow price gaps among differing sulphur content fuels and rising levy rates.

CL designated areas in Osaka Prefecture feature the highest levy rates in Japan, but, because direct controls such as total pollutant load controls and pollution control agreements are also quite strict, there is not much scope for the operation of CL levy-induced pollution reduction incentives. However, even in areas where levy rates are somewhat low, but where direct controls are also relatively weak, an anti-pollution effect rather greater than that seen in the Osaka region may be expected.

NOTES

* This chapter is a revised and translated version of the chapter entitled 'Kokenhou-fukakin (Compensation Law load levy)' which is Chapter 4 of the book, Ueta, K., T. Oka and H. Niizawa (eds) (1997), *Economics of Environmental Policy*, Nihon-Hyoron, pp. 79-96 (in Japanese).

1. Other causal factors in SO_x reduction include government assistance programmes for pollution prevention investment such as policy-tied financing, special depreciation, accelerated depreciation, but, in the case of the steel industry for example, the effect of subsidy policies is deemed to have been slight. See Matsuno (1997a, b).

2. Here, only the functions of the CL levy system are considered. An outline of the establishment of and influences on the system will be the subject of a future study, but refer to Matsuno (1996).

3. The Compensation Law stipulates Class 1 (air pollution) and Class 2 (water pollution) areas. Here, the discussion is limited to the levy system for the former. For more on the composition of the system, see Kido (1975).

4. A straightforward comparison of similar sorts of system in other countries is complicated by differing purposes behind the systems and differing country conditions. For reference, however, if tax (or similar instrument) rates on SO_x emissions and sulphur content in fuel are comparatively aligned with CL levy rates (unitized as [¥/SO_2-kg]), Sweden has a sulphur tax rate of 339 (1991), Norway has a sulphur tax rate of 299 (1988), France has an air pollutant emissions surcharge rate of 3-4 (1985-90) and the USA has an average SO_2 emissions permit price of 17 (1994), 12 (1995). Meanwhile, Japan has rates of 741-1877 (for designated areas, as of 1987) and 110 (for non-designated areas, 1987); levy rates in CL-designated areas can be seen to be quite high compared to charges in other countries. Figures for Sweden, Norway and France are from Ishi (1993); for the USA from *The New York Times*, 1996, March 23, p. 35; and for Japan from the Kankyo-Cho [Environment Agency] (1994). Yen exchange rate conversion is according to arbitrated and standard rates of exchange in The Bank of Japan (1996), *Economic Statistics Annual 1995 Edition*.

5. This sudden fall of LNG prices is mainly due to the introduction of Indonesian LNG in 1977 based on the long-term contract between KEP and an Indonesian public corporation and does not imply a radical fall in international prices for LNG.

6. There is, of course, the issue of the allotment of power generation among power stations, but it is assumed that this issue was decided upon without particular regard to anti-SO_x measures, given thermal efficiency of each power station and the prices of fuel consumed there.

7. Here, cost is the sum of the cost of fuel and the cost of desulphurization (when desulphurization stack-scrubbers are installed). The cost in cases where low-sulphur fuel is

used is represented for various fuel types (according to sulphur content) converted to price per kl of heavy oil. With regard to reductions in emissions of SO$_x$ by means of desulphurization, the cost was calculated based on the sequential introduction of desulphurization stack-scrubbers at the eight generation units of Sakaikou Power Station, together with change-over to low-sulphur fuel. It was thereby found that the least costly method of reaching specified emissions targets was as follows. Desulphurization stack-scrubbers were needed when SO$_x$ emissions of under 12.6 [Nm^3/kl] were required. Desulphurization stack-scrubbers are introduced for each unit sequentially, equipped units using 3 wt per cent C heavy oil and non-equipped units using 2 wt per cent C heavy oil. After all units had been fitted with scrubbers, lower-sulphur than 3 wt per cent C heavy oil fuel is introduced for equipped scrubbers. This was found to be the most cost-effective procedure. In Figure 10.4 (number of units with desulphurization stack-scrubbers, heavy oil conversion sulphur content of fuel, fuel used for equipped unit) from the right (4/8 units, 3 wt per cent, C heavy oil), (8/8units, 3 wt per cent, C heavy oil), (8/8units, 2 wt per cent, C heavy oil), and (8/8units, 1 wt per cent, combination of C heavy oil and crude oil) are represented by the four X points.

8. As the power plant utilization rate (that is, the amount of fuel used) is fixed, annual SO$_x$ emissions and average S content are synonymous.

9. When a line joins the points representing the least costly means of achieving the values for SO$_x$ emissions in Figure 10.4, absolute values for the slopes of the line segments is the vertical axis SO$_x$ marginal abatement cost shown in Figure 10.5. However, within the dotted line labelled 'With desulphurization stack-scrubbers' in Figure 10.5, the section from 1.89–12.6 [Nm^3/kl] is not realized continuously, and only seven points (making the eight segments) can be established. Although emitters cannot tell the following year's rate, as the rate is higher than that of the previous year, the conclusion which rejects the effectiveness of the levy is reinforced.

REFERENCES

Hamada, K. (1977), *Songai baisho no keizai bunseki* [*Economic Analysis of Casualty Compensation*], Tokyo: Tokyo University Press (in Japanese).

Horiuchi, Y. (1995), 'Kigyo no kankyo seisaku' ['Environmental policies of enterprises'] , *Hosei Daigaku Keiei Shirin*, **31** (4), 39–52 (in Japanese).

Imura, H. (1988), 'Iou sankabutsu taiki kankyo kaizen no gen'in kozo ni kan suru kenkyu; osen fuka-ryo fukakin no koka' ['Research on the causative structure of sulphur oxide atmospheric environmental improvement; pollution load levy incentives'], *Kankyo-Kagaku-Kai-Shi*, **1** (2), 115–25 (in Japanese).

Ishi, H. (ed.) (1993), *Kankyo-zei* [*Environment Taxes*], Tokyo: Toyo Keizai Shinpo-sha (in Japanese).

Jesinghaus, V.J. (1988), 'Instrumente der Umweltpolitik: Vergleich Japan/ Bündesrepublik', *Spektrum der Wissenschaft*, February, 43–4.

Kankyo-cho [Environment Agency] (ed.) (1994), *Kogai kenko higai hosho/yobo no tebiki* [*Handbook for the Prevention of and the compensation for Pollution-Related Health Damage*], Tokyo: Shin Nihon Hoki Shuppan (in Japanese).

Kido, K. (1975), *Chikujo kaisetsu Kogai Kenko Higai Hosho Ho* [*A Point by Point Explanation of the Pollution-Related Health Damage Compensation Law*], Tokyo: Gyosei (in Japanese).

Matsuno, Y. (1996), 'Kogai kenko higai hosho seido kakuritsu katei no seiji keizai bunseki' ['Political economic analysis of the process of establishment of the Japanese compensation system of pollution-related health damage'], *Keizai-Ronso* [*The Economic Review*], **157** (5, 6), 51–70 (in Japanese).

Matsuno, Y. (1997a, b), 'Tekko-gyo ni okeru iou sankabutsu haishutsu sakugen he no kakushu kankyo seisaku shudan no kiyo (1) (2)' ['How much were policy instruments effective in reducing sulphur oxides emission by steel mills in Japan? (1) (2)'], *Keizai-Ronso* [*The Economic Review*], **159** (5, 6), 100–20, **160** (3), 19–38 (in Japanese).

Tsukatani, T. (1983), 'Hiyo futan to PPP oyobi inga kankei' ['Cost bearing, PPP and causal relation'], *Kogai Kenkyu* [*Research on Environmental Disruption*], **12** (3), 21–3 (in Japanese).

Weidner, H. (1995), 'Reduction in SO_2 and NO_2 emissions from stationary sources in Japan', in M. Jänicke and H. Weidner (eds), *Successful Environmental Policy: A Critical Evaluation of 24 Cases*, Berlin: Edition Sigma, pp. 145–72.

Weizsäker, E.U. (1994), *Earth Politics*, London: Zed Books.

11. Assessing the efficiency of economic instruments: reforming the French *Agences de l'Eau*

Bernard Barraqué

During the past 30 years, important changes in French water policies have taken place; they are increasingly environmentally oriented. This must be stressed since in France, the environmental issue seems more controversial than in most other European Union (EU) member states. It has often been pointed out that the environment did not have a high priority on the political agenda. However, this is, in fact, a flawed observation. Environmental policies are not marginal, particularly not in their contribution to a significant change in policy styles. For several years now, environmental policy research has been devoted to understanding this relative originality of the French case, and to show how appropriate governance formulas had to be found beyond the traditional liberal public versus private confrontation, despite its particular salience.[1] This can be illustrated through the discussion of the two major characteristics of French water policy, giant water companies operating through delegation rather than privatization, and the *Agences de l'Eau*, which are, in fact, both rooted in a very specific history. In France, environmental policy is relatively weak because environment is largely another word for common property; and common property has a low status in the French constitutional set-up. The *Agences de l'Eau* are notable exceptions, and there is thus a controversy concerning their constitutionality. Focusing on the *Agences de l'Eau* is thus justified, all the more so because recent assessment reports drafted by economists, have criticized the economic inefficiency of the *Agences* and of all French water policy. These developments have generated a controversy on reform of the *Agences de l'Eau*. The issue is: should economists alone assess common property institutions, and what can policy analysts contribute to the discussion?

This section starts with a simple observation: the two specific traits of French water policy are not linked to each other by chance: the levies of the *Agences de l'Eau* are put on water bills, which are collected for the most part by the large private groups who deliver about 80 per cent of drinking water sold in France. The companies then transfer the portion of the bill corresponding to the (small) abstraction levy and to the (bigger) pollution discharge levy to the *Agences*. In turn, aid granted by the *Agences* from the levies collected are often given back to the same companies indirectly, since they also control the public works in the water industry. Some observers contend that this is a typical case of non-transparency, corruption and so on. Others argue, on the contrary, that private companies offer the advantage of concentration, and that they have a strong innovation potential. However, many also argue that public management (direct labour) is necessarily inefficient. Yet, for the policy analyst, the real issue lies beyond this 'public versus private' controversy.

The success of water companies is largely due to the French political system, which relies on fiscal and economic centralization while maintaining the political sovereignty of local authorities. Delegation of local public services provision (that is, privatization of operations but not of infrastructure capital) to private companies has often been the consequence of the financial constraints set by central government on local public accounting. Many towns, and also many suburban independent communes, preferred to contract out services operation to a private company rather than merge it in supra-local joint boards. Strikingly, the result combines a very large number of undertakings with a high degree of concentration of the operators. There remain, however, many small water supply services operated by direct labour, and that is where quality or financing problems tend to occur. Requests for compliance with a growing number of EU standards induce a slow but growing concentration process, in particular under the leadership of the *départements*. Still, very large undertakings operated with direct labour or in mixed economy companies do remain, and they offer a competitive alternative to the private groups. This is a bottom-line explanation for the success of the French model of 'regulation without regulator' (Lorrain, 1995). Since water authorities are small and scattered, while operators are highly concentrated, there should be many cases of capture of the first by the second, and the profits of water companies should be very high. Yet, profits remain much more moderate than in Britain, where there is supposed to be strict control of the privatized water companies by national level regulators (Office of Water Services (OFWAT), Environmental Agency). Lorrain then hypothesizes that the permanent and multiple contracts re-negotiation allows a practical benchmarking. Besides the groups are very sensitive to their image. Thus there is a 'regulation without regulator' superior to the system set up by the British. Contrary to Lorrain, it has been argued that it is difficult to assess the British privatized model after only a short period of existence on the background of the long-term characteristics of investments in the water sector. It has also been argued that, although less visible, central state regulation remains important in France due to the tradition of strict control with the lending and debts of local authorities, but also through the practical unification of the water industry's professional practices under the leadership of the French corps of engineers.

It is difficult to assess the different 'models' of water services provision in Europe, but the British model remains relatively controversial, and the question whether the liberal model, which subjects private provision of public services to public control, is suitable for water policy, needs to be raised. This issue is discussed below in our appraisal of the *Agences de l'Eau*. However, it must be immediately recalled that what is expensive in water services is not water (and this holds all over Europe), but money (that is, interest rates of loans), and also the information needed for a rational policy; in particular, in the present move towards demand-side management. Now that water supply and waste water collection and treatment infrastructures have been built, the future challenge is their long term, sustainable management in a new context where government subsidies have been phased out.

Long term bank loans are needed in water services, but even with rather low interest rates, debt services are very costly[2] and have a potentially serious impact on the water bills; this happens in practice as soon as local authorities undergo a fiscal crisis or have become indebted. If they have to adopt a formula of BOT (build-operate-transfer), the cost of the service will be burdened by the interest rates which private companies have to pay. This is why the 'French model' is sustainable in the long run, operation is privatized and companies are in charge of keeping the infrastructure in good order. However, capital remains in the hands of local authorities, and they have retained the duty to do the investing. This is what is called in French the *affermage* contract; there are BOTs for building or rebuilding sewage works, but this is marginal compared to the costs of maintaining and extending the sewers themselves. Local authorities can more easily get low interest loans or subsidies for investments, and this keeps water prices down. They are even authorized to subsidize investments in water services every time loan reimbursements would bring water prices up to socially unacceptable levels; and, of course, the threshold of unacceptability is not precisely defined. What is needed, then, particularly after the disclosure of some corruption affairs, is more transparency and more accountability to the consumers, but not structural change.

This is also why the revolving fund of the *Agences de l'Eau* is so important: it not only provides incentives to water users to improve their environmental record, but also helps keep water prices from increasing too much despite important investments, since aid is provided at zero interest rate. Yet, this is not necessarily perceived by all economic reviewers, who usually focus on the direct incentive of the levy which generated the fund; and, obviously, the rates of the levies in France, as in many other countries, are too low to provide a polluter-pays-principle (PPP) type of incentive.

THE ISSUE OF THE *AGENCES DE L'EAU*

In 1997 the *Commissariat Général du Plan* (CGP) published an assessment of the *Agences de l'Eau* at the request of both the Ministry of the Environment and the Treasury. The report stirred up a recurrent controversy on the efficiency of the *Agences*, which is not easy to understand for the French, and even less so for other Europeans. Of course, part of the issue was due to rumours that 'the *agences* were failing to deliver'.[3] The report was leaked to the press before publication, and it was published without the usual annexes in which the assessed organizations, that is, the *Agences de l'Eau*, would be offered the opportunity to answer, and on this background the Minister of the Environment, Ms Voynet, proposed a reform of water policy. Yet, the CGP assessment was rather positive, and observers wondered who, through a biased press disclosure, wanted to manipulate its content and why. The authors of the report, who are economists, only contended that the whole system of levies and aids was not as efficient as it could be, since it did not adhere to environmental economics principles, that is, the polluter pays and abstractor pays. The levies are considered too small to provide a proper incentive, and their mode of calculation has become increasingly complex over the years, resulting in an inequitable situation: two neighbouring communes can end up with very different levy rates and it has become difficult for water suppliers to explain this discrepancy to consumers.

The funds of the *Agences de l'Eau* also appear (in the eyes of central government experts) to be spent in a non-transparent manner within communities of water users operating in an overly mutualist way, which should induce irresponsibility. The report suggested that the levies and aid system be operated in a more decentralized manner, in order to induce increased responsibility in water users; to create new levies on diffuse pollution from agriculture and on impervious surfaces (to better tackle nitrates-pesticides and flood control issues); at the request of a minority of policy analysts among a scientific committee consisting of civil servants and economists, it was also proposed to find a legal way out of the unconstitutionality issue (the *Agences* levies are taxes and their budget should, therefore, be annually reviewed by the Parliament. They are now set by the basin boards on a five-year basis, under the sole review of the two ministries mentioned above). On the whole, however, the report stressed the fact that the *Agences de l'Eau* were not the most deficient part of French water policy: the poor level of regulation enforcement by central government services was once again quoted as the most serious problem.

It is no surprise, however, that the government did not hear that part of the message and that the press tried to 'sell papers' through a simplification of the assessment, making the *Agences* the scapegoat. However, from a research point of view, the whole issue repeatedly raises three valid questions: is the system of the *Agences de l'Eau* efficient or not? Should water policy be only (economically) 'efficient'? And if it is, why does the French water policy community refuse to acknowledge that?

GENESIS AND DEVELOPMENT OF THE *AGENCES DE L'EAU*

The answer to these questions makes it necessary to recall a few elements of history of the *Agences*. When they were created, in a 1966 Decree of the 1964 law, the PPP was still an unknown or unpublished economic principle. The model that French water administrators were trying to set up was a combination of British, US and German experiences of integrated river management. They adopted a basically mutualist system with cost recovery principles, that is, a system close to the Dutch *Waterschappen* or the *Ruhr Genossenschaften*, where the users convene and vote both an action programme and the levies they will have to pay to implement this programme. The difference from institutions mentioned above is that the *Agences* are not directly responsible for implementation: at that time, government and local water actors did not want to establish institutions which would be redundant and compete with traditional authorities in charge of building dams, sewers or treatment facilities. Even today, after a renewed debate during the preparation of the 1992 law, the *Agences* do not manage investments directly; they merely fund those who are willing to make investments to improve the environment. The cost recovery principle is then supplemented with some degree of hypothecation: the *Agences* and the basin boards are increasingly unwilling to fund projects which are not good for the environment; for instance, upstream reservoirs supposedly built to protect constructions in flood plains, which is not necessarily efficient, are in many cases more expensive than to remove the constructions from the flood plain; this is also the case with many irrigation projects that dramatically increase the risks of the rivers drying up in summer, while being usually uneconomical. However, since enforcement of water regulations and issuing of permits are not in the hands of the *Agences*, they can only try to persuade water users to increase the level of their efforts through the investments they subsidize. This has resulted in the funding of depollution or summer flow increases rather than reducing discharges or water demand. It was obviously very efficient in the early phases of water environmental policy when everybody agreed on the first investments needed; but it might end up less and less efficient when point source pollution is controlled, thus creating a need for a more sophisticated integrated policy.

The PPP was popularized at the beginning of the 1970s, in particular by Michel Potier and Jean-Philippe Barde at the Organization for Economic Co-operation and Development (OECD), when the *Agences de l'Eau* came into operation. *Agences* were set up by a 1966 decree, but delays in the launch were inevitable: not only was there a need for a preliminary assessment of programmes and funds needed, but water users were initially opposed to the levies. The PPP was then eventually used as a sort of moral argument to force cities and industry to accept playing their part in the basin boards, and thus to pay their share. Later on, the PPP was also used to help convince water users that the rates of levies should be increased. In turn, the *Agences* appeared to be one of the early implementation cases of the PPP, which was later a source of misunderstanding.

The new water policy based on economic incentives managed to overcome the initial oppositions. Indeed, the French association of Mayors had initially rejected that communes should be liable to payment, as being initial abstractors and final polluters (managers of sewer outlets). They argued that their populations were, in fact, responsible. A compromise was reached, with the inclusion of the levies in domestic water and sewerage bills.[4] Premises non-connected to public sewers, which represent an important proportion in a low density country like France, accepted to pay if the total amount of taxes would not be higher than the total amount of taxes in cities. This was a highly efficient political decision, in absence of the information needed to refine the taxation mechanism. Also, the most polluting industrial branches, who argued that varying levels of taxes among the *Agences* would distort competition within the branches, managed to partially escape the system through the development of 'branch contracts' at the national level: the concerned industrial federations would bargain the pace at which premises were to clean up their discharges; the Ministries of Industry and the Environment would then mobilize subsidies, including some of the *Agences* money at national level, in a more favourable arrangement. This policy was condemned by the European Commission as maintaining equal opportunity domestically at the expense of equal opportunity at the European level, and it was, therefore, abandoned. However, it was probably very useful at the beginning to help industry learn about water pollution and economic incentives and make industrial polluters accept the *Agences*. The branch contracts were, however, totally inconsistent with the PPP.

During the 1970s, the *Agences* became more significant because they were able to compensate for the decline in government subsidies to water policy. In addition, this also altered the original principles: initially, the *Agences* were supposed to fund public works in the common interest, not in the private or in the collective interest: that means they could fund sewage works (common interest of the basin) but not sewers (collective interest of the concerned city). However, they soon obtained the possibility to raise more funds through a 'collection multiplier' and an 'urban density multiplier' (applying proportionally to the size of cities), enabling them to fund sewage collection projects. All this happened in a subtle bargaining process between local authorities, the Ministry of the Environment and the rest of central government, in particular the Treasury which would have liked to limit the rise of the *Agences*, as representing a most important tax revenue which escaped its own services.

In the 1980s a socialist government came into power. The new political personnel were distrustful of a system which they tended to associate with the private water companies, and that they had hoped to nationalize, but in vain.[5] They blocked the increase of water prices and the rates of the levies. In 1982, with the law on prevention of natural catastrophies, they chose insurance companies rather than the *Agences* to manage the superfund generated by a compulsory 9 per cent increase of all premiums and so on. This resulted in an increasingly awkward situation, and a crisis in the *Agences* which were stuck with their initial target of point-source pollution control. At the end of the 1980s, the discussions at the European level on the new proposed Directives and the renewed need to push for catchment planning led to the preparation of a new framework law, and thus to a discussion of the new role that the *Agences* were to play.

Still, a reader of the 1992 law will not find a single word on this issue, a fact which indicates a stalemate situation. Opponents to the *Agences* had indeed threatened to mobilize the official statement of the constitutional court, arguing that the *Agences* levies were taxes and thus should be subjected to review by the Parliament. Supporters of the *Agences* had long been accustomed not to formally confront their opponents, and rather to win their skirmishes in the day-to-day bargaining and through the support of the water users in the basin councils. That is to say, they were, and still are, accustomed to playing 'a minor role'. This is fundamentally linked to the weak status of subsidiarity in a centralized political system (Barraqué, 1995; 1997a; 1997b). Water policy actors generally have a positive opinion of the *Agences*, but a majority do not wish to see their role extended. They are afraid to lose their own competencies and powers, and they tend to use the *Agences* as scapegoats for problems that seem to result from what they have not allowed the *Agences* to manage! And this is where some economists are unfortunately useful: they have discovered that the *Agences* do not adhere to the PPP and, therefore, must be inefficient. This is apparent from two documents discussed below.

ARE SUBSIDIARY POLICIES NECESSARILY INEFFICIENT?

The first publication is an article by Yves Martin (1988), who is a respected environmental economist. Engineer in the Corps of Mines, he is one of the founding fathers of the *Agences*, and he was the first director of *Agence de l'Eau Artois-Picardie*. The Ministries of Industry and Environment have charged him with writing various assessments, for example, on groundwater management, and he is well known for his independence of thought. In 1988, when the discussions on the future of the *Agences* began, he took the position that they needed to be modernized. According to Martin the *Agences* are too big, and the levies are, therefore, not sufficiently differentiated (for instance, the problems of Brittany are very different from those of the Loire) which, in turn, diminishes their incentive capacity.

Second, as regards groundwater abstraction and pollution, there was no levy system and, therefore, no incentive policy. The only way to limit the trend towards over-exploitation was to refuse new permits, which implied providing privileges to former permit holders at the expense of economic efficiency. Martin particularly thought of farmers who used to be subsidized by the *Agences* to develop irrigation schemes, although this type of water use was very inefficient compared to most other uses, particularly drinking water. Martin also proposed that there should be a new levy created on those responsible for accidental pollution. He further argued that the *Agences* were 'captured' by water users, providing cheap money for investments that were less and less useful, while not spending anything on making operations more efficient, and on the demand-side issue. All this would be covered by a lack of knowledge of water quality and a reluctance of *Agences* to monitor this quality, and to track responsibilities in the ongoing poor quality of rivers.

Most of these criticisms were not directed towards the *Agences* themselves, but rather the government, and they were and are shared by many water professionals and administrators. However, the paper contains a specific criticism of the *Agences* that is controversial. Martin contends that if the economic incentive tool is not as well-performing as it could be, it is because the levy system is not operating according to the individual responsibility principle, that is, the polluter pays. He claims that the *Agences* have become mutualist or cooperative institutions (and seems to ignore that they have always been cooperatives, in accordance with the initial Ruhr model) and writes that a mutual organization is a tool allowing to externalize internal costs, that is, to transfer individual costs onto others; therefore a mutual organization is an institution which edges out individual responsibility of its members, while the levies should make polluters individually responsible *vis-à-vis* the community. This position is in contrast to the traditional position, that in an investment-focused policy, as in the water sector, there is a permanent need for members of the community to average out the high individual investment costs.

The tradition of community and subsidiarity in water management is prevalent, for example, in the Netherlands, Denmark and Germany, while liberal states with a long tradition of centralization like Britain and France are more at odds with it. So far liberalism has failed to prove its efficiency in environmental policy. In particular, in France, it has been seen how centralization, which was meant to impose the same responsibility rules on all polluters, has induced a specific form of policy-making called cross-regulation: the more stringent the rules imposed on industry or local authorities, the more they will ask for government subsidies or local pass through (Grémion, 1976; Duran and Thoenig, 1996). The case of branch contracts is very illustrative of this state of affairs. Because they exert control a priori, it is more difficult for centralized states to enforce regulation than federal or subsidiary governments, which control a posteriori. Centralized systems end up bargaining in closed policy communities, which is not beneficial to the enforcement side of any policy that is not high on the political agenda (Lascoumes, 1994). It could just as well be argued that the system of the *Agences* does, in fact, not at all edge out individual responsibility, but on the contrary, helps to get out of non-transparent crossed regulation types of policy-making; it helps to learn to live without the state and to develop collective learning processes between users for increased mutual responsibility. The progressive opening of the basin councils to other types of water user (ecologists and consumers) also helps to develop integrated water policies and 'harder' consensus.

In fact, the economic incentives are not used to replace traditional regulations, as assumed in the economic theory, but to supplement them. Besides, after 30 years of collective learning about integrated water management, it appears that it is possible to successfully sue a polluter, even the mayor of a city, for repeated violation of his permit. It was not the case in the 1970s.

Another assessment of the performance of the *Agences de l'Eau* was published by Mikael Skou Andersen (1994), based on a survey conducted in 1992 shortly after the passing of the framework law. Andersen did not find information on the real reasons why the organization of the *Agences* had been 'forgotten' in the law amendments. However, he found statistical information from the OECD compendiums which were eventually provided by the French. The data showed a rather good performance of the policy towards industry, but poor records on sewage collection and treatment by local authorities. After so many FF billion invested in pollution control, only 52 per cent of the French population seemed to live in houses connected to sewage works, which was hardly better than ... East Germany! And this was indeed surprising for a country with leading water industry and institutions. Comments by 'normal' environmental economists tended to confirm the low efficiency of the system of levies in the case of local authorities.

The only problem is that the statistics were misleading, since the actual figures for sewage treatment were not appropriately reported, neither in OECD nor French sources! At the time Andersen came to France, LATTS-ENPC and IFEN (environmental statistics institute) were in the process of analysing some as yet unexploited answers to the communal survey of 1988, acording to which 79 per cent of French people lived in homes connected to sewers, and 70 per cent in homes connected to sewage works. Most of the others will never be connected and remain on decentralized sewerage, since they live in very low density areas. The 1992 law has even made it possible to create local public services for the management of septic tanks, despite the fact that such tanks are private facilities.[6] Even if technological choices have not always been well adapted, the funding mechanism of the *Agences* has made it possible to multiply the number of sewage works by 10,[7] and to almost complete water supply and sewer systems where they were needed. Some problems do remain because the French are the only Europeans that have relied extensively on separate sewers, which were not always carefully designed, and which also imply the development of a specific policy on storm water control (quantity and quality).

Now, observers increasingly find that 'the number of people connected to systems and works' can only be an indicator of very traditional supply-side policies. There is a need for a much more refined set of indicators to assess water policy efficiency, even though assessing performance on many pollution indicators is quite complex. Everybody knows, for instance, that improving records on carbonated and toxic pollution reveals the overfeeding into water bodies of nutrients, and furthermore, that diffuse pollution control requires different policies and source controls.

In fact, the data used by the OECD and other international bodies had not been updated, because of the low institutional status of the *Agences*, and because central government monitoring capacities were reduced after the decentralization laws of 1982. However, the fact that nobody checked that the data had remained unchanged since around the 1960s also tends to reveal the ideology of water engineers and economists: they are so easily convinced of the superiority of corporate management over local authorities, which they consider to be congenially inefficient. This is of particular importance, since local authorities remain in charge of water services everywhere in Europe, except in England and Wales. The British regionalization and privatization is probably adapted to the situation of water stress experienced there but, as a model, it also appears to have been appraised without sufficient precaution by a liberal world under neo-marginal economics influence. On the continent, there is no particular reason to get rid of local authorities' responsibilities in water systems, provided that appropriate averaging-out schemes are designed to solve the problem resulting from the impact of investments on water bills.

THE NEED FOR COMMON PROPERTY ECONOMICS

The explanation above may be stated in another way: the French system of *Agences* is efficient because it relies simultaneously on the levies system and on the basin councils. However, the model can only be efficient in the long term. If one or the other component were taken alone, as often performed in countries trying to imitate the so-called 'French model', it will not work due to the lack of a learning process. A basin council without economic incentives or powers is bound to 'talk policy'; an incentive mechanism without a users' board will eventually turn technocratic, and Treasury people will be tempted to merge the funds raised with the general budget. Conversely, having the two together ensures that the levy system will hesitate between cost recovery and hypothecation in favour of the environment, depending on the type of learning and consensus reached between members of the community (soft or hard). However, the level of levies will probably never reach the PPP incentive.

There are several reasons for this, as explained by Colin Green, a socio-economist working at Middlesex University in London. In a paper on economic instruments for water pollution control, written in response to a consultation by the DETR, the British Ministry in charge of the Environment, Green (1998) argues that the underlying assumptions for applying Pigouvian taxes are not met in the case of water: natural monopoly means that the assumption of a perfect competitive market is far away. Economic valuation cannot catch all the dimensions of the value of environmental assets (and this is a recurrent problem for contingent valuation methods). Marginal costs and benefits and the cost of pollution abatement need to be knowable and known in order for economic incentives to perform better than regulation. However, investments are made in a long-term perspective, and they are very heavy. Marginal costs are, therefore, not significant and difficult to know with any degree of certainty due to the permanent change of context and innovation: 'it has been argued (Green, 1997), that efficiency is a wild goose chase, in that pollution abatement requires long term capital investment; so that, by the time the investment has been made, both the marginal costs and the marginal benefits of pollution abatement have changed' (Green, 1998).

In order to correctly levy a Pigouvian tax, there is a need for much more accurate information on the state of rivers and pollution discharges. The required monitoring system is very costly, and probably more costly than the revenue potential of the information! This is also the case at the level of water supply: while it is theoretically efficient and equitable to have separate meters for each home, the fact is that the inelasticity of indoor water use and the cost of metering renders the extra information provided by individual meters more expensive than sharing one meter between several neighbours,[8] even for those who consume the least. And, for social reasons, it is impossible to raise water prices to the point where there would be elasticity. Conversely, since the price is largely determined by the investments, a successful campaign on water saving by users will often have a short-term negative consequence, that is, to raise the unit price for the sake of the supplier being able to reimburse the loans! Only in the long run will a water saving strategy pay, which implies educating the consumers so they understand the sophistication of the situation in which they are placed.

The transaction costs are thus too high for either traditional regulation or economic incentives to succeed. Put another way, saying water is common property and, therefore, requires common property institutions, so as to first lower the transaction costs through a learning process. For the same reasons, Green is dubious about privatization of water rights and considers tradable permits are bound to fail in the case of water: privatization of water resources makes their subsequent reallocation difficult, which was the very goal of the policy. Not enough traders have a stake, in contrast to the case of air pollution. In another paper, which is part of a previous Eurowater research, the history of water law and institutions in Europe was analysed, and it was found that the member states had something in common beyond the variation of their situations (Correia, 1998). At least some of the water is considered common property, and the traditional state regulation, planning and permit systems, which were 'top-down', are increasingly supplemented, not by the affirmation of private property rights, but by the development of subsidiary and community-type water institutions at regional or basin level, in order to generate 'bottom-up' decision-making processes. The state still has a role to play, but it is more that of warranting the democratic character of water sharing between water users than the one of mastering the resource (Burchi, 1991). The days of big hydraulic works are gone, and water management is 'a natural case for cooperation' (Green and Tunstall, 1998).

The evolution of French water policy in the last 30 years fits into the general European evolution towards complex water services structures and water resource management. Both at the level of public services provision and water rights, the ancient policy structure contrasting 'public' and 'private' is giving way to a more 'community-based' approach. The delivery of water services within an environmental approach requires the development of complex links between elected representatives, operators and the public (which must participate to reduce the crises of systems). As regards water resources, a new structuration appears which balances contractual, bottom-up and consensual approaches to integrated water management on the one hand, and a generalized permits and regulation system at the national level, on the other. This will hopefully maintain a balance between efficiency and equity in water management, without neglecting constitutional principles: *égalité des citoyens devant la loi et devant les charges publiques.*

However, French water policy-makers need to take one more step towards the acceptance of subsidiarity, advocacy coalitions and policy networks (Sabatier and Jenkins Smith, 1993; Bressers *et al.*, 1995; Le Gales, 1995). They also need to find appropriate solutions to the development of land use based water policies, which have so far been limited by the traditionally strong confrontation between state and private property. It is argued that the incentive mechanisms of the *Agences* could be used to help develop compensation mechanisms for land use easements, which are traditionally not accepted by the government; zoning entails no compensation, which makes land use control difficult: *L'État est au dessus des citoyens, mais la propriété privée est bien défendue.*

The most recent project to modernize water policy thus appears disappointing: rather than modernizing and developing the *Agences de l'Eau* system, in particular in the field of diffuse pollution, it seeks to take money from the *Agences* to subsidize the government itself! For many years now, the aim of the Ministry of the Environment has been to fund a better enforcement of water regulations; however, in a 'Maastricht criteria' budget control context where small ministries have less access to money or staff, the Ministry of the Environment is tempted to take something away from the *Agences*. In the context of Agenda 21, a general ecotax reform[9] was put on the table, but instead of creating a green tax on energy or fuel and gas for vehicles, the outcome of the bargaining between the Ministry of Environment and the Treasury was that all existing levies on solid wastes (toxic, special and household), noise from aircraft and so on, have been taken away from the direct management by ADEMEs,[10] and is to be screened first by the ministries of Environment and Finances.[11] And the levies of the *Agences de l'Eau* were supposed to be included, starting in 1999.

Other provisions in this project seem to indicate a recentralizing trend. This is why there is indeed a raging controversy about the proper assessment of *Agences de l'Eau* efficiency. All basin councils have expressed a clear opposition to the project and have, of course, been quite ironical *vis-à-vis* this strange wedding between a green minister and the Treasury. Water policy analysts and economists have organized meetings and conferences to discuss the *Commissariat Général du Plan's* report on the *Agences*, and have disclosed elements of proof that the existing levies and aids system was, in fact, having a real incentive effect (*Académie de l'eau*, 1998). However, the momentum for constructive reform of the *Agences* has apparently been lost, and the most realistic outcome is that they will be maintained unaltered, without the desirable elements of efficiency improvement.

Such an outcome could be considered a 'policy lesson' for academic economists, who have challenged water policies and advocated that the efficiency of the *Agences* be improved through further decentralization and economic rationality based on individual responsibility (the PPP). A Ministry of Finance and a government can choose to misinterpret such recommendations, and on basis of claims that water policy is inefficient and inequitable, they, in fact, chose to implement a policy that goes exactly the other way, essentially because it better fits the sovereign interests of such a Ministry.

The strongest and apparently most legitimate government argument is that French citizens pay very different water bills and that, for equity reasons, there should be an averaging out mechanism at the national level ... but only between water supplies. But this social decision is controversial, because it would lead to the subsidising of inefficient undertakings by efficient ones. Besides, and worse, one of the reasons why water bills rise is that there are non-transparent transfers in favour of industrial premises connected to public sewers and, of course, towards agriculture, via fertilizers' and pesticides' removal. The *Agences* were in the process of making these tranfers more transparent and to organize learning and bargaining processes. They were only blocked by the unwillingness of the government to create new levies, in particular on diffuse pollution from agriculture. The present policy controversies will probably not help water users to better understand why their water bills are rising and may, in fact, increase their feeling of distrust towards water services and their pricing.

NOTES

1. This study is, in fact, the result of several years of confrontation between the water policies of the various member states in Europe. In particular, insight has been gained through the Eurowater project. Eurowater is the name of this research partnership funded by DG XII, LAWA in Germany, the NRA in Britain, the French *Agences de l'Eau* and the Gulbenkian foundation in Lisbon. The partners were Tom Zabel and Yvonne Rees of the WRc in England; Jan Wessel and Erik Mostert in River Basin Administration Centre in Delft T.U. (the Netherlands); R. Andreas Kraemer and his colleagues at Ecologic, an environmental policy consultancy in Berlin; my team within LATTS, a social sciences laboratory at the Ecole Nationale des Ponts et Chaussées; under the leadership of Francisco Nunes Correia, hydrology and environmental policy professor at Lisbon's civil engineering faculty. The results of the first two years of research are published at Balkema, Rotterdam, and a second phase, Water 21, has just been finished, with the same teams.
2. In a review of some 60 different sewerage services of small and medium-size cities (Alexandre and Grand d'Esnon, 1998), water engineers involved in auditing procedures have shown that the average production cost was around FF8/m^3, consisting of FF4 for amortization costs, FF3 for operation costs, and FF1 for interest rates. However, they

hypothesize that, if all the reviewed infrastructure had been built without subsidies, but financed by 30-year-long loans at 5 per cent interest, the debt services would now amount to FF8/m³, which would quasi-double the price of the service. Their model, of course, could and should be refined, but it can already clearly be understood why local authorities support the *Agences de l'Eau*. In all member states in northern Europe, cost recovery is now more or less the rule. However, everybody tacitly considers that the initial investment, which was indeed subsidized, does not have to be repaid. Imposing the full cost pricing onto southern member states, where initial investment is still going on, would not only be unacceptable to the people served; it would be unfair compared to the northerners.

3.   *'La faillite d'une politique'* was a subtitle in a one-page article in *Le Monde*, 14 November 1997.

4.   The result is that French domestic water users pay the water levies via their bills, but their local authorities are reimbursed with the bonus in proportion to the performance of their sewage works. Some observers think that this should be changed. Many argue that consumer associations should be given more seats in the basin councils.

5.   It must always be recalled that even communist mayors prefer to deal with a private giant group rather than Electricité de France, the state company.

6.   The *Agences* already have budgets to support the improvement of decentralized sewerage. However, they depend on the projects that water users are willing to undertake, and since water professionals, mayors and people everywhere in Europe still massively support classical supply and sewer systems, despite the costs, the *Agences* have followed the general trend.

7.   There are now approximately 14 500 public sewage treatment plants in France, which is the highest figure in Europe, due to the low average population density.

8.   This does indeed correspond to the pragmatic approach to metering in France: all single family homes obviously have a separate meter, since outdoor use is elastic. In small and older condominiums, there is usually one meter for the whole building, and water bills are spread proportionately to the floor area of flats. Large high-rise apartment buildings built after the second World War have individual meters because hot water is metered for each individual flat, and it was not very expensive to install and operate a separate meter for cold water.

9.   In French, *taxe générale sur les activités polluantes* (TGAP).

10.   Agence de l'Environnement et de la Maîtrise de l'Énergie.

11.   Hopefully, the share of the TGAP will be limited to 8 per cent of the *Agences'* budget in the coming five years (to 2005).

REFERENCES

Académie de l'eau (1998), *Les institutions françaises de l'eau à l'épreuve de la théorie économique et de la science politique*, Proceedings of the Conference held in Paris, Cité Universitaire, 18 November 1998. (www.oieau.fr/academie)

Alexandre, Olivier and Antoine Grand d'Esnon (1998), 'Le coût des services d'assainissement ruraux', in *Techniques Sciences Méthodes (TSM-l'eau)*, **7-8**, 19-30.

Andersen, Mikael Skou (1994), *Governance by Green Taxes: Making Pollution Prevention Pay*, Manchester: Manchester University Press.

Barraqué, Bernard (1995), 'Water rights and administration in Europe', in F.N. Correia (ed.), *Water Resources Management in Europe, Institutions, Issues and Dilemmas*, vol. II, Rotterdam: Balkema, 1998, available in German in F.N. Correia and R. A. Kraemer, *Eurowater, Institutionen für Wasserpolitik in Europäische Länder*, vol. II, 1997.

Barraqué, Bernard (1997a), 'Gouverner en réseau en France: les Agences de l'eau', in

Gariépy Michel and Marié Michel (eds), *Ces réseaux qui nous gouvernent?*, Paris: L'Harmattan.

Barraqué, Bernard (1997b), 'Subsidiarité et politique de l'eau', in Alain Faure (ed.), *Territoires et subsidiarité, l'action publique locale à la lumière d'un principe controversé*, Paris: L'Harmattan.

Barraqué, Bernard (1998), 'Aspects institutionnels et juridiques de la gestion durable de l'eau en Europe', in H. Zebidi (ed.), *Water, a Looming Crisis?*, Proceedings of the UNESCO Conference, International Hydrological Programme, UNESCO, Paris.

Bressers, Hans, Larry O'Toole and Jeremy Richardson (eds) (1995), *Networks for Water Policy, a Comparative Perspective*, London: Frank Cass.

Burchi, Stefano (1991) 'Current developments and trends in the law and administration of water resources: a comparative state-of-the-art appraisal', *Journal of Environmental Law*, **3** (1), 69–91.

Commissariat Général du Plan (1997), *Evaluation du dispositif des Agences de l'Eau*, report to the Government, La Documentation Française.

Correia, Francisco Nunes (ed.) (1998), *Selected Issues in Water Resources Management in Europe: Eurowater, vol. II*, Rotterdam: Balkema.

Duran, Patrice and Jean Claude Thoenig (1996), 'L'Etat et l'action publique territoriale en France', in *Revue Française de Science Politique*, Summer, 580–623.

Green, Colin (1957), 'Water, the environment and economics: what does experience teach us so far?', *Canadian Water Resources Journal*, **1** (22).

Green, Colin (1998), 'Economic instruments for water pollution: a response to the DETR consultative paper', Middlesex Flood Hazard Research Centre, 22 pages.

Green, Colin and Sylvia Tunstall (1998), 'Water management: a natural case of cooperation?', in H. Zebidi (ed.), *Water, a Looming Crisis?*, Proceedings of the UNESCO conference, International Hydrological Programme.

Gremion, Pierre (1976), *Le pouvoir périphérique, bureaucrates et notables dans le système politique français*, Paris: Le Seuil.

Lascoumes, Pierre (1989), 'La formation juridique du risque industriel en matière de protection de l'environnement', *Sociologie du travail*, **3**.

Lascoumes, Pierre (1994), *L'écopouvoir, environnement et politiques*, Paris: La Découverte.

Le Gales, Patrick (ed.) (1995), *Les réseaux de politiques publiques*, Paris: L'Harmattan.

Lorrain, Dominique (ed.) (1995), *Gestions urbaines de l'eau*, Paris: Economica.

Martin, Yves (1988), 'Quelques réflexions sur l'évolution des agences de l'eau', *Annales des Mines*, July-August, 117–19.

Sabatier, Paul and Hank Jenkins-Smith (eds) (1993), *Policy Change and Learning: An Advocacy Coalitions Approach*, Boulder, CO: Westview Press.

12. The Danish waste tax: the role of institutions for the implementation and effectiveness of economic instruments*

Mikael Skou Andersen

1. INTRODUCTION

According to the authors of a recent OECD report, 'ex post analysis of the performance of economic instruments in environmental policy is able to provide more firmly-based evidence about key responses affecting the environmental and economic effectiveness of economic instruments than can be obtained on the basis of considering theoretical arguments or ex ante forecasts' (OECD, 1997, p. 32).

Although a number of green taxes and levies have been introduced in Denmark since the mid-1980s, such *ex-post* evaluations of the effectiveness of economic instruments remain rare. Their absence is at least partly explained by methodological and statistical difficulties.

Three previous attempts have been made to evaluate the waste tax. In 1989, only two years after its introduction, the waste consultancy GENDAN produced a mini-evaluation for the Danish Environmental Protection Agency, but it was difficult to draw firm conclusions due to limited implementation experience (Holmstrand *et al.*, 1989). In 1990/91 the Environment Agency itself attempted to produce an evaluation, but apart from a memo to the Parliament's Environment Committee, resources were insufficient (Miljøstyrelsen, 1991a). Finally, in 1992 a research institute was asked to prepare an evaluation, but their report, which was made within a very narrow time frame, suffered from statistical and, to some extent, also methodological shortcomings (Christoffersen *et al.*, 1992).

This chapter summarizes the findings of a comprehensive evaluation of the waste tax prepared for the Environmental Protection Agency in 1996/97 (Andersen *et al.*, 1997). The evaluation covers the period from 1987 to 1996, that is, 10 years, which is sufficient to allow for more firm conclusions. At the same time important statistical problems were clarified. The Environment Agency and the Tax and Customs Agency provided access to their data on the proceeds from the tax, as registered quarterly by individual waste sites. A monitoring group consisting of officials from the two agencies, as well as independent experts, was established to follow the evaluation and to comment on the results. However, the conclusions of the report were drawn independently by the authors who had access to all materials that were deemed to be of relevance to the evaluation, including internal documents of the Environmental Protection Agency and the regional Tax and Customs inspectorates. The research was funded by the Environmental Protection Agency.

Section 2 of this chapter describes the theoretical and methodological approach used in the evaluation. Section 3 presents and explains the design of the waste tax. Section 4 outlines the operation of the waste sector and how prices and tariffs are established. Section 5 assesses the developments in waste quantity on the basis of available statistics, including those of the Tax and Customs Agency. Section 6 provides a brief discussion of the methodological difficulties associated with *ex-post* analysis, in particular the disentangling problem. Section 7 reviews the findings of an in-depth survey among 16 companies and firms in six different sectors. Section 8 summarizes the findings of a survey of Denmark's 277 municipalities and their refuse collection authorities. Section 9 briefly discusses the experiences attained in municipalities using different fee principles, in particular those using weight-based fees. Finally, section 10 offers various conclusions and further research questions.

2.   THE ROLE OF INSTITUTIONS FOR THE EFFECTIVENESS OF ECONOMIC INSTRUMENTS

In theoretical terms, the use of economic instruments for environmental policy is based on the principles of environmental economics (Pearce and Turner, 1990; Baumol and Oates, 1975 [1988]). This discipline is rooted in neoclassical economics, with rather strict assumptions regarding the criteria for Pareto-optimal solutions. Its microeconomic perspective on the utility-maximizing behaviour of firms and individuals assumes that a general equilibrium can be reached.

For reasons that are explained in further detail in Part I of this book, there is a considerable discrepancy between the ideal requirements for the design of economic instruments for environmental policy and the actual designs that are seen in practice. It remains the exception that environmental taxes are based on a valuation procedure[1] and they are often designed under more pragmatic circumstances and employed in a mix with other policy instruments.

Institutions, understood as institutionalized practices of public regulation, may affect the design of economic instruments for environmental policy (Andersen, 1994a).

In this study the implementation experience with such instruments is in focus. It is a well-known shortcoming of environmental economics that it does not treat the interplay between economic instruments and other policy instruments, in particular legal instruments. It may, however, find inspiration in the new institutional economics, associated mainly with North (1990), in order to expand the theoretical horizon of environmental economics without challenging its assumptions too profoundly.

Markets cannot exist or operate without institutions (Coase, 1988). The term 'institutions' can be broadly understood as 'rules'. In the law and economics tradition the focus is on rules for property rights and liability which define the ownership and responsibility of market actors, and on the basis of which transactions take place. The polluter pays principle may be said to assume that responsibility lies with the polluters, while the victim pays principle indicates the opposite. The Coasian focus on property rights is rather narrow and erroneously implies that market failures can be avoided through the assignment of property rights.

According to North there are both formal and informal institutions. The formal institutions are administrative and political institutions and they, in turn, settle the economic institutions. The informal institutions are the history, culture and norms which have been established over time. The merit of formal and informal institutions is that they may reduce transaction costs, both in the economic and the political system, through their established procedures and conventions. By developing certain institutionalized practices, actors can avoid undertaking a complete evaluation of the costs and benefits of every transaction and rely on their standard operating procedures. However, institutions may also cause rigidities. There is a path-dependency between former and present choices, and the framework of present choices may rely on the outcome of choices made in the past.

Economic instruments for environmental policy imply the provision of incentives to market actors. A tax on a polluting activity will give polluters an incentive to reduce their emissions, and it will offer a signal to the consumers to choose products that involve the lowest possible emissions. However, the desired incentives to be provided by economic instruments can be obscured by institutional impediments which filter or even neutralize the desired price signal.

There are many such institutions at play. It is important not to confuse institutions with interest groups. An institution can be the result of pressure from interest groups, and sometimes even from interest groups not presently active, but interest groups of the past.

When it is necessary to investigate the impact of economic instruments for environmental policy, a map of the institutions that are in play on the market, or in the context where the incentives are provided, needs to be drawn. A comprehensive and holistic approach is hence required. It cannot be assumed that the tax, *in casu* the waste tax, is the only incentive aimed at the target group. The economic instruments operate at the margin, but at the margin of what? Not only of price signals but also of other incentives, motivations and practices.

In the present evaluation study the idea has been to understand how the waste tax operates in the broader context of waste regulations and waste policy. In addition, the behaviour of firms and individuals in relation to the institutions that influence their behaviour needs to be analysed. A firm has institutionalized ways of responding to its surroundings, and they are not always strictly rational. The same can be said of individuals. In an institutional perspective, and taking into account transaction costs, it may actually be rational for firms and individuals not to respond to the incentive provided by the price signals of economic instruments. An environmental economist might want to express such behaviour in terms of elasticity, but that would be to underestimate the significance of institutions. It is a more sociological approach that can cast light on the responses to economic incentives. The methodology of the present study can be blamed for being unnecessarily 'soft' and 'qualitative' and for relying too much on statements and not enough on figures. It is important to understand, however, that the study seeks to employ quantitative data as far as possible – limited by what is available among the target groups. However, these target groups often do not compute their costs and benefits (at the margin) in accordance with the assumptions of environmental economics. They seem to rely also on practices, codes of conduct and a glance at what the neighbour does.

3.   THE INTRODUCTION AND DESIGN OF THE WASTE TAX

The Danish waste tax was introduced on 1 January 1987 after a decision by the Danish Parliament. It was the first fiscal emission tax in Denmark, and had been conceived by the Environmental Protection Agency already in 1985 (Miljøstyrelsen, 1985).[2] It applies both to household waste and industrial waste.

The tax is weight-based and is levied on all waste which is delivered to or processed at landfills and incinerators. Incineration is widespread in Denmark, and about 70 per cent of residual[3] household waste is incinerated. Approximately 50 per cent of total residual waste is incinerated (Miljøstyrelsen, 1996).

The background for the tax was an acute lack of landfills, especially in the greater Copenhagen area, exacerbated by problems with dioxine emissions from incineration. The tax was also seen as a means to support the Action Plan for Waste and Recycling, the target of which is an increase of recycling. According to then Minister of the Environment, Lone Dybkjær (Social Liberals), the waste tax was to be a 'locomotive' for the action plan (Folketingstidende 1989/90, del F, sp. 3056).

During the 10 years of its existence, the tax has been increased several times (Figure 12.1), and the tax base broadened. The original rate was a uniform DKK40 per ton. By 1 January 1997 the tax reached DKK335 per ton for waste to landfills, DKK260 per ton for waste to incinerators and DKK210 per ton for waste to incinerators with electricity production (in addition to the usual heat production). The tax base has also been broadened. Originally, the tax was only levied at waste sites (landfills and incinerators) that received waste from municipal collection systems. From 1 January 1990 the tax base was broadened to comprise the smaller landfills, as well as various private and industrial waste deposits. All waste sites must register with the tax authorities, and an officially approved scale is used as a basis for calculating the tax.

The successive increases of the tax have been based on a mix of environmental and fiscal reasons. In 1989 it was decided to increase the tax to

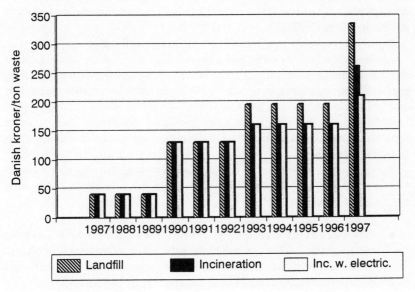

Note: 100 kroner = 13.50 euro.

Figure 12.1   The Danish waste tax

DKK130 per ton in support of the Action Plan for Waste and Recycling, proposed the same year. In 1992 the differentiation between landfills and incineration was introduced, and the rates were increased to DKK160 and DKK195 per ton respectively.[4] In 1993, as part of the green tax reform (Andersen, 1994b), the waste tax was further increased to DKK285 per ton for landfills and DKK160–210 per ton for incinerators with/without energy recovery. This increase was scheduled to become effective from 1997. In 1996, however, when the Parliament was negotiating the state budget, it decided to increase the waste tax by a further DKK50 per ton.

The anticipated environmental effects of the tax were only specified before the increase in 1990 (a 15 per cent decrease in total waste). The other increases were based on a more general reference to the Action Plan for Waste and Recycling. The increases introduced in 1993 and 1997, however, were more fiscally motivated. The differentiation between landfills and incinerators introduced in 1993 was, for instance, not sufficiently high to make landfilling the most expensive solution, as user charges levied by landfill operators were rather low. The increase from 1997 was part of the green tax reform in which taxes were shifted from income to pollution.

Some types of waste are exempted from the tax. The most important are hazardous waste, waste from hospitals, sewage sludge that is clean enough to be distributed on fields, fly ash, clean soil, straw and clean wood waste. In quantity, the most important exemption has been the one that applies to fly ash (terminated from 1998).

Reused or recycled waste is not liable to the tax, as the purpose of the tax is to promote such activities. For the same reason, there is a general reimbursement mechanism, so that the tax is refunded for waste that is removed from registered waste sites. This is mainly relevant for construction and building materials, which can be reused, but it also allows the operators of landfills to have other recycling activities within their domain. There is also a separate exemption mechanism for recycling sites that generate residual waste from their activities.

The tax cannot be said to be targeted at preventing or minimizing waste. However, at the national level there are other more preventive economic mechanisms, notably:

- beer and soft drink packaging: the producers must establish a deposit refund system. Although the regulations were introduced in the early 1980s the system has been in place since the last century and, therefore, does not affect the evaluation of the waste tax;
- the deposit-refund system is supported by taxes on packaging containers for all drink products which supports reuse and penalizes disposable containers (introduced before the waste tax);

- tax on disposable tableware (introduced before the waste tax);
- rechargable batteries: until 1995 there was an agreement with the producers to collect these, but due to a poor rate of compliance a separate tax was introduced;
- a raw materials tax to regulate the exploitation of sand and gravel pits, and support reuse of building materials for construction. This tax was introduced in connection with the waste tax.

4. PRICE SIGNALS IN THE WASTE SECTOR

The difficulty with employing a price mechanism in the waste sector is that the prices of transactions in this sector only bluntly reflect actual costs. There is a tightly knit set of regulations which govern and rule the management of the various waste streams. Also the operators in the waste sector are rather tightly regulated.

Only public authorities are permitted to operate landfills and incinerators – new private operators are not allowed. The municipalities are responsible for refuse collection from households, a responsibility that dates back to hygienic regulations from the last century. Although the municipalities may tender out the collection and transport of waste, it remains in the hands of municipal operators in many places. The municipalities are also responsible for recycling activities and there is, in practice, both horizontal integration between waste collection and waste recycling, as well as vertical integration between waste collection and waste processing.

The waste sector is comprised of a complex network of actors, who find themselves in relatively well-defined positions in relation to each other, and whose transactions are institutionalized through the regulations of the waste sector. The market for waste management, therefore, does not have free competition and full transparency but is, rather, dominated by regional and local monopolies and subject to a complex planning system.

The municipalities are formally responsible for waste collection, through either direct collections or instructions to the waste producers, and the main dividing line in the legislation is between 'collected waste' and 'instructed waste'.

Collected waste Direct collections are mandatory in areas with more than 1000 inhabitants. Collection systems may comprise both private households and companies. It is mandatory to use these systems, also for the private companies. Apart from the environmental/hygienic reasons, this is also thought to provide the citizens with an economically effective system of waste management. The municipalities have in many cases formed intermunicipal, regional waste utilities. Most of the regional waste utilities are formed around an incinerator or, less frequently, common landfill facilities, and they may also be responsible for the collection and transport of waste. The structure and tasks of these regional waste utilities, of which there are about 35 in Denmark, vary considerably. Despite municipal responsibility for collection of waste, there are many private operators in the field who are subcontractors to the municipal authorities.

Instructed waste In more sparsely populated areas the municipality may abstain from refuse collection, and instruct its citizens about where to deliver their waste. These instructions are found in the municipal waste regulations. The municipal authorities will normally also issue instructions regarding other types of waste than regular household waste. There will be specific regulations concerning individual waste streams, such as paper/cardboard, glass, building waste and so on. These instructions will normally apply to industrial waste other than the residual waste, and inform the companies about where to bring certain types of waste. In case of instructed waste, the waste producer will normally use a private transporter to bring it to the waste site.

The main dividing line between collected and instructed waste is important in order to understand how the tax works in relation to the price mechanisms in the waste sector.

Pricing of Collected Waste

The collection of waste must take place in accordance with a non-profit cost-coverage principle, whereby the municipal authority can charge the citizens for refuse disposal based on the actual costs associated with this service. The main cost components are normally collection, transport, processing – plus the waste tax and VAT. The waste tax component differs among municipalities and depends on a number of variables, such as the efficiency of the local refuse collection, recycling facility efficiency, share of apartment buildings, share of incineration and so on, so it is not possible to provide a general figure.[5]

However, the national regulations do not specify exactly how the municipality should charge its users, as this is left to local discretionary decisions. Normally a general fee, which covers all types of waste facility both for disposal and recycling, is charged. The fee is normally proportional to the volume of a waste bin, and there are limited opportunities for choosing the size of a waste bin or the frequency with which it is collected. The incentive of the waste tax, which is charged on a weight basis is, therefore, watered down by municipal user fees that are charged on a per volume basis. For most households an increased recycling activity will thus not be reflected in a lower refuse collection fee.[6]

The designers of the waste tax were well aware of this problem, and the argument behind the tax was not to influence the individual households, but 'to make it more profitable for the municipal refuse collection authorities to establish recycling and sorting systems'. In the legislative text it was thus argued that 'For every ton of waste delivered to recycling, the refuse collection authority will be able to save the corresponding tax' (Folketingstidende, 1985/6, L176, FT, sp. 4426). The implicit assumption was that it would be possible to make the local and regional waste utilities optimize their behaviour, disregarding their monopoly and the possibility for simply passing on the tax to the consumers.

Pricing of Instructed Waste

As regards instructed waste, municipalities normally instruct waste producers about which site they should use.[7] According to the Environmental Protection Agency, waste producers are free to bring their waste products to any recycling site of their preference while they are obliged to use the landfills and incinerators assigned by the municipality (Miljøstyrelsen 1994a, p. 62).

However, few waste producers transport their waste to the waste sites themselves. They normally contract with specialized transporters. There is often a tendering procedure in which the least expensive tender is identified. The waste tax is then integrated in the bill of the transporter. The tax may not always be visible to the waste producer, although it may constitute nearly half the bill for getting rid of the waste. However, some transporters present the tax bill from the waste site in order to prove that the waste has been legally disposed of.

The designers of the waste tax argued that 'a tax on depositing and incineration of commercial waste will directly affect the individual company, which can save the tax and reduce its refuse disposal costs, by sending its waste for recycling or by changing the production processes, to produce less waste' (Folketingstidente, 1985/6, L176, FT, sp. 4426).

As regards instructed waste, the price incentive is more likely to have a direct impact on the decisions of the waste producers than is the case with collected waste.

The Waste Disposal Infrastructure

The possibilities for improving recycling depends on the facilities available in the municipality. For some waste streams national regulations oblige the municipalities to provide a recycling option. Other waste streams are unregulated at the national level, meaning that it is up to the local municipalities to decide whether or not they should provide recycling opportunities.

The following waste factions are, or were until recently, subject to specific regulations:

- paper/cardboard and glass: the municipalities are obliged to establish collection systems according to ministerial decrees first introduced in 1986. These collection facilities can vary from one or a few central collection units or to many decentralized units in the neighbourhoods;
- food waste from large kitchens: the municipalities are obliged to establish separate collection from kitchens that produce more than 100 kg/week.

Other waste streams are not regulated by national guidelines, such as:

- organic waste from households;
- garden waste;
- bulky refuse;
- building materials;
- plastics;
- scrap and metals.

For these waste streams it is up to a local decision whether a collection option should be offered.

The municipalities should be able to meet the target of the Action Plan for Waste and Recycling of a 54 per cent recycling ratio of waste, and in principle they, therefore, recycle as much as possible. However, especially where the municipalities run their own incinerators they may have an interest in not improving recycling to a level that would create an overcapacity. Less than 15 per cent of the municipalities presently meet the target of the plan (Larsen, 1996).

5. THE ENVIRONMENTAL PARAMETER: ASSESSING OUTCOME

The Overall Development: a Reduction in Waste

On the basis of the data compiled by the Tax and Customs authorities on the proceeds of the tax, consistent time series for the waste quantities delivered to registered sites in the period 1987–96 are now available (Figures 12.2a, 12.2b and 12.2c).[8]

Because of the change in the tax base in 1990 (fills and deposits), it is crucial to differentiate between pre-1990 and post-1990 registered waste sites.[9] The pre-1990 sites are generally the larger municipal waste sites, whereas the

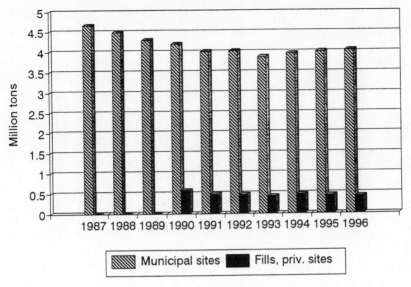

Figure 12.2a   Gross delivered waste 1987–96: landfills and incinerators

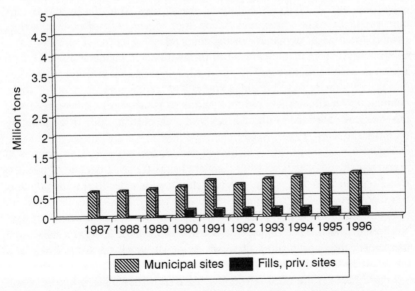

Figure 12.2b   Out-weighed waste 1987–96: landfills and incinerators

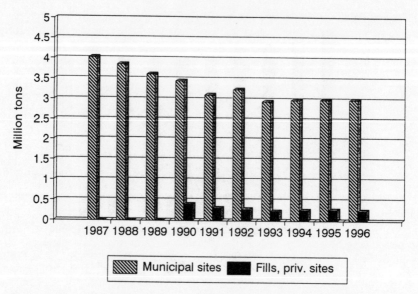

Figure 12.2c   Net delivered waste 1987-96: landfills and incinerators

post-1990 sites are smaller, and both private and public. Ninety-three sites were registered pre-1990; in 1990 another 68 sites were registered. In recent years a further 25 sites have been registered. Post-1990 registration took place somewhat incrementally as additional waste sites were discovered by the authorities. In some cases registration took place only after legal cases, notably for deposits at manufacturing companies.

Because of strict municipal control of landfills and incinerators there is no reason to assume that waste was moved from taxed to non-taxed waste sites during 1987–89. In fact, a detailed analysis of the costs and benefits of waste commuting for all sites showed that the tax of DKK40 per ton was generally too small to cover the additional costs of transport in cases of commuting (Holmstrand *et al.*, 1989).

Figure 12.2a shows gross delivered waste, for pre-1990 and post-1990 registered sites. For the pre-1990 registered sites we see a decline of 605 000 tons from 1987-96. For post-registered sites there is a decline of 150 000 tons from 1990-96.

Figure 12.2b shows out-weighed waste, that is, the waste for which a refund has been obtained. These figures include reloaded waste. There is a substantial increase in the out-weighing of waste, some of which consists of slag and cinders from incinerators.

Figure 12.2c is the most interesting because it shows net delivered waste (that is, gross delivered waste minus out-weighed waste). The net in-weighed waste is the most appropriate indicator, because the figures for gross in-weighed waste are blurred by slags and cinders that have been weighed twice – first as solid waste and later as ashes. It can be seen from Figure 12.2c that a considerable decline in waste took place at the pre-1990 registered sites from 1987 to 1996, from a total of about 4 million tons in 1987 to 3 million tons in 1996. At the post-1990 registered sites there has been a net decrease of 0.155 million tons (39 per cent).

The decline by 1 million tons is equivalent to a decline of 26 per cent, which is a remarkable figure. The decline took place in the period from 1987 to 1993. From 1993 to 1996 the amount of net in-weighed waste was more or less stable, a development which is perceived to be connected with the positive economic development in this period. The effect of the substantial tax increase effective from 1997 could not be included in the analysis (but a follow-up report will be published in 2000).

Identifying the Reductions

Waste has been reduced, but which types of waste? The evaluation is complicated by the lack of good waste statistics in Denmark. The Environmental Protection Agency operates with three different data sources:

1. The 1985 waste planning data, compiled by the Counties (Miljøstyrelsen, 1991b, 1991c).
2. The so-called material surveillance statistics, compiled for 1987–93 by RENDAN (RENDAN, 1991–94),
3. ISAG – the new information system on waste and recycling, compiled from 1993–95 by the Environmental Protection Agency (Miljøstyrelsen, 1996).

The latter source is the most detailed, and is expected to provide more reliable waste data in the future. For the present purposes the ISAG statistics cannot be used because of the short time series and lack of compatibility with other sources. The 1985 data is the most unreliable, in many cases based on raw assessments.

The RENDAN statistics provide a reasonable time series, although only of gross delivered waste. The figures were reported to RENDAN on a quarterly basis. During the first years the data only comprised the larger waste sites, but as part of the evaluation, the data from the missing, smaller, sites have been modelled on the basis of the tax and customs data in order to estimate the development of waste from different sources. There has been a decline mainly in building waste (−64 per cent) and in household waste (−16 per cent), whereas waste from manufacturing industries has increased (+8 per cent), (Figure 12.3a).

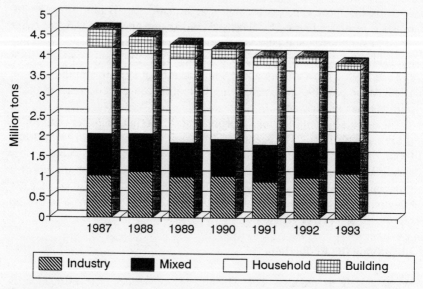

Figure 12.3a   Origins and types of waste 1987–93 (of gross delivered)

The three data sources quoted above refer to the waste sites, but data is also available from the recycling sites. There are relatively few such sites and they have been registered by RENDAN who has collected data from these sites in recent years; they also provide a detailed and reliable assessment of the waste streams. The data do not in all cases correspond to the period since 1987, but still provide a basis for an estimate.

As can be seen from Figure 12.3b, the recycling of scrap and metals – a heavy waste type – has hardly increased since the introduction of the waste tax. There was a market for such waste products, but this was not able to expand, as about 90 per cent was already reused in 1986.

Paper recycling has been increased from 300 000 tons in 1986 to about 500 000 tons annually in 1994, with a total potential of 1 million tons. Within the same time span, glass recycling has been increased from 70 000 tons to 105 000 tons, with a total potential of 158 000 tons.

Building and construction waste is one of the largest categories, with a total amount of 2.2 million tons, of which only 230 000 tons were brought to the waste sites in 1993. About 1.2 million tons consist of asphalt, tile and concrete which is processed by professional 'crushers' and reused, for example, for road-building. 250 000 tons are reused as deposits for noise-baffles for roads and toboggan runs. The RENDAN figures show that the increase in reuse of building and construction materials since 1990 amounts to approximately 5-600 000 tons.

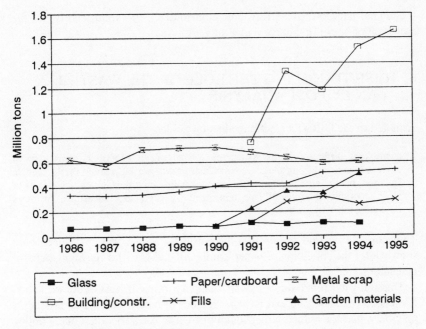

Figure 12.3b   Recycling statistics

Composting of organic household waste and garden waste has increased considerably in recent years by about 500 000 tons, from a level of only 86 000 tons in 1990. This composting takes place at central units organized by the municipalities or regional waste utilities. However, some of this garden waste may have previously been burned by the households, so that it was not hitherto registered.

In sum, it is assessed that the reduction in waste by 1.3 million tons at the pre-1990 registered waste sites consists of the following reductions: paper 200 000 tons; glass 35 000 tons; building materials minimum 600 000 tons and composting 250 000 tons,[10] and possibly a transfer to post-1990 waste sites of up to 100 000 tons. These figures are admittedly estimates, but they are based on the recycling statistics and are the best available. Especially the figure for the reuse of building and construction waste is conservative and may be underestimated.

It is nevertheless interesting that some of the most significant reductions have occurred in waste streams that have not been subject to regulations or decrees at the national level, that is, building waste and the composting of garden waste. These are also among the heavier waste types, expectedly most sensitive to a weight-based tax. Despite the strong emphasis placed on the recycling of paper and glass, and the visibility of containers in streets, the 'command-and-control' effort has contributed less significantly to the reduction of waste in this particular area.

6. DISENTANGLING THE ROLE OF THE WASTE TAX – AN *EX-POST* ANALYSIS

As noted in the OECD's (1997) evaluation guide:

> a frequent difficulty in assessing the effects of an economic instrument in environmental policy is that economic instruments are in practice rarely used in isolation, but are combined in a 'package' of policy measures. Often, the effects of new economic instruments are reinforced by regulatory measures, or other measures, taken at the same time.

This can also be said to describe the waste tax which was introduced only shortly after the collection of paper, cardboard and glass for recycling became mandatory.

This study has relied on 'backward mapping' of the impact of the waste tax. It cannot a priori be said exactly what reasons or motives the waste producers may have had for reducing their output of waste (or not), when many policy instruments are in play, as in the waste sector, but they can be surveyed. This is basically a sociologically oriented case study method. One can then combine quantitative data with more qualitative interview data. For the evaluation of economic instruments for environmental policy this method was first applied by Schuurmann (1988) and later by Andersen (1994a).

The designers of the waste tax regarded manufacturing companies and the municipal refuse collection authorities as the most important target groups for the incentives accruing from the tax, and in the course of the evaluation study two sub-studies were carried out. A number of manufacturing companies in different industrial sectors were interviewed in depth about their waste management practices, and a postal survey was carried out among all municipal waste management units in Denmark.

7. THE RESPONSE FROM FIRMS

A possible caveat associated with the backward mapping methodology should be mentioned. Using this methodology one must carefully avoid 'strategic answers'. When environmental and company ethics are in focus, the firm may wish to present its behaviour as being more altruistic than is the case. Asking companies and firms about how they assess the impact of a green tax on their own behaviour may imply that the investigator does not expect the firm to do anything for the environment for its own good. In order to avoid strategic replies, the interviews conducted with firms in this evaluation were hence designed relatively broadly, and took their starting point in waste management practices in general. Questions about the waste tax were raised at a later stage in the interview in order to minimize the possible bias in the answers.

Sample

In this mini-survey 16 companies within the following sectors were interviewed about their waste management practices:

- iron and steel industry (4);
- breweries (2);
- newspaper printers (4);
- supermarkets (3);
- tele-services (1);
- public education/university (1);
- rail transport (1).

The firms were generally large and well-esteemed companies, but it was not a criterion that they should be environmentally certified. They were sampled from different parts of the country.

Waste Reductions

Three of the sixteen companies had not taken any specific initiatives to reduce their waste or to increase recycling, but they did actually recycle such items as paper or metals.

The remaining 13 companies had actively tried to increase recycling, and these activities ranged from very simple reuse initiatives to more sophisticated production integrated waste minimization measures. The rail transport company recycles more than 50 000 tons of broken stone from the rails. One of the newspaper printers had introduced thinner paper. One of the iron and steel companies had had their suppliers change the format of steel-plates in order to minimize scrap losses. However, the companies generally relied more on recycling and reuse than on making demands to their suppliers. The recycling activities of the firms were mapped in detail, cf. the report.

Motivations

The companies were asked what factors had been essential for their decision to improve recycling and reduce their residual waste, and they were allowed to mention up to three reasons. Table 12.1 shows the results of this motivation analysis. Ten companies pointed out possible income from waste products and eight had concerns about reducing their waste bill. However, there were also many companies that pointed to requirements in the municipal waste regulations (7) and the desire to improve the green profile of the company (8). Fewer pointed to requirements made by their customers (2) or the environmental permit procedure (4).

Table 12.1   Results of motivation analysis

What factors have been significant for the decision to reduce waste	Number
Municipal waste regulations	7
Environmental permit requirements	4
Earnings by selling spill products	10
Costs of waste management	8
Demands from clients/customers	2
Improve green image	8
Other	6

Although possible earnings from waste products and a desire to reduce the waste bill was indicated by eight companies as important, only two companies pointed to the waste tax as being significant for their decision to reduce waste. Six companies did not ascribe it any influence on their actions.

As part of the green tax reform the waste tax was scheduled to be increased by 1 January 1997, and as the interviews were carried out shortly before this date, the companies were asked what changes they would undertake in response to this increase. Four companies had planned changes in their waste disposal. Eight companies had not taken any initiatives, and some were not even aware of the scheduled increase.

Assessment

There were interesting differences among the various types of firm. Generally speaking, the breweries, the iron and steel industries and the railway company were the most professional, and had the most comprehensive knowledge about their waste products and recycling costs. The newspaper printers were in the middle group, positive towards recycling and adhering to the guidelines, but they knew little about the costs and benefits involved. The supermarkets, the tele-service company and the university were generally rather negligent about their waste management practices. The latter group did not, however, have smaller amounts of residual waste than the first group. In the case of the university, the annual amount of residual waste is about 1000 tons, or twice as much as the largest iron and steel companies. However, it may play a role that the total amount of waste, before recycling, is much larger in the first group than in the latter.

Knowledge about the costs and benefits of various waste disposal options is limited in many of the companies. Typically, the physical responsibility for waste management is separated from the accounting unit, and the two units are not in contact with each other. Despite two or more requests to the companies, information about waste management costs were difficult to obtain because the companies themselves did not have an overview, and the figures were scattered across the accounting books. Waste costs seldom account for more than 0.5 per cent of the turnover of a company, and waste management seems to figure even lower in the cost-consciousness hierarchy than energy or transport costs. The exception were the breweries, who had very extensive knowledge, but did not wish to reveal it to the research team. They regard precise cost information as a company secret.

8. THE RESPONSE OF THE REFUSE COLLECTION AUTHORITIES

Sample

A postal survey was carried out among the 277 municipalities in Denmark in order to map the extent of the recycling opportunities offered to the inhabitants, and to question them about their motivations for offering various recycling options. The infrastructure and division of tasks among municipalities and regional waste utilities is very complicated, but in practice the municipalities simply passed on their questionnaire to a regional waste utility if they found that the regional organization was better able to answer the questions. In the survey an 'experienced person' in the municipality's environmental division was asked to fill out the questionnaire, and requested to indicate the name and telephone number of the respondent so that answers could be clarified. The response rate to the survey, which was carried out in December 1996–January 1997, was 68 per cent, which is very satisfactory.

Recycling Facilities Established

It was noted above that only paper/cardboard and glass recycling is mandatory, and as can be seen from Figure 12.4 practically all municipalities

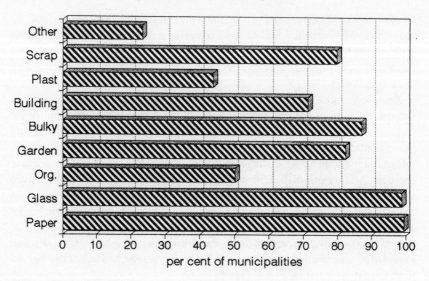

Figure 12.4   Recycling facilities available for various waste streams

have established this. Facilities for recycling or reuse facilities for scrap, bulky waste, garden waste and building waste are also widespread.

It was also asked what year the municipalities established the various systems, as indicated in Figure 12.5. Different 'waves' in the recycling efforts of the municipalities can be seen. The first wave, pre-1987–90, was paper and glass, the second wave, 1987–92 was garden waste, bulky waste and building waste, whereas the third wave, 1993 and later, seems to have led to an increase in composting of organic household waste.

Motivation Analysis

The local authorities may have had different motives for establishing the recycling facilities, and it cannot a priori be assumed that they were established because of the waste tax. As already indicated the recycling of paper and glass is mandatory according to the national waste decree.

The questionnaire contained a list of the following eight motives (Table 12.2), and the respondents were asked to identify the three most significant for each of the recycling options available. A category of 'other' reasons was included to allow for other answers than those stipulated, but the limited use of it is an indication that the motives listed represented a reasonably comprehensive menu.

The survey showed that the political variable, the desire of the Municipal Council to improve recycling, was the most important factor for the majority

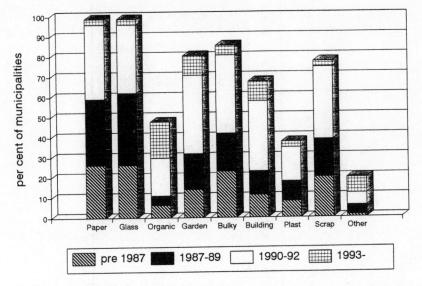

Figure 12.5   Introduction of local recycling systems: various waste factions

of the nine waste factions included in the survey, and mentioned by 50–70 per cent of the municipalities (Table 12.3). The cost variable was generally the second most important factor, but depended on the waste faction. For garden waste and building waste it was the most important factor after the political variable. The reason seems to be that the municipalities can avoid their citizens becoming liable to the waste tax if they offer recycling facilities for these heavier waste types.

Figure 12.6 shows how the respondents estimate the significance of the waste tax for the economy of their various recycling systems. It shows that the

Table 12.2   Motives for offering recycling facilities

Legal	Requirements in law or decree
Plan	Target in National Action Plan for Waste
Capacity	Shortage of landfill or incineration capacity
Costs	To reduce waste processing costs, including the waste tax
Citizens	Demands from the citizens
Regional	Demand/proposal from regional waste utility
Subsidy	Subsidy from the Recycling Council
Political	Desire of Municipal Council to improve recycling
Other	

Table 12.3 Motives indicated as significant by municipal waste officers for choosing to offer recycling facilities (per cent of respondents)

	Legal	Plan	Capacity	Costs	Citizens	Regional	Subsidy	Political	Other
Paper	66	34	10	34	14	19	24	60	2
Glass	56	36	9	33	16	21	22	59	2
Organic	21	48	16	37	11	24	9	72	0
Garden	15	31	25	45	27	21	1	61	4
Bulky	27	36	18	25	33	25	2	57	4
Building	28	41	19	42	20	37	1	55	2
Plastic	29	46	15	29	7	28	3	51	11
Scrap	27	31	17	32	25	31	1	58	4
Other	50	33	14	17	22	31	0	39	6

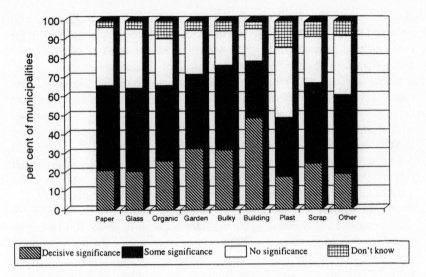

Figure 12.6   Significance of waste tax for economy of recycling

element of the waste tax is most significant for rendering the recycling of garden waste, bulky waste and building waste profitable. In these cases more than 70 per cent accord the waste tax 'some' or 'decisive' influence. For building waste nearly 50 per cent accord the waste tax 'decisive' influence.

Assessment

The municipalities have been active in offering recycling facilities to their citizens. The most important reason has been the political desire to improve recycling, but also the cost component played a role. For the more heavy waste factions the waste tax is seen as significant for the cost-effectiveness of these systems. When this information is linked to the evidence of the waste statistics, it is not difficult to disentangle the effect of the waste tax from the other policy instruments that were listed. The greatest reductions have taken place because of increased recycling of garden and building waste, and these waste factions are not subject to national decrees about recycling.

9.   THE IMPACT OF WEIGHT-BASED WASTE FEES

In Section 8 it was shown that the municipalities have established many different facilities for recycling. However, as previously mentioned, only 15 per cent of the municipalities have been able to achieve the target set by the

National Action Plan for Waste of a 54 per cent share of recycling. It may well be asked, then, whether recycling facilities would be better utilized if the municipalities were to charge their waste fees on the basis of weight, rather than a flat rate with only few levels for different volumes.

There are 8–10 municipalities in Denmark who have introduced weight-based waste charges. The experiences of some of these municipalities have been analysed and compared with the recycling ratio in other municipalities without weight-based waste charges (SBI, 1996). The figures are drawn from ISAG, the environment agency's waste statistics.

Figure 12.7 shows the amount of 'residual waste' (that is, waste after recycling) per capita in 10 Danish municipalities before and after the introduction of new waste management systems with recycling facilities. The two municipalities with the most significant reductions in waste are Tinglev and Bogense. Here residual waste has been reduced to about 100 kg/capita, whereas waste has remained at 200–250 kg/capita despite the introduction of new systems in places such as Århus, Kolding and Albertslund. When the waste reductions in Tinglev and Bogense are matched with the recycling statistics it can be seen that the waste has not disappeared into nature or otherwise been disposed of illegally – it is being recycled.

In the cases of Tinglev and Bogense, two smaller rural communities, a system of weight-based fees has been introduced. In Tinglev each household

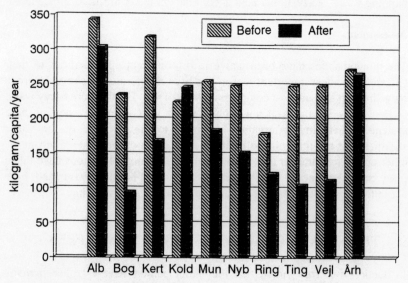

Figure 12.7   Residual waste in 10 municipalities before and after new recycling schemes

pays a small flat rate plus a weight-based rate (Miljøstyrelsen, 1994b). The refuse collection vehicle has a weight which registers the amount of waste in the waste bin. An electronic identity tag is attached to the top of the waste bin, which is read by a scanner, and the data of the identity of the owner and the weight of the contents is recorded on a disk. At the end of each year the waste bill is totalled, minus the instalments collected with the property tax.

Only the city of Vejle is able to display waste reduction on the level of Tinglev and Bogense. Vejle has a very comprehensive recycling system in which most of the waste fractions are collected at the doorstep, and the Vejle system is seen as the leading Danish system. However, the Vejle system is very expensive. Despite a DKK50 million subsidy from the environment agency, the per household waste fees in Vejle are more than twice as high as in Tinglev and Bogense.

It is not possible in the context of this study to go into further detail concerning the admittedly rather intricate comparisons, but interested readers are referred to the report and its references (Andersen *et al.*, 1997).

The experiences with weight-based waste fees seem to suggest that if waste fees were made up on a weight basis, as to better reflect the intention of the waste tax, it would then be possible to avoid the blurring of the incentive accruing from the waste tax, and hence to meet the target of the National Action Plan for Waste, possibly in a more cost-effective way. However, it may not be possible to operate weight-based refuse collection in larger towns and cities. Bogense and Tinglev are smaller rural communities of about 5000 inhabitants and mainly individual houses.

In the context of this study, the practical implications for waste management are less important than the more principal implications regarding the transformation of the price signal from an environmental tax to the polluters through the environmental management system. The evidence of the experiences of the weight-based systems may, therefore, be seen as an indication that, despite the impressive 26 per cent reduction in taxed waste from 1987 to 1996, institutional constraints still remain on the incentives from the waste tax which prevent it from reaping the full benefits.

9. PERSPECTIVES AND CONCLUSIONS

A 26 per cent reduction in taxed waste was achieved from 1987 to 1996 at the municipal waste sites. This development was the result of a comprehensive waste policy consisting of many different policy instruments, including a waste tax.

There was a command-and-control effort towards glass and paper recycling. However, these two waste streams account for only a smaller share of the total waste reduction, about 230 000 tons out of a total waste reduction of 1 200 000 tons. The 'unregulated' waste streams, such as building and construction waste and garden waste, account for the remaining – and greater – part of the reductions. The survey of the municipalities showed that the facilities for the reuse and recycling of these waste streams were offered both for political reasons and out of economic considerations. Especially in the case of building and construction waste, the waste tax was seen as an important factor in rendering recycling profitable.

Where did the waste go that was not brought to landfills and incinerators? According to the statistics of the recycling facilities it seems reasonable to assume that it was used for other purposes. Especially in the building sector, new equipment has been introduced for the reuse of tile, concrete and asphalt. Garden waste is being composted at municipal sites. Despite rumours in the press that waste is being disposed of illegally, on the basis of various incidents, the environmental surveillance of the counties has not detected general problems of illegal disposal.

The waste statistics do not allow us to draw many conclusions concerning developments among manufacturing industries and other companies, but it seems reasonable to assume that their waste was not reduced significantly. It is not known what the baseline scenario would have been, and it might be that waste quantities would have increased in the absence of the waste policy and the waste taxation. However, from the in-depth interviews of a limited sample of companies it seemed that some of these were neither too aware of the waste tax, nor of the possible savings to be gained from a more active waste policy. Some companies, in particular breweries and some iron and steel manufacturers, had more precise estimates, but did not wish to unveil them.

The environmental economist might not be surprised that the waste tax led to substantial reductions in the most heavy waste fractions, such as building and construction waste and garden waste. The waste tax is not expected to lead to waste reductions across the board, but only where the marginal treatment costs of recycling are lower than the waste tax rate. As the waste tax was increased not only building waste but also garden waste became recycled.

However, due to the institutional set-up in the waste sector, the waste producers were not always confronted with the incentive of the waste tax. It was primarily a signal to the municipal refuse collection authorities who, in return, relied on more altruistic recycling behaviour among their customers and users. The refuse collection authorities seem to have been more responsive to the waste tax than many manufacturing companies. This is quite a paradox in relation to conventional economic theory, which would predict a pass-on behaviour from regional utilities to the customers, and greater responses from firms.

Explaining this paradox is in itself an interesting research question which deserves considerable attention. In the context of this study the hypothesis is put forward that the refuse collection authorities were more sensitive to the waste tax because it fell within their primary business domain. Among manufacturing companies the most active response was found among breweries and iron and steel plants with a long tradition for selling their waste products, whereas supermarkets and tele-services' companies were quite negligent. For all companies, and in particular the latter, waste management is outside their primary business domain and, therefore, figures as an insignificant issue in their business attention hierarchy. In institutional terms this can be explained by the path-dependency of company behaviour. There are informal institutionalized practices about 'how to make money' which lead the companies to focus their attention on the issues that traditionally are likely to yield benefits.

This is regarded as a competing institutional hypothesis to be tested against the 'economic man behaviour' assumed by environmental economics. The latter assumption might simply explain the negligence shown by some firms as being due to high transaction costs. However, the in-depth interviews often pointed to circumstances which did not confirm the assumed rational behaviour by firms. In a future research project, financed by the Danish Strategic Environmental Research Programme, it is hoped that these two hypotheses will be analysed in greater depth and will bring further evidence to the discussion.

As a final remark to the effects of the waste tax, the experiences with weight-based fees gained in the municipalities Tinglev and Bogense seem to indicate that the potential of the present waste tax, which is the highest in Europe, has not yet been fully exploited. At the present, the institutional set-up of the waste sector, for example, the autonomy of the municipalities to set flat-rate fees, filters the incentive from the waste tax. If the private waste producers were more systematically exposed to the price incentive accruing from the tax, by having to pay their fees on a per weight basis, a further reduction in waste by increased recycling seems to be within reach.

NOTES

*   This is based on a report prepared for the Danish Environmental Protection Agency. Research assistants Niels Dengsø and Stefan Brendstrup contributed to the project.

1. The only known examples being the UK landfill tax and possibly Taiwan's future waste water tax.
2. Environmental taxes as distinct from energy taxes and transport taxes.
3. The term 'residual waste' denotes the amount of waste after reuse and recycling, that is, the amount exclusively for landfills or incinerators.
4. There was also a need for revenue to compensate for the former milk packaging levy that had been abandoned for social (and lack of environmental) reasons.

5. For a household of four persons and a per capita waste production of 250 kg/year, the waste charge is normally DKK1500–2000 annually, of which the waste tax consitutes an average of DKK250, or 12.5–16 per cent.
6. For experiences in Danish municipalities with weight-based waste fees, see below.
7. Legal experts have questioned their competence to do so, see Basse (1995), p. 288.
8. Some data problems were encountered, as the Tax and Customs Authorities only keep their accounts for five years. However, the lost data were identified in dossiers of the Environment Agency. Generally, data are available for in-weighed and out-weighed waste at each registered site. Data for out-weighed waste are available only at the aggregate level for 1987.
9. In some cases post-1990 registered waste sites had, prior to 1990, reported their waste as a sub-unit of another site. These sites are counted as pre-1990 sites.
10. According to the RENDAN figures household waste decreased by about 500000 tons from 1987 to 1993. About half of this was paper and glass, and it is assessed that the remaining part is organic/garden waste, which is now being composted.

REFERENCES

Andersen, M.S. (1994a), *Governance by Green Taxes: Making Pollution Prevention Pay*, Manchester, UK and New York, US: Manchester University Press.

Andersen, M.S. (1994b), 'The green tax reform in Denmark: shifting the focus of tax liability', *Journal of Environmental Liability*, **2** (2), 47–50.

Andersen, M.S., N. Dengsø and S. Brendstrup (1997), 'Affaldsafgiften – en ex-post evaluering af incitamenter og miljøeffekter', 'The waste tax – an ex-post evaluation of incentives and environmental effects', Arbejdsrapport fra Miljøstyrelsen (*Report from Danish Environmental Protection Agency* (*DEPA*)), no. 96, Copenhagen. (Available at http://www.mem.dk).

Basse, E.M. (1995), *Affaldslovgivningen - et samspil mellem miljø- og konkurrenceret* (*Waste Legislation: the Interplay Between Environmental Law and Competititon law*), Copenhagen: GadJura.

Baumol, W.J. and W.E. Oates (1975 [1988]), *The Theory of Environmental Policy*, Cambridge: Cambridge University Press.

Christoffersen, H., L.G. Hansen and L.K. Jacobsen (1992), *Affaldsafgiftens effekter* (*Effects of the Waste Tax*), Copenhagen: Amternes og Kommunernes Forskningsinstitut.

Coase, R. H. (1988), *The Firm, the Market and the Law*, Chicago: University of Chicago Press.

Finance Ministry, Environment Ministry and Tax Ministry (1992), 'Budgetanalyse om markedsorientering af affalds- og genanvendelsesindsatsen' ['Budget analysis of the market orientation of the waste and recycling effort]', Copenhagen.

Folketingstidende [The Danish Parliament's Bulletin] (1985/6), 'Lovforslag nr. L176 [Law proposal L176], Forslag til lov om ændring af lov om milørbeskyttelse' ['Amendments to the environmental protection framework act'], fremsat d. 11 February 1986 af Miljøministeren, Folketingstidende, del A, sp. 4413 ff.

Folketingstidende [The Danish Parliament's Bulletin] (1989/90), Miljøministerens [Minister of Environment] (Lone Dybkjær) fremsættelse af Forslag til lov om afgift af affald og råstoffer (Lovforslag no. L100) ['Proposal for law regarding taxation of waste and raw materials'], Folketingstidende, del F, sp. 3056.

Holmstrand, H.C., Ole Kaysen and Tage Mikkelsen (1989), *Vurdering af affaldsafgiftens styrende effekter* [*An Appraisal of the Waste Tax and its Incentives*], vols 1-2, Copenhagen: GENDAN.

Larsen, J.H. (1996), 'Opfylder din kommune målene for affald og genanvendelse?' ['Does your municipality meet the targets for waste and recycling?'], *DN-Kontakt* **5**, 8–13, Copenhagen: The Conservation Society.

Miljøstyrelsen [Danish Environmental Protection Agency] (1985), 'Miljøafgifter' ['Environmental taxes and charges'], Copenhagen.

Miljøstyrelsen [Danish Environmental Protection Agency] (1991a), 'Notat om affaldsafgiftens virkninger' [*Note on the Impact of the Waste Tax*], to the Parliamentary Committee on Environment and Planning.

Miljøstyrelsen [Danish Environmental Protection Agency] (1991b), 'Affald i Danmark – teknisk rapport' ['Waste in Denmark – technical report'], Miljøprojekt no. 175, Copenhagen.

Miljøstyrelsen [Danish Environmental Protection Agency] (1991c), 'Affald i Danmark' ['Waste in Denmark'], Orientering no. 4, Copenhagen.

Miljøstyrelsen [Danish Environmental Protection Agency] (1994a), 'Bortskaffelse, planlægning og registrering af affald', [Removal, planning and registration of waste. DEPA guideline no. 4], Vejledning no. 4, Copenhagen.

Miljøstyrelsen [Danish Environmental Protection Agency] (1994b), 'Vægtafhængig dagrenovation – Tinglev Kommune' ['Weight-based refuse collection in Tinglev'], Miljøprojekt no. 265.

Miljøstyrelsen [Danish Environmental Protection Agency] (1996), *Affaldsstatistik 1995* [Waste statistics 1995], Orientering no. 14, Copenhagen.

North, Douglass C. (1990), *Institutions, Institutional Change, and Economic Performance*, Cambridge: Cambridge University Press.

OECD (1997), *Evaluating Economic Instruments for Environmental Policy*, Paris: OECD.

Pearce, D. and K. Turner (1990), *Economics of Natural Resources and the Environment*, New York: Harvester Wheatsheaf.

RENDAN (1991–94), *Materialestrømsovervågning [Material Stream Surveillance]*, Copenhagen: RENDAN.

RENDAN (1996a), *Affaldshåndbogen 1996 [The Waste Handbook 1996]*, Copenhagen: RENDAN.

RENDAN (1996b), *Bygge- og anlægsaffaldsstatistik [Building Materials Statistics]*, Copenhagen: RENDAN.

SBI (Statens Byggeforskningsinstitut) [State building research institute] (1996), 'Affald i boligområder: Livsstil og affaldsvaner' ['Waste in housing areas: lifestyle and waste habits'], Report no. 261, Copenhagen: SBI.

Schuurman, Jacob (1988), *De Prijs van Water [The Price of Water]*, Arnhem: Gouda Quint.

Index